A QUEER HISTORY OF THE UNITED STATES

FOR YOUNG PEOPLE

A QUEER HISTORY OF THE UNITED STATES

FOR YOUNG PEOPLE

MICHAEL BRONSKI
ADAPTED BY RICHIE CHEVAT

BEACON PRESS ■ BOSTON

BEACON PRESS
Boston, Massachusetts
www.beacon.org

Beacon Press books
are published under the auspices of
the Unitarian Universalist Association of Congregations.

Beacon Press gratefully acknowledges the Unitarian Universalist
Funding Program (UUFP) for its generous support of this book.

22   8 7

This book is printed on acid-free paper that meets the uncoated paper
ANSI/NISO specifications for permanence as revised in 1992.

Text design by Carol Chu and Kim Arney
Text composition by Kim Arney

Front cover images: Victoria Woodhull, Wikimedia; Bayard Rustin, half-length
portrait, listens to unidentified man, 1964, photo Stanley Wolfson, Library of
Congress, Prints and Photographs Division, New York World-Telegram and
the Sun Newspaper Photograph Collection; Gladys Bentley, Ubangi Club,
Harlem, 1930s, photo Sterling Paige, courtesy Visual Studies Workshop,
Rochester, NY; Hemphill Essex, photo Robert Giard, courtesy Robert Giard
Foundation; Emily Dickinson, circa 1848, Todd-Bingham Picture Collection
and Family Papers, Yale University Manuscripts & Archives, Digital Images
Database, New Haven, CT; Kiyoshi Kuromiya, courtesy Peter Lien; Walt
Whitman, 1870, Library of Congress; Harvey Milk, 1970s, Wikimedia; Julian
Eltinge, 1917, Exhibitors Herald, Wikimedia.

Library of Congress Cataloging-in-Publication Data

Names: Bronski, Michael, author. I Chevat, Richie, author.
Title: A queer history of the United States for young people /
    Michael Bronski ; adapted by Richie Chevat.
Description: Boston : Beacon Press, [2019] I Audience: Ages: 12+ I
    Audience: Grades: 7 to 8. I Includes bibliographical references and index.
Identifiers: LCCN 2019004259 (print) I LCCN 2019010317 (ebook) I
    ISBN 9780807056134 (ebook) I ISBN 9780807056127 (pbk. : alk. paper)
Subjects: LCSH: Homosexuality—United States—History—Juvenile
    literature. I Gays—United States—History—Juvenile literature. I
    Sexual minorities—United States—History—Juvenile literature. I
    Homosexuality—United States—Miscellanea—Juvenile literature.
Classification: LCC HQ76.3.U5 (ebook) I LCC HQ76.3.U5
    B6965 2019 (print) I DDC 306.76/60973—dc23
LC record available at https://lccn.loc.gov/2019004259

History is a novel whose author is the people.

—ALFRED DE VIGNY
(nineteenth-century French poet and novelist)

CONTENTS

1969. It was a hot night in early August. Nights in New York City are always hot in the summer—the brick buildings and concrete streets soak up the heat all day and release it after the sun goes down. This night was no different, maybe hotter. Or maybe it just felt that way because I was nervous.

I was twenty years old, going to college, and living with my parents in a New Jersey suburb, but on weekends or at night, I often went into New York City, so I knew my way around. I spent a lot of time exploring Greenwich Village, where I would go to plays, movies, and coffee-houses. On this hot August night, I wasn't going to an Italian film (the kind that never played in New Jersey) or a strange, experimental play (the kind that never played on Broadway). I was on my way to my first meeting of a group that had formed only weeks before: the Gay Liberation Front.

It may be hard for you to imagine how excited I was. On my way to that meeting I had the strange and wonderful feeling that my life was finally going to begin. I didn't know exactly how. All I knew was that just saying—or thinking—the words "Gay Liberation Front" was exciting. Just putting those two words together—"gay" and "liberation"—was magical, something I would never have thought of only a few weeks earlier. Something had changed for me, and for the whole world, on the night of June 27, 1969.

It was the series of events that came to be known as the Stonewall riots, and they changed my life and the lives of people everywhere, forever, both gay and straight.

Stonewall Inn, on Christopher Street in Greenwich Village, was a club where gay men and lesbians would get together, dance, and be themselves for a few hours. The police would often "raid" the place, arresting customers for the crime of being gay.

In the early morning hours of June 28, when the police arrived for another routine raid, they were met with a shock. The women and men inside and many outside on the street, some of whom were drag queens, fought back, throwing bricks, trash, and bottles at the police and even attacking a police car with a parking meter they pried loose from the sidewalk. Large crowds gathered to support them. The street fighting and demonstrations happened again the next night and the night after that. Some women and men on the street that night called it an uprising. Later, the name "Stonewall riots" took hold of the public imagination.

And they were only the beginning. Word of what had happened at the Stonewall quickly spread. Remember, this was long before the internet and social media. The local New York City newspapers ran short news stories. But it was the queer community that really spread the news. Women and men called each other up or talked about the riots when they met on the street or in cafés and coffeehouses. Some handed out leaflets or flyers that called for public meetings or spread the word of the riots. We all wanted to share the exciting news: for the first time anyone could remember, homosexuals (as gay people were called then) had fought back. They had had enough

The facade of the famous Stonewall Inn in September 1969,
three months after the Stonewall riots made it a landmark of LGBTQ history.

of police violence and bullying and decided to take the power into their own hands.

The meeting I was going to, that of the Gay Liberation Front, was formed in the aftermath of the Stonewall riots. It also took place in the context of the protest movements of the 1960s. The rallying cry for many political movements of that time was "Power to the People." This was the queer "power to the people" moment.

African Americans had marched, held sit-ins, and been jailed by the thousands in the civil rights movement of the 1950s and 1960s, as well as in the more radical Black Power movement of the later 1960s. Women had started to form feminist groups—some even calling themselves "radical feminists"—to fight sexism, discrimination, and violence against women. And Americans from all walks of life, but especially young people, were joining national street protests in huge numbers to voice their opposition to the war in Vietnam.

The idea behind the Gay Liberation Front was to form a political group that would fight for the social and political freedom for gay men and lesbians. The organizers saw it as a natural part of the larger freedom movements going on all around them. They called for a series of meetings and a demonstration. Some women and men wrote a leaflet that demanded "the rights of homosexuals to openly love whom we please and to an unharassed lifestyle. . . . We refuse to accept the straight person's guilt about sex." The leaflets asked people to "help bring about the day when we can walk out in the open as first-class citizens."

On July 27, nearly four hundred women and men met in Washington Square Park, a few blocks from the Stonewall Inn. They laughed, joked, sang songs, and talked politics. Four days later, many of these same people met again at a nearby progressive school called Alternate U. to start a new political movement that would fight for the rights of gay men and lesbians.

The people who showed up decided to call themselves the Gay Liberation Front. Many of the people in the room at Alternate U. were already involved in other political movements: radical feminism, civil rights, and the antiwar movement. They chose the name "Gay Liberation Front" to connect themselves, by association, to the National Liberation Front, the North Vietnamese group that was fighting the United States troops in the ongoing war in Vietnam.

I was there on that hot summer night. I had already been heavily involved in protests against the war in Vietnam, but I wasn't thinking about the war that night. I was thinking about a lot of other things. I was thinking that this new political cause was about me: About me being gay and not being able to tell many people. About me being gay and being bullied in high school because other boys suspected it.

And, to be honest, being only twenty years old, I was also thinking of some other things that night as I walked into the small room at the Alternate U. I was really hoping I looked OK and not like a nerd from New Jersey. I hoped that my hair looked alright. (Like a lot of men at the time, I wore mine in a long ponytail.) I hoped that people would like me.

I held my breath as I entered the room. I didn't know anyone and was immediately intimidated. The room was filled with women and men—some older, some my age—who were animated and arguing and laughing and yelling.

It was more like a party than a political meeting. As I began to listen, I realized that everyone was talking about politics and what we were going to do next and how we were going to change the world.

That was fifty years ago. It would be the beginning, not only of a new life for me but of a career as well. That night, in my nervousness and excitement, it seemed that anything—maybe everything—was possible. This meeting was my introduction to LGBTQ politics. (The language we used was different then. "Gay" was a collective term—as in "gay people"—that often meant gay men but also lesbians. Later, our idea of community, and language, grew and the words "lesbian," "bisexual," "transgender," and "queer" were added to make LGBT and, later still, Q.) I knew that I wanted to get involved and "do something" for the new movement. And even though we talked about changing the world, I had no idea then—none of us did—how much the world really would change, and how much I would be a part of that change.

That meeting sent me down a new, exciting path for my life. A year after this, I would move to Boston and become involved with Gay Men's Liberation, the Boston equivalent of the Gay Liberation Front. I went to work on *Fag Rag*, the first national gay men's cultural and political newspaper. After that, I spent close to twenty years working at *Gay Community News*, the first national gay and lesbian weekly newspaper, and for almost a decade I programmed *OutWrite*, a national, annual LGBTQ literary conference. Over these years I was a freelance journalist (who sometimes made money working as a chef in restaurants) and a film reviewer, a theater critic, and a political writer, as well as an independent scholar who studied LGBTQ history and politics and wrote books about them. For the past two decades I've been teaching LGBTQ history and studies at Dartmouth College and then at Harvard University.

■ WHY I WROTE THIS BOOK

If anyone in 1969 had told me that fighting for LGBTQ rights was going to be my future, I would not have believed them. Even in the height of excitement about gay liberation, believing that anything was possible, I am not sure I could have imagined how far LGBTQ people and the movement would come, or how far I would come along with it. In many ways, the movement has been inseparable from my life—it is an essential part of who I am.

In 2011 I wrote *A Queer History of the United States*, the first full history of how America and LGBTQ people helped transform one another over centuries. Writing that book made me think deeply about how LGBTQ people helped make America what it is today—by shaping it, contributing to it, and challenging it. Writing also gave me a new appreciation for the way the LGBTQ community throughout history has given all Americans another perspective on freedom, an alternative example of how to live. I also began to rethink what this history meant to me, not professionally but personally.

James Baldwin, a trailblazing writer, civil rights activist, and an openly gay man at a time when it was not easy to be out, helped shape many of America's ideas about racial justice and freedom in the 1960s and 1970s. In his 1965 essay "The White Man's Guilt," he wrote:

> History, as nearly no one seems to know, is not merely something to be read. And it does not refer merely, or even principally, to the past. On the contrary, the great force of history comes from the fact that we carry it within us, are unconsciously controlled by it in many ways, and history is literally *present* in all that we do. It could scarcely be otherwise, since it is to history that we owe our frames of reference, our identities, and our aspirations.

And he is right. We all carry history in us, around us, with us, alongside of us. Histories of all kinds—national, local, personal, family, sexual, emotional—are part of our lives and shape who we are. As Baldwin writes, they are our "frames of reference, our identities, and our aspirations."

It's easy for Americans to find our "official" national history. We learn it in school; we see it in movies and on television. We hear it told on national holidays and see it enacted in pageants and even carved in stone in statues and monuments from Washington, DC, to small towns across the country.

For LGBTQ people—and especially youth and people just coming out—it's not as easy to find out our true history. It's not taught in schools; it's not on postage stamps; the statues and monuments are only now beginning to appear. Many famous Americans have been LGBTQ, yet when their names appear in textbooks or histories, their sexuality is never discussed. Their love lives—and sex lives—are never mentioned.

If we are erased from the history books, then how can we ever know who we are? This absence, this erasure, denies us the right and the ability to use our history as a guide, to feel pride in the heroism and accomplishments of the LGBTQ people who came before us. And it denies us the ability to use this history as a guide to the future so we can follow in their footsteps.

Think of the opening chapters of J. K. Rowling's *Harry Potter and the Sorcerer's Stone*, in which Harry—a boy with his own secret past and secret powers—is shown to know nothing about his family past or his own history. He only learns about his past, who he is, and his true nature when Hagrid—the trusty Keeper of the Keys at Hogwarts who had been a close friend of Harry's deceased parents—tells him. When Hagrid discovers that Harry's foster parents have kept the information from him because they are ashamed Harry is "not normal," Hagrid explodes with righteous fury: "It's an outrage! It's a scandal! Harry Potter not knowin' his own story."

And it is an outrage and a scandal that LGBTQ people do not know their history—that it has been kept from them.

This book is a series of biographical stories and historical sketches. They begin before there was a United States and move forward to the twenty-first century. You may know of some of these people or have read about them in school, such as poet Walt Whitman or Jane Addams, a social worker and spokesperson for world peace. Others—such as the world-famous early-twentieth-century cross-dresser Julian Eltinge or the African American poet and activist Essex Hemphill—will be new to you. Each of these people, and each moment in history, tells us something very distinct and important about the role that LGBTQ people played in American history.

The world—and America—has changed since I was in high school and college. Many middle schools and high schools have gay-straight alliances (GSAs). There are LGBTQ characters on television, openly gay people now run for political office, and issues such as transgender identity and homophobic school bullying are discussed in the media, the courtroom, and the classroom.

Yet, with all of these enormous changes, many LGBTQ people still face hostility in school and at home. People have a hard time coming out. People face discrimination in the workplace and in the military. The stories in this book will, I hope, show LGBTQ youth, and their friends and allies, that no matter what they face in life, or how they understand themselves, they are part of a long, wonderful history that is not only a queer history but an American history too.

I think about myself in 1969 and how much I thought I knew—and how much I didn't know. When gay liberation came into existence, my compatriots and I thought we could change the world. And we did. The world still needs changing—and that will be up to the readers of this book. My hope is that, unlike the young man I was in 1969, you will know your history and—as James Baldwin writes—it will guide you into the future.

BEFORE WE START, OR, WHAT IS NORMAL?

Any book of LGBTQ history must begin with a discussion of the idea of "normal." This is a word people use all the time. It is a word with a lot of meanings, many of which are vague and misleading. Most commonly, the word is used to convey the idea that "this is the way things are or should be." Used this way, "normal" really means whatever the majority of people in a society agree is acceptable or correct. The bottom line is that "normal" is not a scientific term, it has no set meaning—it's simply a way of insisting that the customs the majority of people follow are somehow "correct" or "natural."

For much of recorded history, gay men, lesbians, bisexuals, and transgender people were considered "abnormal"—outside the accepted norm. They were also labeled with other terms that reinforced this idea. Words such as "unnatural," "abomination," and "unspeakable" were used to make sure that LGBTQ people were not considered worthy of full civil rights, equality, or even simple respect.

These attitudes were, and are, sometimes based on very limited interpretations of verses in the Hebrew Bible and the Gospels. (People consider them limited because many scholars and religious people disagree with these interpretations.) Even today, there are religious leaders who use the Bible as an excuse to call LGBTQ people sinful. Sometimes they say that sexual activity is only natural if it can lead to reproduction. Thus, sex between same-sex couples is "unnatural."

In the past, since LGBTQ people were said to be "sinful" or "unnatural," it was considered shocking or wrong to even mention them, so they were called "unspeakable." Many important legal and medical texts up until the mid-twentieth century used words and phrases such as "unmentionable" or "the unspeakable vice" to describe sexual acts between members of the same sex.

The word "normal" has been used not just to define sex but also gender roles. Society has had strict rules about how men and women should act. For example, when I was young, it was a well-known "fact" that "normal" men and boys didn't cry. Men and women who did not follow the rules were often made fun of, criticized, bullied, and even punished.

People who use the word "normal" to describe human behavior think they are referring to never-changing characteristics. History shows us that what is considered "normal" often changes, sometimes quite rapidly. We can see that right now in the way ideas about same-sex marriage are changing. Many of the people you will read about in this book had to fight against the idea that they were not "normal." Sometimes they even embraced it. By doing so, they changed the way their fellow Americans looked at them and changed the history of our country.

Today most people, in conversation, and in the media, use the words "gay," "lesbian," "bisexual," "transgender," and maybe even "queer" to describe women and men who are attracted to members of their own sex. These words are fairly new. People only began using them starting in the late 1800s. Our language changes all the time, especially when our ideas change. The history of terms for LGBTQ people reflects this.

Words are important because they are not neutral. The word we use to describe something can change the way we feel about it. This is especially true when we use words to describe groups of people. We have to remember that these labels are shortcuts and can never fully describe any individual.

The words that we as LGBTQ people use to describe ourselves can change the way the world looks at us and the way we feel about ourselves. We need to define ourselves in ways that are positive and inclusive and not let others define us in ways that are negative and hurtful.

The organizers of the Gay Liberation Front understood that, and that's why they embraced the word "gay." Using that word was a conscious, political gesture to define ourselves. But it wasn't the end of our attempts to do this.

HOMOSEXUAL: A VERY USEFUL WORD FOR ITS TIME

Before "gay" the word most commonly used to describe LGBTQ people was "homosexual." Though we do not use it very often now, it was a useful word because it had a neutral, scientific sound to it. "Homosexual" was used by doctors, social scientists, newspapers, and everyday people. It was, in many ways, a polite and acceptable word, invented to replace words such as "sodomite," which implied that gay men and lesbians were sinful.

The word dates back to the 1860s and was coined by Karl-Maria Kertbeny, an Austrian man. Kertbeny was a writer and a poet, and he was friends with the fairy-tale writers the Brothers Grimm and Hans Christian Andersen. He was also passionate about social injustice, especially against same-sex loving men and women. In 1868 he published two widely read pamphlets that argued to abolish German behavior laws criminalizing same-sex love. In those pamphlets Kertbeny used the words "homosexual" and "heterosexual." In a short space of time, the terms began to be widely used.

L IS FOR LESBIAN

The word "homosexual" was often only associated with men, so a separate term to describe women who were attracted to women evolved. Writers in the late 1800s began using the words "lesbian" and "sapphist" to describe women who were attracted to other women. Both words refer to the classical Greek poet Sappho.

Sappho lived on the island of Lesbos sometime between 620 and 570 BCE and was famous in her own time. We know almost nothing about her life, and only fragments of her work survived. She wrote love poems to both women and men, and in the nineteenth century, several European poets and scholars described Sappho as a lover of women or perhaps bisexual. They coined the

A painting of the poet Sappho imagining her on the ancient Greek island of Lesbos, 1904.

word "sapphist" to describe a woman who loved women, and in 1897 the heterosexual British sexologist Havelock Ellis first used the term "lesbian"—referring to the island of Lesbos—a word we continue to use today.

G IS FOR GAY: A NEW WORD FOR A NEW ERA

By the early twentieth century, in the United States, "lesbian" was widely used, but few people used the word "sapphist." The term "homosexual" was also in wide use. Same-sex loving women and men weren't happy with these terms and decided they needed their own language. By 1920, both women and men began using the word "gay" to describe themselves.

No one knows exactly why this word emerged. Many scholars think it is because women who were considered "overly sexual" by mainstream society were called "gay." Another reason may have been because "gay" already had an innocent definition meaning "lighthearted" or "fun." This meant it could be used by same-sex loving women and men as a "code word"—that is, a word they could use in public but only they would know the hidden meaning.

The word quickly became popular. In the 1938 Hollywood film *Bringing Up Baby*, the actor Cary Grant (who was bisexual) appears dressed in a woman's satin nightgown because he has lost his clothes. When he is asked why he is dressed this way, he jumps in the air and says, "I just went gay all of a sudden." The lesbian writer Gertrude Stein wrote a story in 1922 about two women who are in love. It was titled "Miss Furr and Miss Skeene," and in the story, Stein repeatedly uses the word "gay" to describe the characters' relationship. In 1968 activist Frank Kameny first used the phrase "Gay is good," and after the 1969 Stonewall riots, the word almost immediately became commonly used by gay and straight people and gradually by the media.

B IS FOR BI

The word "bisexual" is used to describe a person who is sexually and romantically attracted to both genders. People may feel this attraction their entire life or during stages of their life. They may act on it by becoming sexually involved with the object of their attraction, or not. Some bisexual people may be in a committed relationship with one person their entire life and yet attracted to people of the other gender; this does not make them less bisexual. Just as people may identify as heterosexual or homosexual and not necessarily act on that desire, the same is true of bisexual. The word "bisexual" was first used in English in 1892 and was mainly used by physicians, though it became more common during the twentieth century and was frequently used by people and in the media by the 1950s.

Human sexuality is complicated, and all people have the potential for a wide range of feelings and desires. Sigmund Freud, the father of psychoanalysis, noted this in 1905 in *Three Essays on the Theory of Sexuality*. Alfred Kinsey's scientific studies on male and female sexuality in the late 1940s and early 1950s empirically confirmed that large numbers of his interview subjects reported attractions to both genders. Today the word "bisexual" is commonly used, often interchangeably with the term "pansexual," which means a person who is attracted not to *two* genders but to all genders and sexes.

T IS FOR TRANS: GENDER AND SEXUALITY

Even today, in many places in America, any boy who does not act "like a boy" is assumed to be gay. Any girl who does not act "like a girl" is assumed to be lesbian. This is simply not true. Gender behavior is different than sexual preference.

Words such as "homosexual," "gay," and "lesbian" describe women's and men's sexual feelings and how they might act on them. Sexual feelings are complex, and people may experience a wide variety of feelings, which may change over time. This is separate from the complicated concept of gender.

Gender is not the same thing as sexual attraction. Gender is the whole range of behaviors that get associated with being a "man" or being a "woman." It includes how we think people should dress, what kinds of jobs they can do, how they should express emotions, even the kind of movies they are expected to like. The list of gender expectations is endless. They are so much a part of our society that we sometimes make the mistake of thinking they are "natural." (There's that word again.) They are not. They are just customs that have become a part of our society, and like all customs, they are constantly changing.

Here is the reality: most people do not fit into these simple categories. People possess a complex mix—and a broad range—of feelings, impulses, likes and dislikes, and ways of expressing themselves.

There have always been women who "acted like a man," who fought in battle or performed strenuous physical work. There have always men who "acted like a woman" and were caretakers to children or openly emotional when society told them not to be. There is no one way to "be a woman" or to "be a man." Again, gender is not the same thing as sexuality. Here are just two out of an infinite number of examples: Just because a man is extravagant with his hand gestures and interested in fashion does not mean he is gay. Just because a woman likes to play sports and use power tools does not mean she is lesbian.

Some people feel they were born in the wrong body. In the past these women and men might have dressed in the clothing of the "other sex" and even passed as the gender they knew they were. Since the twentieth century, with advances in medicine, these women and men have been able to undergo surgical and hormonal treatments to bring their bodies and identities into alignment.

As we have seen, gender is not a fixed binary—man or woman. Human beings are complex, and in spite of what Western society considers "normal," the ways they live and express themselves are too numerous to list here. The term "transgender" tries to cover this infinite variety. It was first commonly used in the 1990s to describe people who felt that they were not the sex or gender they were assigned at birth. Today it has become an umbrella term to include people who are not comfortable in either the male or female gender role. Some of these people may express their discomfort by cross-dressing, some by undergoing surgery to adjust their bodies to how they feel they should be, and some simply refuse to be classified with traditional gendered terms. Some people feel that traditional pronouns are outdated and don't apply to them. They don't feel they are a "he" or a "she" and instead want to be called "they." Others suggest inventing new pronouns, such as "ze" for "he" or "she," and "zir" for "him" or "her."

I have attempted to be very careful in this book to use pronouns that accurately describe an individual's gender identity. Publick Universal Friend renounced all pronouns and none are used, not even "they," which Friend did not use. Before he transitioned and became Christine Jorgensen, George Jorgensen used "he" to describe himself, and that is done here. "She" is used after the transition to Christine. Albert Cashier always referred to himself as "he." Holly Woodlawn, Sylvia Rivera, and Marsha P. Johnson predominantly used "she" through their adolescent and adult years, as I do here. Historical figures are not identified as transgender as that word did not exist at the time and they would not have been able to use it.

Q IS FOR QUEER

In June 1990, a group of women and men who called themselves Queer Nation passed out a flyer at the New York City Gay Pride March. The headline read "Queers Read This." Some gay people found this shocking because for many of them "queer" had always been used as a slur.

"Queer" was not always a negative term. From the sixteenth century to the early twentieth century, the word meant "quaint" or "odd," as in the title of Frances Eaton's 1888 children's book *A Queer Little Princess and Her Friends*.

One of the first recorded negative uses of "queer" relating to gay people was in an 1894 letter by the Marquess of Queensberry to the playwright Oscar Wilde (whose lover was Queensbury's son Alfred Douglas). Throughout much of the twentieth century "queer" was a very negative, hurtful word. What Queer Nation did in reclaiming the word was to say, "Call us what you want—we are proud of ourselves." This usage caught on, and for many people "queer" is now a powerful word of pride.

PEOPLE, NOT LABELS

Now that we have explored all the terms and words for LGBTQ people, we are going to throw those words out. The people you will meet in this book are all different; no two are alike. They are complicated and complex individuals. They can't be defined by a single word, especially since many of these words weren't invented when they were alive. So we're not going to get hung up about whether a particular person was gay or lesbian or bi or trans. Frequently we don't know the complete answer. As they say on social media, "It's complicated."

America is a complicated country. It was a new country in 1776 when it emerged and broke from the older cultures of Europe. Because it was new, there were endless possibilities, not just for the country as a whole but for the people, in all their amazing variety. The stories in this book represent just a handful of the many Americans who, for whatever reason, were not considered "normal." Each of these stories is a window into the many ways that America inspired LGBTQ people and how these people shaped America.

CHRISTINE JORGENSEN

George Jorgensen was born in 1926 in the Bronx, New York. Like most American men who were of age during World War II, he was drafted. The war ended in 1945, and he received an honorable discharge several years later. By 1950, George, who always knew he was a woman, began exploring how to physically transition to being female. He began taking hormones, and in 1952, he became the first American to have sex-reassignment surgery. The surgery took

Publicity photo of Christine Jorgensen after her "sex-reassignment" surgery.

(continues on next page)

(continued from previous page)

place in Copenhagen, and it was so new that the Danish government had to give the doctor special permission to perform the operation.

When Jorgensen returned to America, poised and very glamorous, and now going by the name Christine, she was met with amazement and doubt and, mostly, good-will. Jorgensen referred to herself, as did the media, as a "transsexual," although today we would probably use the term "transgender." In a 1970 interview she stated: "At first, I was very self-conscious and very awkward. But once the notoriety hit, it did not take me long to adjust." And she did.

Jorgensen, who remained private about her emotional and sexual life, became a nightclub performer and a very public figure. She opened minds in America and around the world to the idea that gender was not fixed. It was the first time most Americans had to consider that being a man or being a woman is about more than the body you have when you are born.

Jorgensen was the perfect spokesperson for how the world was changing. She once noted that she gave the sexual revolution "a good swift kick in the pants." She certainly did.

AMERICA

NEW BEGINNINGS, NEW IDENTITIES

1500–1860

CHAPTER ONE

NATIVE PEOPLES

Different Genders, Different Sexualities

The history of America does not start with the arrival of Europeans, and neither does the history of queer America. The Europeans described this continent as a "new world." Of course, it was only new to them. The Americas, North and South, were already home to numerous tribes of people who had rich, complex cultures, traditions, family structures, and gender identities.

The Pueblo Indians, for example, who lived in what we now call the state of New Mexico, had a very complex civilization. Women were responsible for home life, raising children, and cooking, while Pueblo men dealt with the outside world and were warriors. For women, taking care of the home also meant building them. Men were responsible for supplying the timbers while women mixed the adobe—a blend of earth and other materials—to build the walls.

Women weren't just responsible for household chores—they owned the homes and all of the household items, such as pots and blankets. The house and its belongings were passed down from mother to daughter. Women raised children. When a son got married, he went to live in his wife's mother's house.

The Pueblo traditions gave women a lot of freedom to control their own lives. Under Pueblo custom marriage was not "till death us do part." Couples only stayed together for as long as they wanted to, and often it was the woman who formed a relationship with another man. Traditionally, women chose their own sexual partners, and this freedom was respected by men. The Pueblo also engaged in a wide range of sexual relationships, including sex between women and between men. They accepted all sexual relationships among adults as not only good and holy but as part of nature. They also thought that the human body was sacred and saw little reason to cover it. They felt no shame in walking about their community wearing little, and sometimes no, clothing.

While the Pueblo had an accepting view of a wide range of sexual behavior, they did not have many traditions of *fluid* gender roles. However, many North American tribes did have fluid gender roles as part of their

FLUID GENDER ROLES: MORE THAN TWO

Most people think of gender as a *binary* choice: that there are only two genders, male and female. However, social scientists have come to recognize that in any society, there can be much more than an either/or choice. We now use the term "fluid" to reflect that gender is not fixed into two strict male and female roles; they exist in a whole range of behaviors that can combine different aspects of both.

It's important to remember that gender is not the same thing as sexuality. To give two simple examples: A girl can want to play football, be a police officer, or dress like a "tomboy" and still be sexually attracted to boys. A boy can like to wear makeup, want to be a dress designer, or love to cook and still be sexually attracted to girls. When we speak of gender roles, we are talking about the whole range of behaviors that our society associates with either men or women.

culture. That is, they understood and accepted that some men would act as women and some women would act as men.

In some North American societies, people who did not follow strict binary gender roles were held in great esteem and became religious leaders, shamans, or artisans. For example, anthropologist Will Roscoe notes that among the Crows, "men who dressed as women and specialized in women's work were accepted and sometimes honored; a woman who led men into battle and had four wives was a respected chief."

French explorers and missionaries referred to these women and men as "berdache." This European term is not only an insult but is also incorrect because it confuses sexuality with gender roles. Historians no longer use that word and instead try to use the language of specific tribes to describe people and their traditions. In the language used by the Navajo people, the word used to describe

We'Wha, a Zuni two-spirit person, giving a weaving demonstration, late 1800s.

A sketch depicting a ceremonial dance by a midwestern indigenous tribe in celebration of a two-spirit person, mid-1800s.

individuals of nonbinary gender is "nádleehi." For Mojave people, who speak a variant of the Yuman language (shared by a number of tribes), the word used is "alyha." At a 1994 international anthropology conference held in Chicago, the term "two-spirit" was overwhelmingly agreed upon by indigenous lesbians and gay men.

It is important to remember that there were and are many different Native American tribes with different languages and cultures. It would be wrong to make general statements about all indigenous people and their attitudes towards gender roles. However, it is fair to say that the European explorers, settlers, and missionaries who arrived here almost universally misunderstood what they were seeing when they encountered these tribes. They primarily saw Native Americans through the prejudices and customs they brought with them.

Missionaries found it particularly disturbing that some native cultures allowed women degrees of sexual equality. They were surprised and confused to find that women held any power in society and were often engaged in physical activities such as building houses and, in some tribes, even participating in warfare. Coming from countries in which women's sexual behavior was strictly controlled and officially allowed only within marriage, missionaries found the sexual freedom among tribes not only alarming but sinful. They were also upset at what they considered the lack of modesty among various Native American tribes, of women and men not being fully clothed, as was the European fashion. Missionaries thought this was unnatural and immoral. For the Europeans, the most extreme example of the immorality of native people were the women and men who dressed and behaved, in the missionaries' eyes, as the other sex.

The Europeans tried to impose their own views on native people. For example, Spanish missionary Alonso de Benavides tried to convert the Pueblo to Catholicism. Benavides and his fellow Europeans insisted that to be true Christians the Pueblo had to cover their bodies, give up all sexual activity that was not heterosexual, commit to monogamous marriages, and limit the power women had over their own lives and in society.

Sometimes the indigenous people agreed to this; often they were forced to do so through violence. For example, Pietro Martire d'Anghiera, an Italian historian who documented the military campaigns of Spanish explorers, reported that the explorer Vasco Núñez de Balboa had vicious mastiffs rip apart forty Panamanian men dressed as women who were having sex with other men.

The invasion of European missionaries and explorers, and their terrible treatment of indigenous people, has been well-documented. In the context of queer history, it was the beginning of a tragic pattern that repeated throughout the history of the United States. Again and again, women and men who do not fit the appropriate gender roles, who do not behave in ways that the majority dictates, and who engage in any sexual activities or attractions outside of heterosexual marriage are punished, often severely, denied their basic human rights, and cast out from society.

EUROPEAN MISSIONARIES

Europeans repeatedly made connections—or, rather, jumped to wrong conclusions—between indigenous people's (real and imagined) sexual practices and equated them to European ideas about sin. Jacques Marquette, French Jesuit, noted in his journals of 1673–1677, on his first voyage down the Mississippi, of the native peoples he met:

> Their garments consist only of skins; the women are always clad very modestly and very becomingly, while the men do not take the trouble to cover themselves. [. . .] Some Il[l]inois, as well as some Nadouessi, while still young, assume the garb of women, and retain it throughout their lives. [. . .] They never marry and glory in demeaning themselves to do everything that the women do. They go to war, however, but can use only clubs, and not bows and arrows, which are the weapons proper to men.

(continues on next page)

(continued from previous page)

In a diary from his 1775 trip to what is now California, the Franciscan missionary Pedro Font described how many Christian Europeans viewed indigenous cross-dressing figures. He is also very clear in his intention to change them.

Among the women I saw some men dressed like women, with whom they go about regularly, never joining the men. [. . .] From this I inferred they must be hermaphrodites, but from what I learned later I understood that they were sodomites, dedicated to nefarious practices. From all the foregoing I conclude that in this matter of incontinence there will be much to do when the Holy Faith and the Christian religion are established among them.

CHAPTER TWO

THOMAS MORTON

Free Love Among the Puritans?

It was a beautiful, cloudless spring day in 1627. The harsh New England winter had ended weeks earlier, and the land was now covered with rapidly growing plants, leafing and budding, covering the land in green. Thomas Morton and his friends had a long day ahead of them. They planned to erect an eighty-foot maypole on a hill in their newly formed colony of Merrymount.

Merrymount—the name is a play on words: merriment on the mountain—was located in what we now call Quincy, just a few miles away from Boston, the most populous center of the Massachusetts Bay Colony. The maypole was an old European tradition of welcoming in the spring and had roots in pagan cultures. This one was to be erected on a hill that could be seen by ships at sea, ships that were important to the colonists' business of trading animal furs. Morton and his men nailed the horns of a buck to the top of the maypole and festooned it with ribbons. Traditionally, people would dance around the maypole holding the ribbons, but in this case, they were more decorative, since the eighty-foot pole—as high as a modern multistory building—was far taller than the usual eight feet.

During that week Morton and his fellow colonists—including native people of the Wampanoag Confederation—did dance around the maypole, drinking, partying, and singing songs. They celebrated the Roman goddess Flora, who was thought to usher in springtime and also could guarantee successful pregnancies for people and their animals. This celebration did not please everyone.

William Bradford, the governor of Plymouth Colony (the place where the Pilgrims had landed seven years earlier), wrote that Morton and others engaged in "ye beastly practices of ye mad Bacchanalians." "Bacchanalians" refers to Bacchus, the Roman god of wine, drinking, sexual activity, and fertility. We don't know exactly what made Bradford upset. Was he talking about sexual activity or just a rowdy drinking party with lots of joking and laughing? During the week of festivities, Morton declared himself a "Lord of Misrule." "Misrule" was an

The Merrymount maypole festivities, 1627.

old medieval custom, one that gave people the freedom to behave, for short periods of time, in ways they might not otherwise, including various forms of usually forbidden sexuality. This may have included male same-sex behavior. We know that the men danced hand-in-hand around the maypole and that Morton described them as "Ganymede and Jupiter." This was a reference to the myth that the god Jupiter transformed himself into an eagle and snatched the young man Ganymede to Mount Olympus to be his lover.

Whatever their sexuality, the colonists at Merrymount were not simply having a good time. Their partying was an extraordinary departure from—a revolt against—the way most Bay colonists lived. It was also a challenge to the Pilgrims' views about proper conduct and morality. It certainly goes against our common view of the Puritans' society as religiously strict and harshly controlled.

To understand why Thomas Morton founded Merrymount—and why it quickly came under attack and was disbanded—we need to understand a little about how people thought about sexuality, culture, and religion in sixteenth-century England under Queen Elizabeth I.

This Elizabethan period was, despite what was taught in the churches of the time, quite open-minded. The popular plays of William Shakespeare were filled with suggestive sexual humor. A wide range of sexual behaviors was tolerated and even accepted. Christopher Marlowe, a noted playwright and poet, openly discussed his sexual activity with men and was widely quoted as saying, "All they that love not tobacco and boys were fools." Although homosexual activity between men was illegal, these laws—which were also the laws of the colonies and later were adapted by the American states—were only selectively enforced. Gender roles were also fairly loose, and women were allowed more economic and social freedom than in the past.

Elizabeth's father, Henry VIII, broke away from the Roman Catholic Church because the pope would not grant him a divorce from his first wife. When this split occurred, Henry started the Church of England, making himself its head. This was also a time of great religious upheaval throughout Europe, with many Christians splitting from the Catholic Church and starting new Protestant denominations. This period, spanning the 1500s and early 1600s, is called the Protestant Reformation.

Some in England felt that the tenets of Henry's church were still too similar to those of Roman Catholicism. Like many Protestants, they longed for a more simple and direct relationship with God, one not controlled, or directed by church officials. Because they desired a more "pure" church, they were called Puritans.

Puritans were very unhappy with the openness and sexual freedom of Elizabethan culture. They would not go to the theater, public fairs, or festivals nor go to taverns to drink. This put them in a minority in England, and their religious views were barely tolerated. So the Puritans, like the Quakers and other English Protestant sects, went to North America, where they could freely practice their religion.

The Pilgrims, who were members of a stricter form of puritanism, planned to live according to the most severe rules of Protestantism and to create what they saw as a truly righteous society here on earth. When they came to the Bay Colony, in present-day Massachusetts, the Pilgrims attempted to create their ideal society and passed many laws governing belief and everyday life. These included strict laws against any kind of differences in sexual or gender norms. Homosexual relationships were strictly forbidden. Cross-dressing or any behavior that didn't fit society's norm—including marriage to non-Puritan people or people of other races—was forbidden and could be punished.

Thomas Morton, a trader and lawyer, sailed to Plymouth, from England in 1624, with his friend Captain Richard Wollaston. We don't know why they picked that colony, but we do know that when they arrived, the two men quickly found that they could not get along with the Puritans. Morton, Wollaston, and other men with them had different views that were less strict. They quickly left Plymouth Colony and in 1625 founded Merrymount. After a short time, Morton and Wollaston had a falling out because Wollaston believed in slavery and Morton did not.

Life at Merrymount was about as different from that of Plymouth as it could be. Morton and his friends freed their indentured servants (servants who had to pay off the price of their journey to America by working for a certain number of years) and treated them as equals. This was seen by the Puritans as foolish, possibly sinful. Morton and his friends also befriended the local Wampanoag tribe, whose culture they admired. The Merrymount residents urged intermarriage between native women and male colonists, something strictly forbidden not only by Puritans but by most Europeans.

When, in 1627, the colonists erected the eighty-foot-
tall maypole, here's how Morton described his celebra-
tions (his spelling is changed here to our modern usage):

> They brought the Maypole to the place appointed,
> with drums, guns, pistols and other fitting instruments,
> for that purpose; and there erected it with the help of
> Savages, that came thither . . . to see the manner of
> our Revels. A goodly pine tree of 80 foot long was
> reared up, with a pair of buckshorns nailed on, some-
> what near unto the top of it: where it stood, as a fair
> sea mark.

THE END OF MERRYMOUNT

Governor Bradford was furious at the founding of
Merrymount. After a second maypole celebration,
in 1628, his troops attacked Merrymount and arrested
Morton, who was brought back to Plymouth and put
in the stocks—restraints made of wood that were used
for public punishment and humiliation—there. Then, in
1629, Morton was sent back to England. Bradford and
the Puritans understood that life at Merrymount—which
presented people with a freer way of living—was a threat
to their dream of a strict religious colony. That threat had
to be stamped out. After Morton's exile, Merrymount
survived for a year, but it was finally destroyed by the
Puritans, and its community dispersed. In 1637 Morton published a book called *The New English Canaan*,
three volumes that mapped out a utopian vision of how

the new colonies might be organized along the lines of Merrymount.

Thomas Morton's vision lasted only a short time before the civic and church leaders crushed it. Throughout history, societies have made laws that pushed aside and persecuted groups considered to be "unclean." When societies feel that they are in danger from outside, unclean forces, they tend to group together and become stronger. Historians call this the theory of the "persecuting society."

Merrymount lasted a very short time. Yet the *idea* of Merrymount—that there can be a place of more personal, sexual, racial, and economic freedom and equality—has always been present in the United States and is with us today as well.

WHAT IS MEANT BY "SODOMITE"?

From the Middle Ages onward, in Europe and later in colonial America, a man who had sex with another man was called a "sodomite." "Sodomy," a word derived from Sodom, a city in the Bible, was considered a sin and became an illegal act. The Italian Renaissance artist Leonardo da Vinci was accused of being a sodomite in 1476. In America during the colonial era, antisodomy laws were passed that prohibited sex between members of the same sex. In 1982 Michael Hardwick, a gay man in Atlanta, Georgia, was charged with sodomy and fought his conviction to the Supreme Court. He lost, but the decision was reversed in 2003 in *Lawrence v. Texas*.

CHAPTER THREE

JEMIMA WILKINSON

The Surprising Life
of Publick Universal Friend

At age eighteen Jemima Wilkinson dedicated herself to religion. Born in 1752, in Cumberland, Rhode Island, she attended Quaker meetings with her family and also went to the more mainline Protestant New Light Baptist church. Through dedicated studying, she became well-versed in both the Hebrew scriptures and the Gospels.

In 1776 the warship *Columbus* docked in Providence, bringing with it the often deadly disease typhus, which Wilkinson caught. Like many infected people, she developed a high fever and became very ill. As frequently happens with a high fever, Wilkinson had visions. Her visions were religious in nature. She saw "archangels, descending from the East, with golden crowns upon their heads [proclaiming] room, room, room in the many mansions of eternal glory for thee!"

We do not know whether Wilkinson's vision was truly mystical or the result of a fevered hallucination. But when she recovered from typhus, Wilkinson had changed. She told her friends and family that Jemima Wilkinson had died and that she was a new person, neither male nor female. She took the name "Publick Universal Friend."

From that day onward, Friend refused to use the self-describing words "she" or "he."

Instead of women's clothing, Publick Universal Friend chose to wear long robes like a priest or monk. The robes hid the body underneath, and in them, Friend looked like neither a man nor a woman. Newspaper accounts of the time show that most people thought Friend was a man.

One of the few existing images of Publick Universal Friend in robes, late 1700s.

Publick Universal Friend began to preach a message of universal friendship, speaking out against slavery and alcohol and urging everyone, even married couples, to refrain from sex. A tall impressive figure with a strong voice, Friend had absolute faith in these beliefs. Friend's sermons were reported on and published in newspapers, leading to fame and inspiring a following of well-educated men and women. Writers at the time still wondered if Friend was male or female, although the many people who listened to and followed Friend did not seem to care.

Perhaps Friend's refusal to be seen as male or female was what attracted followers from throughout Rhode Island, Pennsylvania, and Massachusetts. Many people loved Publick Universal Friend, whom they saw as a messenger from God. However, others found Friend's message and gender-free appearance disturbing, and on at least one occasion, they confronted Friend in the street.

After a decade of preaching, Publick Universal Friend decided to start a colony, named Jerusalem, in central New York State—a place where "no Intruding foot could set." So, in 1788, Friend and followers set out for land west of the Genesee River in New York. At that time, most of northern New York was home to the Haudenosaunee Confederacy (sometimes called the Iroquois). Friend had no worries about relations with Native Americans and befriended them. Preaching universal love and tolerance, Friend and Friend's followers supported many of the Native people's basic rights and stood with them against other colonists by insisting that signed treaties be honored. The Native Americans called Friend the "Great Woman Preacher."

Ironically, Publick Universal Friend's success became a problem. The colony did so well at building and farming that more and more unbelievers came to share the wealth. Because of the prohibition on sexual activity, the colony had no new children. Slowly, the religious colony dwindled as Publick Universal Friend's followers died. Friend died in 1819.

Publick Universal Friend appeared at a pivotal moment in American history, right in the middle of the American Revolution and the start of a new country. The United States was evolving and growing in exciting ways, and gender roles were also changing. For many men, this meant highlighting aspects of traditional, heterosexual masculinity. The image of the frontier woodsman or the revolutionary fighter was an important identity to separate American men from what they saw as the "sissified" British man. Daniel Boone, a former Revolutionary War soldier whose exploits as a hunter, trapper, and explorer became folklore, exemplified the rugged "new" American man.

For women, changing gender roles often meant exploring new, more independent ways of behaving. Abigail Adams, the wife of Founding Father John Adams, for example, ran the family farm, invested their money, conducted the family business (and raised the children) when he was at the Continental Congress, the group of delegates from each colony that governed the newly formed United States during the Revolution. Women were free to enter political debates and sign petitions.

Publick Universal Friend viewed gender in a totally different way, by breaking out of the traditional expectations. Being "neither male nor female," Friend felt free to behave without meeting the gender expectations of the time. Publick Universal Friend preached and practiced sexual abstinence, so the words "homosexual," "gay," or even "queer" do not apply. All we know of Friend is through the preaching and writing. It would be inaccurate to use any modern terms here in a description.

How can we think about Friend's gender? What words do we use? Words are important. In the case of Friend, the lack of language is also important. Words not only express what we want to communicate but also influence how we think and how we see and construct the world around us. We all feel we know what the word "red" means: we can see the color in our minds. On the other hand, it is not as simple as that. There are many words for different shades of red—"crimson," "carmine," "scarlet," "rose," "ruby," "vermillion," "cardinal," "claret"—all of which are similar yet distinctly different. The same is true for how we think about people and gender. It might be useful to think of Friend's gender as a shade of gender and—as Friend's followers did—not worry too much about it.

We don't know if any of Friend's followers followed Friend's gender-free example. We can guess, based on diaries and letters, that large numbers of people were intrigued with the idea that gender was not fixed. Maybe they understood that the traditional ideas about gender were limiting. Or maybe they were fascinated by the idea that someone could be as bold to break from firmly established conventions. Perhaps in this new country, where so much seemed possible, the traditional limits of gender were also up for reinvention.

Publick Universal Friend's life and ministry spanned the years at the very beginning of the United States. For many colonists, political freedom meant freedom from the British Crown. It meant not paying taxes to the king, and it meant being able to make your own laws. For some people, though, like Friend, it meant the freedom to break out of the usual roles in which society placed you.

DEBORAH SAMPSON

Patriot, Soldier, Gender Rebel

Deborah Sampson (sometimes spelled Samson) was born in 1760, eight years after Publick Universal Friend, in a small town outside Plymouth, Massachusetts. She was the oldest of seven children. Sampson's family was poor, and like many female children, she worked at jobs that were considered appropriate for young women. Growing up she worked as a servant, taught school in the summer, and wove fabric in the winter.

In 1781, when she was twenty years old, Sampson struck out on a different path. She was fairly tall—five foot nine, when most women were five feet tall—and realizing that she could pass for a man, she began dressing as one, calling herself Robert Shurtleff.

The American Revolution was nearing its climax, but fighting was still going on. The next spring, Sampson, at age twenty-one, enlisted in the Light Infantry Company of Captain George Webb's Fourth Massachusetts Regiment. Very soon after, her regiment was called to protect the Hudson Highlands at West Point in New York from the British. Sampson fought bravely in her first battle by the banks of the Hudson River near the area known as the Tappan Zee, where the river widens. During the battle, Sampson was wounded by a British saber but refused to

An engraving of Deborah Sampson in *The Female Review*, 1797.

be treated, knowing that a doctor would quickly discover she was a woman. She dressed her own wound and went back into battle.

A few weeks later, in another battle, Sampson was wounded again. This time, she was hit in the leg by two musket balls. Her comrades insisted that she go to the hospital, but Sampson managed to fool the doctors by showing them her old saber wound. She dug one of the musket balls out of her own leg and recovered.

After their battles in New York, Sampson's regiment was sent to Philadelphia. There, she worked briefly for General Henry Knox until she became sick with a high fever. Once again, she was taken to the hospital. This time, she was unconscious and a Dr. Binney discovered, to his surprise, that this brave soldier was not a man.

Dr. Binney explained the situation to General Knox. The general told his commanding officer who, finally, told General George Washington. All these men agreed that though they thought women should not serve in battle, they also believed that Sampson was a fine soldier and a patriot. General Washington ordered that Sampson should be honorably discharged. She was asked to leave the army but was given high praise for her service. In 1783 Sampson was presented with letters from three generals praising her career as a soldier. Before leaving the military, she put on a dress and stood with General John Patterson as the Fourth Infantry marched in review.

Sampson was denied her army salary because she was a woman. In 1792 she petitioned the Commonwealth of Massachusetts for it, and was granted the money. Governor John Hancock even wrote a declaration that stated: "Deborah Sampson exhibited an extraordinary instance of feminine heroism by discharging the duties of a faithful, gallant soldier, and at the same time preserving the virtue and chastity of her sex unsuspected and unblemished and was discharged from the service with a fair and honorable character."

Two years after leaving the military, Sampson married Benjamin Gannett, a farmer from Sharon, Massachusetts, and had three children. She lived quietly with her family until 1797. While Sampson was proud of her service as a soldier, she was frustrated because, unlike her fellow male soldiers, she was not allowed to receive her military pension (money paid to soldiers who were honorably discharged from the army).

Herman Mann, a writer and educator, heard of Sampson's tale and of her frustrations. Together, they wrote and published the story of her adventures as a soldier as *The Female Review: Life of Deborah Sampson, the Female Soldier in the War of the Revolution*. The book was based on Sampson's life as a soldier, but much of it was fiction. Sampson and Herman Mann intended for it to be an exciting story—the public was fascinated by a woman soldier dressed as a man—and its purpose was to gain public support for Sampson's attempts to be awarded her military pension. Many people thought she deserved the money, as well as the honor, including Revolutionary War hero Paul Revere.

In 1802, Sampson began giving a series of lectures about her life to promote her case against the army's decision to deny her pension. She always began her lectures by announcing—no doubt to make some audience members comfortable with her gender masquerade—that she couldn't explain why she chose to cross-dress and join the Continental army. She also praised traditional gender roles for women. Yet, at the end of every presentation she would exit the stage and return dressed in her army uniform and then proceed to do a series of complicated and difficult military drills.

Sampson's lectures were extremely popular in Boston and throughout New England. They, along with her book, gained her the support she needed to gain her pension. In 1816, after more than fifteen years of petitioning, Deborah Sampson Gannett was finally awarded the pension she sought from Congress.

Sampson died in 1827. Her grave is in Sharon, Massachusetts. On one side of her tombstone is written "Deborah, wife of Benjamin Gannett, died April 29, 1827, aged 68 years." On the other side of the stone is written "Deborah Sampson Gannett, Robert Shurtleff, the Female Soldier, Service 1781–1783."

Years after Sampson's death, her husband petitioned for pay as the spouse of a deceased soldier. His petition was granted. The Congressional Committee on Revolutionary Pensions wrote that it "believe[s]" it is "warranted in saying that the whole history of the American

Revolution records no case like this, and furnishes no other similar example of female heroism, fidelity and courage . . . [and] there cannot be a parallel case in all time to come."

Sampson's family was descended from the Pilgrims who arrived in America on the *Mayflower*. (Her mother was a great-granddaughter of Governor Bradford, who dismantled Merrymount.) In 1906 the Daughters of the American Revolution, a very politically conservative group made up of *Mayflower* descendants, created a plaque in Sampson's honor. They also started up a chapter of the DAR in Brockton, Massachusetts, called the Deborah Sampson Chapter. In 1944 the US Navy commissioned a battleship named the SS *Deborah Sampson Gannett*. In 1983 Sampson was declared a Massachusetts State Heroine by Michael Dukakis, the state's governor.

■ ■ ■

Publick Universal Friend (born Jemima Wilkinson) and Deborah Sampson deliberately chose to behave in extremely "unwomanly" ways. They were not alone. When it came to gender and relationships, many of America's founding fathers and founding mothers behaved in ways that were outside of the mainstream. As we've seen, gender and sexuality are not the same. After serving in the army as a man, Deborah Sampson married a man and had children and lived as woman. There is no evidence that she had homosexual relationships.

The terms we use today for LGBTQ people did not exist back in 1781. If we had to choose a word to describe Deborah Sampson, we might choose "queer." This term is used today with pride as an umbrella term for anyone who does not fit into mainstream rules about sexuality or gender.

Deborah Sampson never heard the word "queer" used in that way, nor did anyone else at the time. However, there is value in using it to describe her, because it helps us understand that throughout history there have been people who did not fit into the molds society tried to force them into. Deborah Sampson certainly was one of those people, and in that sense, she certainly was queer.

CHAPTER FIVE

NINETEENTH-CENTURY ROMANTIC FRIENDSHIPS

BFFs or Friends with Benefits?

When we think about LGBTQ history—or any history—we rarely think about friendship. We all know what friendship means today. There are varieties of friendships: close friends, fast friends, work friends, school friends, best friends, casual friends, childhood friends, BFFs, ex-friends. In the seventeenth, eighteenth, and nineteenth centuries, there was a type of friendship we no longer have. It was called "romantic friendship." Understanding these relationships is key to grasping the full scope of relationships in the eighteenth and nineteenth centuries.

In the 1800s, women and men often did not mix in public. They tended to exist in social worlds that revolved around their own gender. Women, for example, were not allowed in many public places, such as bars, and generally were not allowed in restaurants, in theaters, or at public lectures without a male escort. Women were expected to occupy what was called "the domestic sphere." This was the home itself, as well as anything related to family and children. Men often socialized with one another in men's clubs, work spaces, and the military. Working-class women and men often had fewer restrictions on their

Two men enjoying each other's company, 1800s.

behavior—women, for example, often had to work to help support their families—but even their social worlds were still constructed around gendered norms.

Because of this strict social separation, it was difficult for women and men to form friendships with each other. That is one reason they often formed intense friendships with people of the same gender. These friendships were so close that to our modern eyes they seem like they must have been sexual relationships. A romantic friendship may or may not have involved sexual attraction or interaction. It may have just been a very close friendship, or it may, indeed, have been a sexual relationship. Often we have no way of knowing if it did or not.

We can easily find evidence of "romantic friendships" in the lives of both famous and everyday people. Historians have uncovered—in letters and diaries—extensive, complex networks of friendships in the eighteenth and nineteenth centuries. Some of these documents could easily be mistaken by modern readers as love letters. In a sense they were; love does not always mean sex.

For example, in the early 1800s, Eunice Callender of Boston, lovingly wrote many letters to her cousin and friend Sarah Ripley:

> Breathe forth the sentiments of my soul. [. . .] Oh could you see what rapture . . . all of your epistles are open'd by me . . . then would you acknowledge that my Friendship at least equals your own, and yours I believe is as true as a flame as ever warmed the breast of any human Creature.

Were Callender and Ripley in love? Or did they just love each other as friends? We don't know. We do know that Ripley married later in life and that Callender, judging from her diary entries, was a deeply religious woman.

This passionate language was common in male romantic friendships as well. In 1804 the twenty-two-year-old Daniel Webster, who later became a famous lawyer, US senator, and statesman, wrote to his college classmate James Harvey Bigham:

> Yes, James, I must come; we will yoke together again; your little bed is just wide enough; we will practice at the same bar, and be as friendly a pair of single fellows as ever cracked a nut.

Webster married a woman later in life, and there is no evidence that he and Bigham were lovers. There is also no proof they were not. The fact that they shared a bed is not proof one way or another. It was a common practice for same-sex friends or mere acquaintances to share beds throughout the 1700s and 1800s.

Beginning in the later 1700s, it was perfectly acceptable for friendships between women and between men to be intense and deeply committed. They could express their devotion and love for one another in the most passionate language, and we would be wrong to assume this implied a sexual relationship.

Such an intense friendship can be seen in the letters of the Marquis de Lafayette and George Washington. Washington, as you know, led the Continental army in the fight for independence from Great Britain and was the first president of the United States. Today he is revered as a principled and heroic figure.

Gilbert du Motier de Lafayette was the teenage son of a French aristocrat, and his title was marquis. As was customary for male French nobility, the marquis was educated by tutors and became an officer in the king's army at the age of thirteen. In 1775, at the age of eighteen, Lafayette heard about Washington and his army at a dinner party. As an idealistic young man who believed in democracy, he made the decision to fight with the colonists against the British. Because his family was powerful and had many connections, Lafayette was able to make his dream come true. Two years later he landed in America, now as a major general of the French army.

At first, Washington, who was forty-five, saw this young Frenchman as an annoyance. However, he quickly became fond of Lafayette and admired the younger man's intelligence and bravery. Within a month, Lafayette and a small group of Washington's closest military staff were living at Washington's home in Mount Vernon. Lafayette became one of Washington's close aides and rode alongside the general when reviewing the troops. Later, when

Gilbert du Motier, the Marquis de Lafayette, as a lieutenant general, late 1700s.

George Washington after victory at the Battle of Princeton during the Revolutionary War, late 1700s.

Lafayette was wounded at the Battle of Brandywine, Washington sent his personal doctor to care for him. Soon after, Washington himself nursed Lafayette back to health. Lafayette spent the winter of 1778 with Washington at the Valley Forge encampment and then returned to his homeland to ask his fellow French citizens to support the fight for American independence.

What was this friendship all about? Was it, as some historians say, a father-son relationship? Or was there a romantic or sexual connection? We know that both men were married and that Lafayette had children. We also know that they were very close throughout their lives.

On June 12, 1799, many years after he had left America, Lafayette wrote to Washington:

> My Dear General, [. . .] There never was a friend, my
> dear general, so much, so tenderly beloved, as I love
> and respect you: happy in our union, in the pleasure
> of living near to you, in the pleasing satisfaction of
> partaking every sentiment of your heart, every event
> of your life, I have taken such a habit of being insepa-
> rable from you, that I cannot now accustom myself to
> your absence, and I am more and more afflicted at that
> enormous distance which keeps me so far from my
> dearest friend.

Like any relationship, "romantic friendships" could be complicated and not always smooth, as we see in this letter, written a few months after the previous one, from Lafayette to Washington.

> My dear general . . .
>   From those happy ties of friendship By which
> you were pleas'd to unite yourself with me, from the
> promises You So tenderly made me when we parted
> at [F]ishkill, I had Such expectations of hearing often
> from you, that Complaint ought to be permitted to
> my affectionate heart—not a line from you, my dear
> General, is yet arriv'd into My hands. [. . .] My
> ardent hopes of Getting at length a letter from Gen-
> eral Washington . . . have ever been unhappily disap-
> pointed. [. . .] Let me Beseech you, my dear General,
> By that mutual, tender and experienced friendship, in
> which I have put An immense part of My happiness, to

be very exact in inquiring for occasions, and Never to Miss these which may Convey to me letters that I will be so much pleas'd to Receive. . . .

Oh, My dear General, how happy I would be to embrace you again! With Such an affection as is above all expressions any language may furnish I have the honor to be very Respectfully My Good and Beloved General Your Affectionate friend

Lafayette

Today, Lafayette's second letter to Washington reads to us like a note from a hurt lover. We have no definite evidence that George Washington and the Marquis de Lafayette were involved as lovers—nor evidence that they were not. Did they just have a deep emotional friendship? Are there sexual overtones here? Clearly, Lafayette's relationship with America's first president was emotionally intense.

Lafayette named his only son Georges Washington, and when Lafayette was buried, in France, he requested that his grave be filled with soil from Washington's estate at Mt. Vernon.

We also must remember that Washington and Lafayette were soldiers who served together and were united by their strong feelings about democracy and their common cause. This is another reason their friendship was so intense.

■ ■ ■

The 1700s and 1800s are a very long time ago. Our lives today are both more, and less, complicated, and our customs and expressions of emotion are different from those of that time. The contemporary idea of the nonsexual "bromances" describes a closeness between men. But would they write letters to one another such as Lafayette wrote to Washington? Women, in our culture today, are allowed more freedom to express their emotions. They may be able to write letters that resemble Eunice Callender's to Sarah Ripley. It is important to look for similarities to the past, and as important to be mindful of the differences. If we are careful, we may be able to learn from these letters something of how people felt and acted hundreds of years ago, and what that means to us today.

CHAPTER SIX

THE MYSTERY
OF EMILY DICKINSON

Passionate Attachments
and Independent Women

E mily Dickinson is one of America's most famous poets. Yet in her lifetime, and for many years later, no one outside her family circle and a small number of friends knew her name or her work. Few of her poems were published during her life. (She died at age fifty-five, in 1886.) The poems that were published by her family after her death were radically changed in ways that hid their meanings, truly original style, and even content. In 1955, when scholars had restored the poems, readers could see Dickinson's original vision. Only in the late 1960s did people began understanding that some of her poems and letters were clearly about intimacy and sexual desire between women. Today, Dickinson is regarded as one of the greatest American poets.

Emily Dickinson was born in 1830—half a century after the end of the Revolutionary War and over thirty years before the Civil War began. The Dickinson family had come over to America with the earliest Puritan settlers in the mid-1600s. They were moderately well off and respected in their town of Amherst, Massachusetts.

Emily's grandfather was the primary founder of Amherst College, which today is still a very prestigious liberal arts school. Her father, Edward, was the treasurer of the college and a state legislator for many years. Her mother, Emily Norcross, was highly educated and suffered from bouts of depression. Dickinson had two siblings, William Austin and Lavinia, and they lived in a large family home—some in Amherst even called it a mansion—overlooking the Amherst cemetery.

Dickinson was a well-behaved child who loved music. She and her siblings were well educated, but there was something different about Emily. She was called "melancholiac" (we might now use the term "depressed") in her teen years, and by the age of twenty she began exhibiting some peculiarities. She became increasingly reclusive, rarely leaving the house. At the same time, her mind and poetry began to thrive.

She wrote many poems and letters to people, and in particular to Susan, or Sue, Gilbert, a family friend with whom she was extremely close. Sue Gilbert was well educated, a mathematician, and a teacher. She wrote poems, essays, and biographies, and was considered one of the most intellectually sophisticated women in western Massachusetts. In 1856 Gilbert married Dickinson's brother, Austin. Dickinson's feelings for her were deep, loving, and probably complicated.

In 1852 Dickinson wrote to Gilbert:

June 11, 1852

Susie, forgive me Darling, for every word I say—my heart is full of you, none other than you in my thoughts, yet when I seek to say to you something not for the world, words fail me. If you were here—and Oh that you were, my Susie, we need not talk at all, our eyes would whisper for us, and your hand fast in mine, we would not ask for language—I try to bring you nearer, I chase the weeks away till they are quite departed, and fancy you have come, and I am on my way through the green lane to meet you, and my heart goes scampering so, that I have much ado to bring it back again, and learn it to be patient, till that dear Susie comes.

Gilbert was very supportive of Dickinson's writing, and the two corresponded frequently. Dickinson wrote over three hundred letters to Gilbert, even though for some time they lived next door to each other. Eventually, Gilbert pulled away from Dickinson. Perhaps Dickinson expected too much from their friendship. At the same time, Gilbert's marriage to Austin was unhappy. (In 1880 Austin began a very public affair with the younger Mabel Loomis Todd.)

A few years later, in 1859, Dickinson met Kate Scott Turner, an old school friend of Sue Gilbert. Turner was a widow whose husband had died after only a year and a half of marriage. Dickinson and Turner quickly became deeply attached. For several years they had a relationship in which Turner traveled frequently and then visited Emily in Amherst. While she was away, Dickinson wrote her poems and letters. In these letters Dickinson worried incessantly that she and Kate were not as close as she wanted them to be.

During this time Dickinson withdrew almost completely from the world, spending more and more time alone in her room. She also began dressing only in white

A daguerreotype possibly of Emily Dickinson (left) and her friend Kate Scott Turner, c. 1859.

and wearing her hair in an old-fashioned style. At the same time, she was incredibly productive as a poet. Between 1858 and 1865 Dickinson wrote more than eight hundred poems, which were only discovered after her death. In all, she wrote over 1,800 poems during her life.

Some of these poems were love poems, prompted by her affection for either Sue Gilbert or Kate Turner. It's clear that Dickinson's emotional and sensual attraction to these women was her artistic inspiration. Here's one:

> *Her sweet Weight on my Heart a Night*
> *Had scarcely deigned to lie—*
> *When, stirring, for Belief's delight,*
> *My Bride had slipped away—*

If 'twas a Dream—made solid—just
The Heaven to confirm—
Or if Myself were dreamed of Her—
The power to presume—

With Him remain—who unto Me—
Gave—even as to All—
A Fiction superseding Faith—
By so much—as 'twas real—
    (poem number 518; written circa 1862)

Turner was very attached to Dickinson and carried one of her letters with her until her death. In 1866 Turner married John Hone Anthon and then visited Dickinson infrequently. In 1860 Dickinson wrote to Turner:

Distinctly sweet your face stands in its phantom niche—
I touch your hand—my cheek your cheek—I stroke
your vanished hair, Why did you enter, sister, since you
must depart? Had not its heart been torn enough but
you must send your shred? Oh, our condor Kate! Come
from your crags again! Oh: Dew upon the bloom fall yet
again a summer's night! Of such have been the frauds
which have vanquished faces—sown plant by plant the
church-yard plats and occasioned angels.

Much of Emily Dickinson's life is shrouded in mystery. Why did she keep to herself? Why did she wear white? Why did she share so few poems with others, even her family? What exactly were her relationships with Gilbert and Turner? Was she in love with them? Did she want to be in a sexual relationship with them?

What is clear is that she had a passionate attachment to both of these women. I don't use contemporary language to describe people throughout history as that would be historically inaccurate. At the time, some people used the word "sapphist" to describe a woman who experienced same-sex female attraction, but the word "lesbian" was not in use. However she may have thought of herself, Emily Dickinson was certainly a woman who loved other women.

Maybe Emily Dickinson withdrew from society so that she could have complete freedom of the imagination. Perhaps, with no one looking over her shoulder, she felt able to express the full range of her feelings and her desires. That she turned to other women for the inspiration tells us of the importance of same-sex attraction not only in her work but in the nineteenth-century culture of romantic friendships.

We can also say with certainty that Emily Dickinson, Susan Gilbert, and Kate Scott Turner Anthon were all remarkable women. Dickinson was a brilliant poet, and Gilbert and Anthon traveled, wrote poems, essays, commentary, and biographies, and were engaged with the world. For women in mid-nineteenth-century America, the world was opening in new ways, yet it was still closed in others.

They lived in a country that did not grant them full rights—women could not vote until 1920, when the Nineteenth Amendment was passed. It was illegal in some states for married women to own property or to freely dispose of their own inherited income. Many states forbade women to serve on juries. Women like Dickinson,

Gilbert, and Turner had a degree of privilege because they were white, had access to either their own or their husband's money, were able to get an education beyond a grammar or high school, and had social position. This allowed them to be travelers and writers and to comment on the issues of the day. Women without this privilege did not have these options. Yet, as the century progressed, we see many women of poorer economic status, impoverished immigrants from Europe, and women of African heritage (many of whom were slaves until 1865) also bravely making decisions about their lives, often with the help of other women, that radically changed America.

CHAPTER SEVEN

JULIA WARD HOWE, SAMUEL GRIDLEY HOWE, AND CHARLES SUMNER

Complicated Relationships and Radical Social Change in Very Proper Nineteenth-Century Boston

Julia Ward was born in 1819 to a wealthy New York family. She was tutored at home, and as a young woman she was well-read on a vast array of topics. She socialized with the novelist Charles Dickens, who was visiting from London, and with American thinkers such as Margaret Fuller, who was a founder of a new philosophy called transcendentalism. At seventeen, Ward was publishing essays on philosophy, and she continued to write for the rest of her life.

Perhaps you've heard the song "The Battle Hymn of the Republic"? It begins "Mine eyes have seen the glory of the coming of the Lord; He is trampling out the vintage where the grapes of wrath are stored." Julia Ward Howe, as she was known then, wrote those words in 1861 to be sung by soldiers in the Union army.

In 1841, when she was twenty-two and visiting Boston, Julia Ward met the charismatic Samuel Gridley

Howe. He was a well-known social reformer and activist, and also eighteen years older than she.

Born in Boston, Samuel Howe dedicated his life to social change. After graduating Harvard Medical School in 1824, he went to volunteer in the Greek revolution against the Ottoman Empire. He fought as a solider and also served as a doctor. His bravery was so great that he was called "the Lafayette of the Greek Revolution." In 1830 he continued his medical studies in Paris and took part in an antimonarchist revolt that was known as the Second French Revolution.

Upon returning to Boston in 1831, he founded the Perkins School for the Blind, which was the first of its kind in the country and the first to print books in braille. Later, in 1848, he led the founding of America's first public institution to help the mentally disabled.

Ward and Samuel Howe shared a passion for social justice, especially the cause of abolition—ending slavery. They married two years after they met and over the next fifteen years had six children. Despite his many liberal attitudes, Samuel Howe held very traditional ideas about the role of women. He welcomed Julia's support for his work, yet he was unhappy when she became publicly active herself. These attitudes raised difficulties between them. In 1854, after twelve years of marriage, Julia Ward Howe published *Passion-Flowers*, a book of poetry that clearly reflected her unhappiness with their relationship.

The Howe marriage had other problems. In 1837, several years after Samuel Howe returned from France, he became intimate friends with Charles Sumner, a

Julia Ward Howe and her husband, Samuel Gridley Howe, 1816.

leading abolitionist. Sumner was born in 1811 to an old Boston family. He became a lawyer, and in 1845 he argued a case—*Roberts v. City of Boston*—in the Massachusetts Supreme Court that challenged segregation in Boston public schools. Though he lost the case, many of his arguments were used over one hundred years later in the 1956 case *Brown v. Board of Education*, which ended segregation across the United States. Later, as a US senator, Sumner was a leading voice against slavery.

Julia Howe; her husband, Samuel; and Charles Sumner shared many political views. Samuel and

Sumner's relationship, however, went much deeper. Their very close relationship was so public that one mutual friend wrote, ironically, to another that Sumner was "quite in love with Howe and spends so much time with him I begin to feel the shooting pains of jealousy."

Sumner, for his part, was jealous of Julia Howe. In 1843, while on his honeymoon with Julia, Samuel responded to a letter from Sumner:

Samuel Howe's intimate friend, Charles Sumner, 1846.

> You complain of your lonely lot, & seem to think your friends will lose their sympathy with you as they form new ties of love, but dearest Sumner it is not so with me and in the days of my loneliness & sadness I never longed more for your society than I do now in my joy & in the whirl of London life: hardly a day passes but [I] think of you & long to have you by my side.

In 1841 Howe wrote Sumner about an evening they planned to spend together, that they "might make a night of it . . . as we have done, oft and again in interchange of thought and feeling." Were Samuel Howe and Charles Sumner lovers? Was theirs just a "romantic friendship" or was it a sexual relationship?

Julia was friends with Sumner and deeply respected his political work. She was also aware of her husband's relationship with him. In a letter to Sumner, Samuel describes the situation quite plainly:

> When my heart is full of joy or sorrow it turns to you
> & yearns for your sympathy; in fact as Julia often
> says—Sumner ought to have been a woman & you to
> have married her.

In her diary in 1842, just after she and Samuel were married, Julia wrote: "What shall I do? Where shall I go to beg some scraps and remnants of affection to feed my hungry heart? It will die, if it be not fed."

Julia was troubled by feelings of loneliness for most of the marriage. In 1846 she began working on a novel titled *The Hermaphrodite*, which she never finished and was not published in her lifetime. "Hermaphrodite" was an early medical term used to describe people who have some male and female genital and secondary sexual characteristics. Today we would use the term "intersexed." There are many famous Greek and Roman statues of hermaphrodites—Julia had seen them on her honeymoon in Europe—and in Greek mythology they are not seen as abnormal or defective, just different.

In Julia's novel, the main character, Laurence, is both woman and man. Another character, a woman named Emma, falls in love with Laurence. She describes him/her this way: "bearded lip and earnest brow . . . falling shoulders, slender neck, and rounded bosom." Laurence describes himself as "I am as God made me."

The bi-gendered Laurence is often confused but is filled with enormous emotional and sexual energy. Although Emma calls Laurence a "monster," Howe's attitude to the character is kind. Later in the novel, Laurence falls in love with a sixteen-year-old boy named Ronald, and Howe describes the relationship sympathetically.

Hurt by her husband's relationship with Sumner, Julia Howe was committed to finding a way to explain it to herself that made emotional sense. *The Hermaphrodite* was her attempt to think about personal problems. It also shows how she viewed the society she lived in, one that had limited gender roles and also strict rules about nontraditional sexual relationships.

At that time in history there was no specific language for a person who was capable of loving both a man and a woman—a person we might call bisexual today. Howe imagines a man-woman, a hermaphrodite, as the ancient Greeks would have imagined, who is capable of loving both. Despite her unhappiness, Julia and Samuel remained married for thirty-three years until his death, at seventy-four, in 1876. She died at the age of ninety-one, in 1910. Julia Ward Howe never finished *The Hermaphrodite*—we do not know why; perhaps it was too personal or she sorted out her feelings with what she had written. The manuscript of four hundred pages, in disjointed chapters, lay in a manuscript box in an archive at Harvard University. It was discovered nearly a century and a half after Howe's death by a literary scholar who fitted the pieces together and published it in 2004 for an audience who might understand it more clearly.

■ ■ ■

Julia and Samuel Howe and Charles Sumner lived at a time of great upheaval in US society: the fight for abolition, waves of European immigration, women's suffrage, progressive reforms to help the disadvantaged. These struggles for basic rights and equality laid the basis for great changes in the way Americans thought about sexuality. And these struggles were about to break into open warfare with the coming of the Civil War.

AMERICAN FREEDOM BEGINS TO BLOOM

CHANGE AND THE CIVIL WAR

1860–1875

CHAPTER EIGHT

THE AMAZING LIFE
OF ALBERT D. J. CASHIER

Transgender War Hero

In 1914 the American Civil War had been over for
almost half a century. The soldiers who had survived,
from the North and the South, were now facing old age.
Many were still dealing with wounds they received in
battle. Some were re-experiencing the traumas they had
endured during very bloody combat. Most were just con-
tending with the problems of aging.

That year Civil War veteran Albert D. J. Cashier, age
seventy-one, was admitted to the Watertown (Illinois)
State Hospital for the Insane (at the time, the word "insane" was loosely used to describe people with a range
of mental and emotional problems) with signs of senility, which means declining mental and physical abilities.
Cashier had been living in a home for old soldiers in the
town of Quincy, Illinois. He had been a Union soldier
in the army for the northern states in their fight against
the Confederate States of America, those southern states
that had withdrawn—seceded—from the United States of
America and had fought in the battles of Nashville, Mobile, and Vicksburg. The last battle marked an especially
important Union victory and helped turn the tide of the
war against the Confederacy.

Over 2.75 million people fought in the Civil War, but even with the war's high fatality rate, there were close to half a million veterans still alive in the first decades of the twentieth century. Albert Cashier was different than most of them. When the Watertown hospital doctors examined him, they discovered that Cashier had been born with female genitals, yet he had lived as a man for more than half a century.

Albert D. J. Cashier was born on December 25, 1843, as Jennie Hodgers in Killabush, Clogherhead, a small fishing village on the northeast coast of Ireland. His parents, Sallie and Patrick Hodgers, were most likely fishermen and also had a small farm. This was a time when many Irish emigrated to England, Australia, and the United States, forced from their homes by starvation caused by the Irish Potato Famine.

We don't know if this is why Cashier came to the US. We do know, however, that he arrived sometime in the early 1860s, a young teenager unable to read or write. It is not known if Cashier called himself Albert before or after he arrived in America. Certainly being in a new country gave him a freedom he would not have had in the village in which he grew up. After he arrived in the United States he settled in Belvidere, Illinois, and on August 6, 1862, a year after the war started, he joined the Union forces in the Ninety-Fifth Illinois Infantry.

For three years Cashier fought bravely. His first battles were in the Red River campaign in Louisiana in May 1864. Then his regiment fought and won an important battle in the Franklin-Nashville Campaign. He also fought in one of the Civil War's last battles at Mobile, Alabama. President Abraham Lincoln issued a commendation to

Woman Soldier in 95th Ill.

ALBERT D. J. CASHIER
OF
COMPANY G, 95TH ILLINOIS REGIMENT

Photographed November, 1864

ALBERT D. J. CASHIER
OF
COMPANY G, 95TH ILLINOIS REGIMENT

Photographed July, 1913

Albert D. J. Cashier in his Union uniform during the Civil War and his later civilian life.

the Union forces in that battle, noting their bravery in a pivotal part of the conflict. Albert Cashier was a Civil War hero.

Throughout all of this, Cashier presented himself, and was accepted by his fellow soldiers, as a man. He was smaller than the other men and had little facial hair. No one noticed this, though, as there were many soldiers in their teens and even younger in both the Union and Confederate armies. After the war Cashier left the army and went back to Illinois. For the next forty-five years he was a church janitor, worked on farms, lighted gas street lamps, and, for a while, ran a small business with an old army friend.

In November 1910 Cashier, now sixty-seven years old, was hit by a car and taken to the nearest hospital with a broken leg. As with Deborah Sampson in the Revolutionary War, when doctors examined Cashier they found he was born with female genitals. These doctors respected Cashier's wishes and his privacy and did not reveal their discovery. After being released from the hospital, Cashier went to the Soldiers and Sailors Home in Quincy, Illinois, to recuperate, and he lived there for the next four years.

Cashier lived into his seventies, which was very old for the time. As he got older he began to show signs of senility and was moved to a state hospital. He lived there until he died.

Tragically, the staff at this hospital were far less understanding about Cashier's male identity than his previous doctors were. They refused to give him men's clothing even though he had been dressing as a man for fifty years. Cashier, already disoriented because of his mental state, found the dresses, women's undergarments, and shoes strange, wrong, and restricting. He often stumbled wearing them and once fell and broke his hip.

Some of his former army comrades supported Cashier's wish to wear the clothing he had always worn. These veterans had fought alongside Cashier and accepted him. Cashier's story spread through some newspaper accounts and word of mouth, and many people became interested in him and his experiences. Unfortunately, Cashier, already confused, became depressed and had great difficulty telling clear stories about his life. He died on October 10, 1915, at the age of seventy-one. He was buried in his regimental uniform and his gravestone read "Albert Cashier" with details of his military service.

What made Jennie Hodgers dress as a man, take the name Albert Cashier, immigrate to the United States, and fight in the Civil War? One theory suggests that when Jennie was a young child, her father made her dress as a boy to obtain work. Others speculate that Jennie took on a male identity in order to travel safely on the long journey from Ireland to America. Neither of these theories explains why Albert would dress as a man and present himself as a man for the rest of his life.

Albert Cashier was not the only cross-dresser in the Civil War. The war called forth extreme actions in many ways and inspired people to do things they might not have considered in peacetime.

The Civil War was also the bloodiest example of debates and struggles going on in the United States. Abolition and states' rights (the ability of individual states to make their own laws, even when they may be in conflict with the Constitution) were the most debated. The war also brought to the forefront many other questions, such as economic disparity between classes or people, issues of immigration, and a growing divide between rural and urban areas. There were also discussions about gender, sexuality, and how women and men were supposed to act and live in this constantly evolving America. These discussions—in books, magazines, lectures, between friends, and in families—were beginning to influence the decisions citizens made in their lives. New definitions of masculinity and femininity—and the sexual identities that may emerge from them—were not just being discussed but also acted upon.

CROSS-DRESSING IN THE CIVIL WAR

There are over four hundred documented cases of women who dressed as men to fight in the Civil War. That means there are probably many more for whom we have no record. Why did these women join the army? Some enlisted with their husbands and fought side-by-side with them. Satronia Smith Hunt joined the Union forces with her spouse, and after he died in battle, she continued fighting. Some, as many male soldiers did, enlisted out of intense patriotism.

Loreta Velazquez, who served the Confederacy as Lieutenant Harry Buford, had enough money of her own to finance her career as a soldier. She must have deeply believed in the South's cause. Sarah Edmonds joined the Second Michigan Infantry as Franklin Thompson in 1861. She fought in some of the bloodiest battles of the war and deserted in 1863 when, after coming down with malaria, she refused to be hospitalized and have her secret uncovered. Unlike Albert Cashier, when the war was over, all of these people returned to the civilian world to live as women.

Loreta Velazquez out of uniform in women's clothing.

Harry T. Buford in his Confederate uniform during the Civil War.

CHAPTER NINE

CHARLOTTE CUSHMAN

American Idol, Lover of Women

On Saturday night, November 7, 1874, in Booth's Theater on Twenty-Third Street and Sixth Avenue, Charlotte Cushman gave her final New York performance as Shakespeare's Lady Macbeth. The audience was filled with anticipation. Cushman, a brilliant performer, was the most praised American female actor of the time. After the play, there was a planned on-stage ceremony with political dignitaries. What was not planned were the twenty-five thousand women and men who marched alongside her carriage with torches as she left the theater until she arrived at her hotel several blocks away. There, as she watched from the balcony, the crowd cheered, sang songs, and saw a fireworks display.

Charlotte Cushman was an American icon, celebrated and famous. She was friends with Abraham Lincoln and socialized with the rich and powerful. She was seen as a living example of American ideals. Yet Cushman never married and had a series of very public affairs with women. How did she do it?

Cushman's family roots went back to the early American colonies. A female ancestor, Mary Allerton, came over on the *Mayflower*. Six generations later, on July 23, 1816,

Charlotte Cushman was born in Boston to Mary Eliza and Elkanah Cushman. Mary Eliza had run a school before she married Elkanah, a prosperous merchant.

The Cushman family lived in Boston's North End, by the harbor. Cushman had younger siblings—Charles, Augustus, and Susan—but she was the most adventurous. Later in life Cushman wrote, "I was born a tomboy."

When Cushman was ten years old her uncle took her to see a play, and she was entranced by it. She wanted to perform and sang at home and in the choir of her Unitarian church, where the young Ralph Waldo Emerson was the assistant minister. (Emerson went on to become a very famous American philosopher and writer.) By 1829, when she was thirteen, the family had fallen on hard times. Her mother thought Charlotte should go on the stage to help support the family. Seven years later, after rigorous training, Cushman became a professional actor in New York.

Charlotte Cushman depicted in her Romeo costume, 1851.

America was in the process of inventing its own culture, and this was easily seen in the differences between

Charlotte Cushman as Romeo with her sister Susan as Juliet, 1846.

Sallie Mercer, Cushman's lifelong companion and friend, 1860s.

American and British actors. The great British actors at the time, who often toured in the US, used broad gestures and spoke their lines in loud and melodramatic tones. Cushman, on the other hand, acted in a new, more realistic American style. Her commanding personality and charisma allowed her to play forceful women in a way that had not been seen before.

Audiences loved this new style of acting. It was so striking and popular that Cushman quickly became a star, playing strong characters such as Lady Macbeth, instead of more "feminine" roles. She was so successful, audiences accepted her in male parts. She played Hamlet and the evil Cardinal Wolsey in Shakespeare's *Henry VIII*. She was world famous for her Romeo, with her sister Susan playing Juliet.

In 1844, while performing in Philadelphia, Cushman hired Sallie Mercer, a fourteen-year-old African American woman, to be her maid. Cushman responded to Mercer's personality and trusted her immediately. Over the rest of Cushman's life Mercer was her personal assistant, confidant, dresser, dialogue prompter, and advisor. Mercer ran Cushman's household and served as a go-between for Cushman's friends and lovers. Cushman was so grateful to Mercer that she bought Mercer's mother a house in Philadelphia.

This close, professional relationship between a white woman and an African American person was almost unheard of at the time. This was before the Civil War, when the debate over slavery was beginning to tear the country apart. Mercer became the center of a growing circle of Cushman's close female friends. Their friendship was also proof of Cushman's support for abolition and equality.

Cushman was an active supporter of the Union side in the Civil War. She held benefit performances to raise money for the US Sanitation Commission, whose job was to create clean and healthy conditions for the Union army. When Cushman toured the South in 1850, she took all possible measures to ensure that Mercer, a free African American woman, would be treated with respect and never detained. Mercer was accepted as part of Cushman's family.

As she became famous, Cushman gained a large following. Her fans avidly read about her personal life in the newspapers, much in the way people today watch shows like *TMZ* or follow a celebrity on Instagram. In 1848, Cushman's fans could read that their idol and a woman named Matilda Mary Hays were a couple. Hays was a British essayist, journalist, and translator who started several magazines dealing with feminist issues.

Cushman and Hays often went out in public wearing matching outfits. Their friends referred to Hays not as

Matilda but as Max or Matthew. Cushman and Hays were so famous that in England, the renowned poet Elizabeth Barrett Browning wrote about them in a letter to a friend: "I understand that [Cushman] and Miss Hays have made vows . . . of eternal attachment to each other—they live together, dress alike . . . it is a female marriage."

Cushman, who frequently toured outside America, moved to Rome with Hays in 1852. She hired a full staff for Sallie Mercer, who ran the large household of family and friends. Their circle included artists such as the French novelist Amantine-Lucile-Aurore Dupin (who wrote under the male pen name of George Sand) and Nathaniel Hawthorne, who wrote *The Scarlet Letter*. Also part of the extended family were three noted sculptors—Harriet Hosmer, Emma Stebbins, and Edmonia Lewis—each of whom was romantically involved with other women.

After ten years together, Cushman and Hays drifted apart. The breakup reached a climax when Hays threatened to sue Cushman. She said that she had suffered professionally by giving up her own career to emotionally support Cushman. To us, it sounds like a modern divorce, yet such a lawsuit was unheard of during this time and certainly not between two women. It is a clear indicator of how close Cushman and Hays were. Both Hays and Cushman went on to have other lovers. Cushman was in a relationship with the sculptor Emma Stebbins for many years until Cushman's death.

How did Cushman, in a culture that criminalized homosexuality, become so publicly loved? By viewing her relationships as nonsexual, "romantic friendships," her fans and the public ignored what might have otherwise been obvious. We know that Cushman's relationships with these women were sexual because of the letters between them. In an 1860 letter written to Emma Crow, a woman with whom she had an affair, Cushman wrote:

> Ah what delirium is in the memory. Every nerve in me thrills as I look back & feel you in my arms, held to my breast so closely, so entirely mine in every sense as I was yours. Ah, my very sweet, very precious, full, full of ecstasy.

Cushman was an independent woman. Her substantial income allowed her to travel, support other women artists, and create her own community. This, and not being bound by the strict gender rules of most heterosexual marriages, gave her freedom not available to other women. Cushman's public life showed that women could be powerful, charismatic, and independent, as well as womanly, charming, and loved. Her fondness for male attire and ability to convincingly play a man on the stage (even a romantic and sexy Romeo) made her the embodiment of a new type of American woman and a role model for other women. In 1858, at age twenty-six, Louisa May Alcott, author of *Little Women*, was so taken with Cushman that she noted in her diary that she "had a stage struck fit." Alcott later based Miss Cameron, a character in her novel *Jo's Boys*, on Cushman.

Cushman died in 1876, at the age of fifty-nine, of breast cancer. At her bedside were Emma Stebbins, Emma Crow, her nephew Edward, and Sallie Mercer. She was mourned by the nation. At her funeral, the Reverend W. H. H. Murray said:

> She was a Samson and Ruth in one. In her the strength of the masculine and the tenderness of the feminine nature were blended. She seemed to stand complete in nature, with the finest qualities of either sex.

CHAPTER TEN

WALT WHITMAN

Poet of the People

The Civil War had changed America. It saw the end to the legal institution of slavery. It radically changed ideas about how women and men should live. One very important way it changed Americans was through their exposure to the incredible violence of mass warfare.

The war was catastrophically brutal. One estimate holds that 750,000 soldiers died and perhaps 500,000 were wounded. In term of a percentage of the population, it would be as if over seven million soldiers died in a war

A dead Confederate soldier on the battlefield during the Civil War in a stereoscopic image.

today. The Civil War, much more so than the American Revolution, tested men's physical and emotional strength on a huge scale. In doing so, it also challenged their attitudes about masculinity. Male soldiers, faced with their own deaths and immense suffering, explored and shared their feelings and emotions in new ways.

They also confronted and explored new ideas about sexuality. We know this through the poems and writings of Walt Whitman, one of the towering figures in American literature. His writing is moving and innovative, and also gives us wonderful insights into how ideas about men, and sexuality, changed at this time.

Whitman's life was, in many ways, an American success story. Born in 1819 to poor parents with nine children, he was raised in Brooklyn and left school at eleven. He worked as an office boy for lawyers and then began doing small jobs at newspapers. At sixteen he was publishing short articles and some poetry, while he worked at various New York newspapers. As he became more established as a newspaperman—writing theater reviews, fiction, and even a health column for men— he realized that he really wanted to write poetry.

Whitman's vision was to write a single poem that would capture the spirit of personal and political freedom in America. Not only that, the poem had to be written in a new and open American style that would reflect and demonstrate that freedom. In

Walt Whitman, 1860s.

1855, at age thirty-six, Whitman published—at his own expense—the first edition of *Leaves of Grass*. Today this is considered a great, foundational work of American poetry. The philosopher and critic Ralph Waldo Emerson wrote to Whitman: "I am not blind to the worth of the wonderful gift of *Leaves of Grass*. I find it the most extraordinary piece of wit and wisdom that America has yet contributed. I am very happy in reading it, as great power makes us happy."

Leaves of Grass also shocked and scandalized some readers with its open embrace of sexuality as a part of human life. It also contained thinly veiled references to same-sex male love and sexual activity. Stanza 5 of "Song of Myself" fancifully describes the poet imagining a physical encounter with his own soul. It contains what was for some people a shocking description of two men in a sexual embrace:

> *I believe in you my soul, the other I am must not abase*
> *itself to you,*
> *And you must not be abased to the other.*
>
> *Loafe with me on the grass, loose the stop from your*
> *throat,*
> *Not words, not music or rhyme I want, not custom or*
> *lecture, not even the best,*
> *Only the lull I like, the hum of your valvèd voice.*
>
> *I mind how once we lay such a transparent summer*
> *morning,*
> *How you settled your head athwart my hips and gently*
> *turn'd over upon me,*

And parted the shirt from my bosom-bone, and plunged
   your tongue to my bare-stript heart,
And reach'd till you felt my beard, and reach'd till you
   held my feet.

An important literary critic named Rufus Wilmot Griswold labeled Whitman a lover of men. In an 1855 review, he wrote that Whitman was guilty of "*Peccatum illud horribile, inter Christianos non nominandum.*" That is Latin for "horrible sin not to be mentioned among Christians" (a sin so horrible it couldn't even be written in English).

Over the years Whitman would revise *Leaves of Grass* many times, adding new poems and editing old ones. This reflected his growth as a poet and also his changing vision of America.

When the Southern states seceded from the Union, Whitman strongly backed the North. His poem "Beat! Beat! Drums!" became a patriotic anthem for the North. Whitman's younger brother George, to whom he was very close, enlisted and went to the front. In 1862 Whitman saw the name "First Lieutenant G. W. Whitmore" on a list of wounded printed in a newspaper. He feared that it might be his brother and quickly went to find him.

To Whitman's relief, he found his brother in a hospital in Washington DC, and discovered that George's wounds were very slight. But Whitman was shocked and moved by the conditions he saw in the hospital. Many of the wounded soldiers had no family to visit them and were housed in very bad conditions. He decided that he would move to Washington and help care for the wounded. Whitman's friend Charley Eldridge helped him obtain a job working part-time for the paymaster of the Union army so that he could stay in Washington and volunteer in the hospital and infirmaries.

Whitman understood that nursing wounded soldiers was a way of helping win the war, save the Union, and abolish slavery. It was also an inspiration to him. In these hospitals Whitman saw the worst that man could do to his fellow man. He nursed men who were missing limbs, physically scarred and emotionally damaged. Separated from their families, they needed a friend and companionship.

In a time of war and loss Whitman was able to show these soldiers that men could also be loving and caring. These sentiments are written down in many of Whitman's 1863 notebook entries of his meetings with wounded soldiers and other young men:

The Army Hospital Feb 21, 1863 There is enough to repel, but one soon becomes powerfully attracted also.

Janus Mayfield, (bed 59, Ward 6 Camp[bell] Hosp.) About 18 years old, 7th Virginia Vol. Has three brothers also in the Union Army. Illiterate, but cute— can neither read nor write. Has been very sick and low, but now recovering. Have visited him regularly for two weeks, given him money, fruit, candy etc.

Albion F. Hubbard—Ward C bed 7 Co F 1st Mass Cavalry/ been in the service one year—has had two carbuncles one on arm, one on ankle, healing at present yet great holes left, stuffed with rags—worked on a farm 8 years before enlisting—wrote letter—for him to the man he lived with/died June 20th '63.

Whitman's wartime writings as a nurse on the battlefield and in a hospital are excellent examples of how a man who loved other men was able to think in a different way about the war. Whitman's "Hymn of Dead Soldiers" (stanzas 6–8) from the 1867 edition of *Leaves of Grass* are a prime example of this:

> *Phantoms, welcome, divine and tender!*
> *Invisible to the rest, henceforth become my companions;*
> *Follow me ever! desert me not, while I live.*
>
> *Sweet are the blooming cheeks of the living! sweet*
> *are the musical voices sounding!*
> *But sweet, ah sweet, are the dead, with their silent eyes.*
>
> *Dearest comrades! all now is over;*
> *But love is not over—and what love, O comrades!*
> *Perfume from battle-fields rising—up from fœtor*
> *arising.*

After the war, Whitman's fame spread. He also began a ten-year-long love affair with Peter Doyle, a horsecar (a street trolley drawn by horses) conductor in Washington, DC, who had fought and was wounded in the Civil War. They met just after the war ended. Doyle was almost twenty at the time and Whitman was forty-six. Whitman's temperament had always been serious, if not melancholy, and his love of Doyle made him happier. He even removed three unhappy poems from *Leaves of Grass*.

Whitman and Doyle were constant companions. They wrote one another often, even when separated a short time. In 1868, after they had been together for several years, Whitman went to visit his family in New York. On September 18, Doyle wrote to Whitman: "I could not resist the inclination to write to you this morning it seems more than a week since I saw you." Seven days later Whitman wrote: "I think of you very often, dearest comrade, & with more calmness than when I was there—I find it first rate to think of you, Pete, & to know that you are there, all right, & that I shall return, & we will be together again. I don't know what I should do if I hadn't you to think of & look forward to." For the month and a half they were separated Doyle wrote his beloved seven times, and Whitman wrote eleven letters.

In January 1873 Whitman suffered a small stroke and stopped working. In May of that year he went to see his dying mother in Camden, New Jersey. He ended up staying there

SEX BETWEEN MEN IN THE NAVY

Few historical records document same-sex behaviors in the nineteenth century, but there are some. In his diaries, Philip C. Van Buskirk, an American marine, details mutual sexual interactions among sailors in the mid-1800s. Some of these relationships are between mature adults, some are between older sailors, often officers, having sexual and romantic relationships with teenage cabin boys.

In 1853 Van Buskirk's diary records an older sailor's opinion about sex between men. While this sailor would punish men who had sex with men on land, he had a different attitude about sex between men at sea: "What can a fella do?—three years at sea—and hardly any chance to have a woman. I tell you . . . a fella must do so. Biles [boils] and pimples and corruption will come out all over his body if he don't."

The open sea, like the mostly all-male spaces of the American West, was often a place where men could escape the social and religious rules of more "civilized" communities. Some scholars have suggested that it wasn't the lack of women that "drove" men in these places into same-sex relationships. Instead, it might have been that men sought out these places in order to have the freedom to do as they pleased.

to recover, and Doyle stayed in Washington, DC. They remained in touch over the years. Even though Whitman's health declined, he produced three more editions of *Leaves of Grass*. He died in 1892, America's most celebrated poet. He not only wrote about the American spirit but also invented a new, American style of poetry. His writing celebrated a new type of American man, who was able to be open and caring and to love other men.

CHAPTER ELEVEN

REBECCA PRIMUS AND ADDIE BROWN

A Nineteenth-Century Love Story

Hartford, Connecticut, in 1836 was small city. Its population was ten thousand. The African American population was even smaller, about seven hundred people. There were numerous African American–owned businesses such as barbershops, restaurants, and funeral homes. These formed the core of a growing, prosperous African American community.

Hartford at that time was also a center of the abolition movement against slavery. The Reverend Lyman Beecher preached against slavery, and his daughter Harriet Beecher Stowe wrote the bestselling novel *Uncle Tom's Cabin*. That book, published in 1852, greatly shaped public opinion in favor of abolition. Harriet and her sisters Catharine and Isabella were also active in the suffrage movement to win the vote for women. Hartford abolitionists fought against slavery for decades. In 1784 they passed an emancipation law that would gradually free Connecticut slaves at the age of twenty-five for men and twenty-one for women. In 1800 there were 951 slaves in Connecticut, and by 1830, only twenty-five.

Rebecca Primus was an African American woman born in Hartford in 1836. Her parents, Holdridge and Mehitable Primus, had deep American roots. Holdridge's grandfather had won his freedom by fighting against Great Britain in the Revolutionary War. The Primuses and their four children were an important part of Hartford's Black middle class. They owned their own home—unusual for an African American family in Hartford—and took in boarders. They were church-going people whose faith informed their view of the world.

Rebecca Primus had finished high school, an accomplishment for any woman or man in early nineteenth-century America. Many children had to work to support their family and often married very young. Primus went on to teach at a school for African American children. She also wrote poetry and essays. Like many educated Northern Black women at the time, Primus was eager to put her religious and political beliefs into action. In 1865, after the Civil War ended, the Hartford Freedmen's Aid Society funded her to go to Royal Oak, Maryland, where slavery had been legal, to teach African American students who were now free. She was twenty-nine.

Primus first taught in a church and later raised funds from citizens in both Royal Oak and Hartford to buy lumber to build a schoolhouse. It was constructed by local African American men and was still standing in 1929.

It is unclear when Rebecca Primus met Addie Brown. It may have been through a church connection, or possibly Brown boarded with the Primus family. Brown was an orphan and for most of her life had worked as a domestic servant in and around Hartford. There was a social and economic distance between the two women, but this did not seem to matter to them, although it may have to other people. There are few official records of Brown's life, although we do know she could read and write and expressed herself extremely well. A letter written from Brown to Primus in 1859 survives, and we can see from it that they were already intimate friends and probably sexually involved.

On August 30, 1859, Brown, who was living in Waterbury, Connecticut, wrote to Primus.

> My ever Dear Friend,
>
> I no doubt you will be surprise to received [*sic*] a letter so soon I think it will be received with just as much pleasure this week as you will nexe [next] my Dearest Dearest Rebecca my heart is allmost broke I don't know that I ever spent such hours as I have my loving friend it goes harder with me now then [*sic*] it ever did I am more acquainted with you it seems to me this very moments if I only had the wings of a dove I would not remain long in Waterbury although we can't allway be together O it tis hard!
>
> O dear I am so lonesome I barelly know how to contain myself if I was only near you and having one of those sweet kisses.

On November 17, 1860, Brown wrote:

> My Cherish [*sic*] Friend,
>
> My head is better today Last night it pain me very hard O My Dear dear Rebecca when you press me to

your Dear Bosom . . . happy I was, last night I gave anything if I could only layed my poor aching head on your bosom O Dear how soon will it be I will be able to do it I suppose you think me very foolish if you do tis all the same to me. Dear Rebecca when I am away from you I feel so unhappy it seems to me the hours and days are like weeks and months.

Brown saw herself in an almost formal marriage relationship with Primus and even signed some of her letters "Addie Brown Primus." This did not stop her from playfully trying to make Primus jealous. On October 27, 1867, when she was working in Miss Porter's School in Farmington, Connecticut, she wrote to Primus:

The girls are very friendly towards me. I am either in they room or they in mine, every night out ten and sometime past. One of them wants to sleep with me. Perhaps I will give my consent some of these nights. I am not very fond of White I can assure you

In some biographies we have to guess about the exact nature of a relationship between two men or two women. In this case, because of their letters, there is no need to guess. There are 120 letters from Addie Brown to Rebecca Primus that survive, and 51 from Primus to her own family. Those are mostly from Royal Oak and concern Primus's daily life and teaching. We do not know how many letters are missing. From the surviving letters, though, we can clearly see that the women loved one another and engaged in loving physical activity.

We know that both Rebecca Primus and Addie Brown married men. Brown married Joseph Tines, whom she had mentioned many times to Primus in her letters of April 1868. Brown died in 1870. After Brown's death, Rebecca Primus married Charles Thomas, who worked for her family as a handyman and a gardener, sometime between 1872 and 1874. Thomas rose up in the world and in 1886 was given the respected job of doorman for the Connecticut State Assembly in the State Capitol. He died in 1891, and Rebecca Primus died in 1932, at the age of ninety-five.

The relationship of Rebecca Primus and Addie Brown is an example of a female friendship and of how complicated relationships between women were at the time. The love that Primus and Brown felt for one another did not have a name—or a clear social identity. Both women felt that they could also marry men, although in her letters Brown always says she is hesitant to do so. Did the two women marry because of social pressure? Would they have lived together as a couple if that had been acceptable?

As the nineteenth century progressed, Americans and Europeans were becoming more open about describing sexuality and relationships. Their understanding of sexual desires and sexual identity was becoming more informed and enlightened, inventing specific words to describe identities. Today we might say that Addie Brown and Rebecca Primus were lesbian or bisexual, words they never used. Those words, however, are just labels. They are categories that may help us make sense of the world—and are often not applicable to people who lived in the past. They can never fully define unique human beings.

SOCIAL PURITY AND THE BATTLE OVER WHO IS AN AMERICAN

The Civil War brought many changes to American society. Millions of newly freed slaves were now citizens, even though they were denied many basic rights. At the same time, after the war, many new immigrants began arriving in the United States. Many people in the white, Anglo-Saxon majority were upset by this.

The entire country was caught up in a debate about what it meant to be an American and who should be allowed to become a citizen. Some of the debate concerned how people should behave in their everyday lives. Many immigrant groups were seen by the majority as having different ideas about sexual behavior or morality, and were demonized for this. Cities, where many immigrants lived, were seen as having a corrupting effect on American culture. Often theaters, and later movie houses, as well as any books that mentioned sex, were seen as detrimental to a mythical, pure vision of American life. We can see echoes of this in modern arguments about "moral values" and national identity.

Those who were fearful of the changes taking place formed political movements with the aim of keeping American "pure." In 1844 a political party, known as the Know-Nothing Party, formed in response to the fear that newly arrived Irish and German Catholic immigrants would take over the country. (The party was called "Know-Nothing" because if members were asked about their movement, they claimed to "know nothing.") In 1865 the Ku Klux Klan formed in response to the freeing of African American slaves and to what they saw as the "dangerous influence" of Catholic and Jewish immigrants. The Klan—through terrorist acts such as cross burning and lynching—used the language of "purification" of American society and "racial purity." These groups promoted, through violent means, an America of and for white Protestants only. They believed in strict rules of segregation, racial identity, and sexual morality.

Ku Klux Klan parade in Washington, DC, September 1926.

There was a nonviolent part of this movement, called the social purity movement. This included groups with names such as the Union for Concerted Moral Effort, the American Purity Alliance, and the National Congress of Mothers, which presented themselves as concerned citizens working for the betterment of American society. Many of these groups were made up primarily of women and focused on drunkenness, crime, sexual behavior, and personal morality, often saying they were trying to help women and children. They also were against prostitution, saloons, and public drinking, as well as urban crime—most of which they saw as brought on by immigrant

"Woman's Holy War. Grand Charge on the Enemy's Works." The "Holy War" was the nineteenth-century crusade for temperance and prohibition. Here a young woman in armor holding a battle-axe leads a group of women to shatter barrels of alcohol, 1874.

(continues on next page)

(continued from previous page)

populations—sexual relations outside of marriage, and "indecent" books, music, and theater. Frequently they placed the blame for these "problems" on African Americans, immigrants, and anyone outside the white Protestant majority.

All of these movements marked a reaction to changes in US culture and population. While the Ku Klux Klan and the Know-Nothings engaged in violence, the other social movements, even when well-intentioned, were profoundly conservative. They attempted to strictly control personal choices, freedom of expression, sexual activity, and even freedom of association by defining what was morally acceptable. By doing this they attempted to limit the idea of who could be an American.

NEW AMERICANS

BOLDLY CHALLENGING SOCIETY

1875–1900

CHAPTER TWELVE

THE RADICAL VICTORIA WOODHULL

First Woman to Run for President

Victoria Woodhull is one of the most surprising and radical figures of the nineteenth century. She believed in, and actively promoted, ideas that would have a great impact on how Americans viewed the place of women in society. And though she was not a lesbian, she fought for the idea of sexual freedom. She led a very public life filled with drama, scandal, and newspaper headlines. In 1872 she became the first woman to run for president of the United States.

Victoria Woodhull was born Victoria California Claflin, in the small frontier town of Homer, Ohio. Her family was very poor. Her mother was unable to read or write, and her father was a small-time crook who made money by selling fake medicine. They had ten children, and Victoria was the seventh. Woodhull had a terrible childhood. She was beaten and possibly sexually abused by her father. She had only three years of schooling and married Canning Woodhull, a local doctor almost twice her age, when she had just turned fifteen. After they were married she discovered Canning was an abusive alcoholic who constantly mistreated her. They had two children and finally Woodhull—shockingly for the time—divorced him.

Deciding to have a new life and no longer be victimized by anyone, Woodhull moved to New York City with her sister Tennessee Claflin, who was several years younger. There they set about making new lives for themselves. After a few years of hard work, and thanks to their ingenuity, intelligence, and some good connections—including befriending millionaire Cornelius Vanderbilt—they founded the first stock brokerage firm run by women. Despite their success, they were denied a place on the Stock Exchange because of their sex.

Through clever trading, during the gold panic of 1869, in which unscrupulous businessmen tried to corner the gold market and caused a stock market crash, Woodhull and Claflin netted $700,000. This would be worth close to $13 million today. In 1870 Woodhull and Claflin founded *Woodhull & Claflin's Weekly*, a national newspaper with a circulation of twenty thousand, in which they called for complete equality for African Americans, the rights of workers, the right for women to vote, the right for women to dress in sensible (and healthy) clothing, the right to use birth control, and the freedom for all people to lead the personal and sexual lives they choose.

In the years following the Civil War, many progressive social change movements flourished in America advocating a broad range of personal and social freedoms. These social change movements were often at odds with the social purity movement. Woodhull embraced many of these progressive movements, including the Free Love movement. The Free Love movement supported a broad range of individual freedoms, including the right to freely choose romantic and sexual relationships, without any interference from the government.

The Free Love movement saw state laws governing marriage as a barrier to personal freedom. In many states a married woman could not own her own property or have a legal right to make decisions about her marriage or children. For this reason, some women embraced the Free Love movement, as well as the suffrage movement, which fought to give women the right to vote. Despite what the name suggests to us today, Free Love groups did not argue that people should have "open marriages" or multiple sexual relationships. Rather, they argued, every adult should be free to choose their own relationships. They believed government restriction on any personal relationships were wrong, including marriage laws and laws prohibiting various forms of sexual activity. These same arguments would be used one hundred years later by feminists and advocates of gay liberation.

Woodhull was a brilliant and compelling speaker who gave many public addresses. On January 11, 1871, she became the first woman to testify before the House Judiciary Committee. She spoke on suffrage and insisted that women *already* had the right to vote under the Fourteenth and Fifteenth Amendments, which were already part of the Constitution. This argument, however, was not accepted by Congress. Later that year, on November 20, she gave her famous speech "And the Truth Shall Make You Free: A Speech on the Principles of Social Freedom" in front of three thousand people in New York City's Steinway Hall. Woodhull argued that, legally and philosophically, the government had no right to regulate sexuality and affection:

Yes, I am a Free Lover. I have an inalienable, constitutional and natural right to love whom I may, to love as long or as short a period as I can; to change that love every day if I please, and with that right neither you nor any law you can frame have any right to interfere. And I have the further right to demand a free and unrestricted exercise of that right, and it is your duty not only to accord it, but as a community, to see I am protected in it. I trust that I am fully understood, for I mean just that, and nothing less!

These sentiments sound bold even now. In 1871 they were controversial yet accepted as part of a public conversation about personal freedom. Woodhull was denounced and attacked by many associated with the social purity movement. On February 17, 1872, *Harper's Weekly*, a prominent national magazine, ran a cartoon that called her "Mrs. Satan." To many women and men, however, she was a hero. Later that year, she was selected by the Equal Rights Party to run for president of the United States, the first woman to do so. The Equal Rights Party promoted women's suffrage, along with other progressive issues.

Woodhull's vice presidential running mate was the noted abolitionist leader Frederick Douglass. The choice of Douglass was important. Although slavery had been abolished, the United States, both in the North and the South,

"Get thee behind me, (Mrs.) Satan!" A political cartoon depicting Victoria Woodhull as the devil. She is shown offering the freedom of "Free Love" to a woman saddled with a drunk husband and several children, only to have her philosophy rejected. The message is that it's better for a woman to suffer than engage in Free Love.

Abolitionist Frederick Douglass as a young man, 1855.

was deeply segregated. This was the first time that an African American man had been on a presidential campaign ticket. This was also an important moment that combined the newly emerging feminist movement with the movement for civil rights for African Americans. The Equal Rights Party ticket did not win. We have no idea how many votes Woodhull and Douglass received because some districts threw them out without even counting them.

After her presidential bid Woodhull spent some time out of the public eye. In 1877 she and her sister Tennessee moved to England. There she lectured, married John Biddulph Martin, a wealthy banker, and eventually become involved in education reform in the English village to which she retired. She died at age eighty-eight on June 9, 1927.

In the later nineteenth century, America was growing up very quickly. Progressive movements—for labor, race relations, and personal freedom—took hold in the public imagination. The Free Love movement promoted ideas about individual freedom, and freedom from the state, but it could only do so on a small scale. Nevertheless, the movement set the stage for a new way to think about personal freedom and what people were allowed to do in their personal lives.

CHAPTER THIRTEEN

JANE ADDAMS

The Mother of Social Work

In many ways, America was at war with itself at the end of the nineteenth century. People held very different views about what behavior was appropriate in private and in public. They argued about what kinds of sexuality should be allowed and what could be written about in books or shown on the stage. They were also debating ideas of "fairness" and "justice" in labor practices and immigration, just as they had since the time of Victoria Woodhull. At the heart of this debate were the questions of who could—or should—be considered an "American" and what "America" even meant. Jane Addams thought she had some very good answers to these questions.

Jane Addams was many things. She was a social reformer who radically changed the way people lived in cities. She sympathized with socialist ideas and argued for fair wages and better lives for working people. She was a pacifist who spoke out against war. She was a supporter of women's rights. She was also a lover of women.

Addams was an unlikely person to take these political positions since she had been raised in what looked like a nineteenth-century picture-book American home. Born in 1860 in Cedarville, Illinois, she grew up in a big house, with servants and farmhands.

Her father, John Huy Addams, was a prosperous businessman who owned factories that produced wool and flour. He traced his roots back to colonial times. In 1854 he was elected as a Republican to the Illinois State Senate and served sixteen years. He was an energetic supporter of the Union and the abolitionist cause and was friends with Abraham Lincoln, who served in the Illinois legislature at about this time. One of Addams's biographers described John Huy as "tall, muscular, and dark-haired, with pale eyes and a grave demeanor that made him seem older than his years."

Yet there was sadness in this storybook life. Addams's mother, Sarah, gave birth to eight children and, tragically, three died before their first birthdays. Another child died at sixteen. Jane was the youngest, but her sister Sarah died when she was two years old. When Jane was four she was diagnosed with spinal tuberculosis, which left her spine curved and made it difficult for her to run and play with other children.

Even as a child, possibly because of her politically liberal father and her disability, Jane saw herself as an outsider. From a young age, she thought about others who were less fortunate. She wrote in her 1910 memoir *Twenty Years at Hull House*:

> I recall an incident which must have occurred before I was seven years old, for the mill in which my father transacted his business that day was closed in 1867. The mill stood in the neighboring town adjacent to its poorest quarter. Before then I had always seen the little city of ten thousand people with the admiring eyes of a country child. . . . On that day I had my first sight of

the poverty which implies squalor, and felt the curious distinction between the ruddy poverty of the country and that which even a small city presents in its shabbiest streets.

Addams was fiercely intelligent and wanted to attend the newly opened Smith College in Northampton, Massachusetts. She intended to become a doctor and help the poor. Her father insisted that she attend a school closer to home. She enrolled in the Rockford Female Seminary in Rockford, Illinois. It was here that she met Ellen Gates Starr, with whom she formed a very close relationship. Over the next few years they exchanged many, many letters. John Huy Addams died in 1881, and most of the family moved to Philadelphia, so Addams and her brother Henry and his wife, Anna Haldeman Addams, could all attend medical school.

Addams's plans changed, however, after her spinal problem became worse, and she could not pursue her studies. She moved back to Cedarville in 1883 and underwent an operation that partially cured her spinal problems. In 1885 she decided to travel to relax and heal. In 1887, after two years in Europe, Addams moved back to Cedarville. While Addams was traveling in 1885, Starr wrote to her:

> My Dear, It has occurred to me that it might just be possible that you would spend a night with me if you should be going east at the right time. If you decide to go the week before Christmas—I mean—what do I mean? I think it is this. *Couldn't* you decide to spend the Sunday before Christmas with me? Get here on Saturday and go on Monday? . . . Please forgive me for writing three letters in a week.

An etching from Jane Addams's memoir, *Twenty Years at Hull House*, 1910.

In 1887 Addams read about a place called Toynbee Hall in the impoverished East End neighborhood of London. Toynbee Hall was a new concept called a settlement house. These were group living situations in poor neighborhoods that brought together women, men, and children from the neighborhood and also included women and men from various economic backgrounds who lived there, as well as teachers, artists, and counselors. They offered education, health care, exercise rooms, arts training, day care, meals, and emotional support for people who were neglected by urban society. Today we might call them intentional living groups. The wealthy people who funded them frequently viewed them as living examples of their Christian beliefs.

Addams visited Toynbee Hall several times, once with Starr, and decided she wanted to start a settlement house in Chicago. In 1889 she and Starr found a once grand, now run-down, mansion built years earlier by the tycoon Charles J. Hull, on Halsted Street. Formerly a neighborhood for the wealthy, the area was now home to small factories, junkyards, cafes, and five-cent movie theaters (called nickelodeons). Many immigrant groups, including Greeks, Italians, the Irish, and Eastern European Jews had moved there as Chicago expanded. This mansion was to become Hull House. Its charter stated that the house was "to provide a center for the higher civic and social life; to institute and maintain educational and philanthropic enterprises, and to investigate and improve the conditions in the industrial districts of Chicago."

As Addams intended, Hull House became a vital part of the neighborhood. It was a meeting place for many community groups; sponsored English lessons; ran vocational training; offered classes in art, sewing, music, and metal work; and ran a health clinic. The house also had volunteers read to community members who stopped by. Hull House eventually hosted a summer camp and gave athletic classes.

Most important, Hull House helped the community organize many new projects, including public baths, playgrounds, labor unions, a juvenile court system, and social groups. Addams insisted that labor organizing was necessary to ensure that workers were safe, worked reasonable hours, were paid fairly, and gained some satisfaction from their work. Many female social activists were attracted to these issues as they affected women and children who were either workers themselves or lived off a worker's wages.

Addams and Starr were the heart of Hull House. They shared a bed and worked together and separately. Addams spoke out against lynching and fought against segregation in Chicago schools. Starr worked on labor issues, often joining women strikers on picket lines. In 1889 Addams wrote to Starr, "I need you, dear one, more

A woman and her four children in a Chicago tenement building, 1949.

than you can realize." Starr remained at Hull House until 1920, though by then she and Addams had drifted apart as a couple. Sometime after 1891, Addams became emotionally involved with Mary Rozet Smith, a wealthy woman who had come to volunteer at Hull House. Addams and Smith soon became a couple and considered themselves married. They always shared a bed, whether they were at Hull House or traveling, and, if apart, wrote one another at least once a day.

Smith provided much needed financial support to Hull House, but more important was her constant backing of Addams. Their relationship was mutually loving and supportive. Addams wrote to Smith January 20, 1897: "I miss you, dear, every time I think of you, which is all of the time."

Hull House influenced a generation, and twenty-five years after the first one was established, the settlement house idea had spread to thirty-two states. Eventually there were close to five hundred settlement houses in cities across the nation. Addams continued her activism and became internationally famous for her work on labor relations and world peace. In 1915 she was involved in the Woman's Peace Party, and four years later with the Women's International League for Peace and Freedom. She won the Nobel Peace Prize in 1931. Addams and Smith were together for forty-three years until Smith's death in 1931, at age sixty-six. Addams died four years later, in 1935, of abdominal cancer.

Addams did an amazing amount of work in her life and transformed American society. Her work on social justice and world peace is important, but her most radical idea was at the heart of the settlement house movement. She envisioned an expansion of the idea of family beyond the heterosexual, biological family to include broader, diverse social groups that came together and "combined" for a common goal.

For a woman to live and work outside the nuclear family structure during this time meant creating a new type of family. For Addams this meant her relationships with Ellen Gates Starr and Mary Rozet Smith.

LILLIAN WALD AND THE INVENTION OF PUBLIC HEALTH

Lillian Wald set out to change America. She was born in 1867 into a comfortable, middle-class Jewish family in Cincinnati, Ohio, who eventually moved to Rochester, New York. Wald was very smart. She applied to Vassar College at age sixteen, and while she had proven she could handle the schoolwork, she was turned down because of her young age. Wald later decided, at age twenty-two, to go to nursing school.

After graduating, she and her close friend Mary Brewster moved to New York's Lower East Side. This was a poor immigrant community. Inspired by Jane Addams and Hull House, Wald and Brewster moved into a tenement building and then into a larger home on Henry Street, which they turned into a settlement house called Henry House.

Wald had the financial and emotional support of many women, and some men, and she formed around her a close network of single women. Wald and Brewster had a complex series of personal friendships and romantic relationships.

Knitting class at the Henry House settlement in New York, 1910.

Some of these relationships were sexual; some were nonsexual "romantic friendships." Mabel Hyde Kittredge, a wealthy New York socialite who spent years working in Henry Street and was an intimate friend to Wald, wrote to her:

> I seemed to hold you in my arms and whisper all of
> this. . . . If you want me to stay all night tomorrow night
> just say so when you see me. . . . Then I can hear you say
> "I love you"—and again and again I can see in your eyes
> the strength, and the power and the truth that I love

Throughout it all, the settlement house was the center of their lives and the focus of their work. The Henry Street settlement became an important cultural and social influence in the city. It's important that this institution, which wove together leisure, work, and politics, was a direct result of homosocial— meaning people of the same gender associating with one another—community building.

CHAPTER FOURTEEN

JULIAN ELTINGE

The Most Famous Cross-Dresser in America

The exact details of the early years of William Julian Dalton are foggy. Some accounts claim he was born on May 14, 1881, in Newtonville, Massachusetts, and that his father was a barber. Other sources state his was born in 1894 in Butte, Montana, where his father was a mining engineer or maybe a gold prospector. In some stories, William—who was called Bill—was born in Newtonville, traveled west, and was then sent back to the Boston area from Montana.

All of this confusion, or mystery, is fitting, because in his later life William Julian Dalton spent a lot of time confusing people. At a very early age, Bill—who eventually took the stage name Julian Eltinge—was an extraordinary and very talented female impersonator. That is, he performed on stage dressed in female clothing and presented himself as female characters. By the 1920s, he was internationally famous and critically praised on the stage and in films as a man who played female characters.

It's unclear how Eltinge started in this career. One, highly unlikely, story has him performing, dressed as a girl, when he was a young boy in saloons in Butte and later being beaten by his father. Another story has him performing as a girl in amateur dance classes or other

Julian Eltinge in costume, early 1910s.

Eltinge out of costume, early 1910s.

performing groups. We know that in 1892, at the age of ten or eleven (if the birth year of 1881 is correct), he was performing the role of a female character in the *Boston Cadets Revue*, an all-male show with boys and young men playing the female roles.

Theatrical records show that young Julian Eltinge was in the Broadway production of a musical titled *Mr. Wix of Wickham*, in 1904. The show only ran forty-one performances, though Eltinge was singled out as a star.

Men dressing as women has a long theatrical tradition. Women were not allowed to be on the British stage until 1660, when King Charles II repealed the Puritan ban on theater (the word "actress" was not coined until 1700). The first Juliet in *Romeo and Juliet* was played by a young man, as were all the female roles in Shakespeare.

After the late 1600s men usually portrayed women on stage as comic characters. Their impersonations were not meant to be taken seriously. What Julian Eltinge did was totally different. In all of his roles he convincingly portrayed well-dressed and glamorous women. These characters displayed the female gender ideals of the day, and Eltinge, as he became increasingly famous, was cited in the media as an example of perfect femininity.

Eltinge's fame grew quickly. In 1906 he made his London debut playing for King Edward VII. He returned to New York the next year an international star. He had a number of Broadway successes and was highly praised for his 1910 show *The Fascinating Widow*. Two years later the Julian Eltinge Theater was built and named after him on Forty-Second Street. For an actor, to have a theater named for you was considered the height of theatrical fame.

Eltinge moved to Los Angeles and, over the next few years, made a series of successful silent movies—often playing both male and female roles. For a time, he was one of the biggest stars in the new movie industry. In 1918 he returned to New York to play the legendary Palace Theater, for which he was paid $3,500 a week, comparable to $63,000 today. That same year Eltinge built a new home, the Villa Capistrano, in the hills of the Silver Lake section of Los Angeles. It was considered one of the most lavish homes of a Hollywood star.

Julian Eltinge touched a deep chord with American audiences because he was both exposing and exploring the new thinking about gender in the country at the time. Throughout the nineteenth century, American women and men had seen many changes in ideas about gender and

sexuality. Women had more freedom than ever before—
and would get the right to vote in 1920—and men understood that there were many different ways to be manly.

What Eltinge demonstrated in his act was that the
traditional trappings of femininity were artificial trappings. What many perceived as a "pretty woman" was
not the result of a natural state but of artfully applied
make-up and attractive clothing. With the right effort,
even a man could be a pretty woman. Eltinge understood
how influential he was, and during his career he published
three separate magazines aimed at a female readership.
In them, he gave advice on beauty, clothing, and running
a household.

Some historians presume that Eltinge was a gay man,
but this is a label he actively resisted. Eltinge spent a great
deal of time in the press promoting the idea that he was
a "real man." He engaged in rowdy behavior, smoked
cigars, got into fights, and physically attacked people—
even audience members—who questioned his heterosexuality. His press agents released numerous stories about his
skills as a poker player, his ability to work on his farm,
and his fishing expertise. He also announced a series of
marriage engagements to women—and even stated that
he had been married once or twice—though none of this
was true. Although Americans loved Eltinge as a man in
a dress playing beautiful women, he understood that he
would not be accepted as a homosexual man who could
love and desire other men. The new openness in American
society had not gone that far.

As Julian Eltinge, and the century, grew older, attitudes about cross-dressing also changed as the practice
became more closely identified with male homosexuality.

Most states passed laws or enforced older laws (some of which were the result of the social purity movements lobbying government officials to ban "indecent" entertainment) that made it illegal for women and men to cross-dress in public. Nightclubs and theaters were often forbidden to feature cross-dressing—now called "drag"—in performance. Eltinge lost a great deal of his money in the stock market crash of 1929, and during the 1930s his career was in decline. By 1940, Los Angeles police had instituted a new rule that required female impersonators to have an "impersonation license" and to undergo an interview with a police department psychiatrist, presumably to determine if they were homosexual.

In one of his last shows, Eltinge was forbidden to dress as a woman, and the act consisted of him, dressed in a tuxedo, singing songs while standing next to a mannequin dressed in the gown he would have worn had he been allowed. He died in 1941 in his apartment after a cerebral hemorrhage he sustained during a nightclub performance.

A NEW CENTURY OF FREEDOM

RADICAL VISIONS, REVOLUTIONARY ACTIONS

1900–1960

CHAPTER FIFTEEN

MARIE EQUI

Fighting for Women, Workers, Peace, and Justice for All

The United States is a nation of immigrants and Marie Equi—nationally famous physician, labor organizer, women's rights advocate, and antiwar activist—was one of them. Her father's family came from Fornaci di Barga, a small town in Italy. Looking for a new life in America, Giovanni Equi, at twelve years old, set sail on the *Gondar*, which arrived in New York in May 1853. He then took a smaller ship to New Bedford, on the southern coast of Massachusetts. There he joined his brother Dominic, who had come to the US ten years earlier.

Giovanni changed his name to John and learned to be a stone mason, like his brother. Thirteen years later, in 1866, he married Sarah Mullins, an Irish immigrant. She had come to America at the age of nine, along with her widowed mother. Her grandparents had been Irish revolutionaries fighting English rule. Marie Diana Equi, born in 1872, was the fifth of their eleven children.

Marie Equi's young life was full of contradictions. Her family was poor yet owned a home and a small lot on which they built an apartment building. Although she was basically healthy, she caught tuberculosis and had to go to Florida to recuperate. She was an excellent student who had to drop out of high school to help support the family by working in a factory. Luckily, Marie had a friend, Betsy Bell Holcomb, who helped her, in 1889, get into the Northfield Seminary for Young Ladies, a private school. Meanwhile Holcomb—who was called Bessie—attended Wellesley College.

Dr. Marie Equi, 1910s.

Within two years both women had dropped out of school. In 1891 Holcomb decided to make the three-thousand-mile cross-country trip from Massachusetts to Oregon. There she bought 122 acres of land outside Portland and became a farmer. In 1892 Equi joined her there as her friend and, eventually, partner.

In Oregon, Holcomb taught at Wasco Independent Academy, a private school, and both she and Equi worked the land. In 1897 the two women decided to move to San Francisco and start new lives. Holcomb wanted to become a landscape painter and Equi wanted to become a doctor. This was a brave decision because at that time, only 6 percent of doctors in the US were women. In addition, Equi had not graduated high school or college.

But Equi passed the medical school entrance exam and in 1899 enrolled in the College of Physicians and Surgeons in San Francisco. Holcomb helped her pay the tuition, $115 a year. In her second year in med school, after ten years together, Equi and Holcomb split up. Equi

An assistant to Dr. Marie Equi with a patient in her office.

became involved with Mary Ellen Parker, a medical student, and Holcomb married a man.

After finishing her coursework in San Francisco, Equi moved back to Portland in 1901, this time with Mary Ellen Parker. They both finished medical school in Oregon and both became physicians with their own practices. Equi's practice focused on women's and family health, which, at the time, was a new field of medicine. The Progressive Era of American politics—which saw the advancement of many social justice issues—had begun, and Equi embraced it wholeheartedly. Seeing how women were disadvantaged politically, she joined the growing suffrage movement in Oregon. Her experience of poverty and doing mill work in New Bedford led her to support labor unions and the fight to improve the lives of working women and men. Equi was a woman of decisive action.

People on Sacramento Street watching the city burn after the San Francisco earthquake of 1906.

On April 18, 1906, San Francisco was hit with a devastating earthquake. The city was in ruins and ravaged with fires. Equi and a group of volunteers from Oregon immediately traveled south to help. Her work was so acclaimed that the *Oregon Daily Journal* wrote that she was "one of the most conspicuous examples of self-sacrifice in [a] desire to aid the suffering that has been seen in Portland."

It was around this time that Equi and Parker broke up. Equi, now thirty-three, soon began a new relationship with a woman she had met a year earlier, Harriet Speckart, who was a decade younger than Equi. By 1907 Equi and Speckart were living together. Speckart wrote to a relative, "Yes, I am very happy single, especially now that I have Dr. Equi. I need no more, she loves me the same as I love her."

By 1913 Equi was known in Oregon, and soon nationally, as a radical. Women still did not have the vote, and she was a vocal activist for women's suffrage and workers' rights. She often spoke out in public, on street corners, and at meetings. When the women at a local fruit cannery went on strike, Equi joined their picket line. Though not a factory worker, she became a leader of the strike and was quoted in the *New York Times* and *Washington Post*. When the police tried to break up the picket lines, she led the workers in resisting them. Because of her fierce activism, she was arrested numerous times and became a national leader for workplace reforms such as the eight-hour day and an end to child labor.

Equi and Speckart were a visible, public couple, and in 1915 they adopted a child, Mary, who called Speckart "Ma" and Equi "Da." Understanding that social justice causes were linked to one another, Equi, like Jane Addams, also became an advocate for world peace and spoke out against the US entering World War I, which was raging in Europe. In 1917 she attended a protest against war preparations. Making the connection between unregulated capitalism, the exploitation of workers, and war profiteering, she carried a banner that read: "PREPARE TO DIE, WORKINGMEN, J. P. MORGAN & CO. WANT PREPAREDNESS FOR PROFIT."

This act of free speech was enough to get her into trouble with the government. Three years later Equi was convicted under the federal Sedition Act, a law Congress passed in 1918 that punished individuals for speaking out against the government or World War I, which was ongoing at that time. Equi was sentenced to three years in San Quentin Prison. This was a moment in American history often called the Red Scare because people with communist, socialist, or just progressive views were targeted and members of the Communist Party were known as "Reds," and the government was intent on discouraging, even criminalizing, political dissent. Equi, who had always voiced her beliefs, as was her right as a citizen, found this very discouraging. She served her prison sentence, during which Harriet Speckart wrote her every day and was the sole caretaker for their daughter, who was now six. Equi was released in 1921 after ten months for good behavior. Life in prison was not easy for Equi, who was only forty-eight years old but not in good health, and after leaving prison she never regained her previous stamina.

Marie Equi returned to her life as a physician and continued to speak out against injustice. She and Speckart separated—the latter doing much of the parenting—and remained friends. Speckart died suddenly in 1927 at age forty-four, and Mary, now twelve, moved in with Equi.

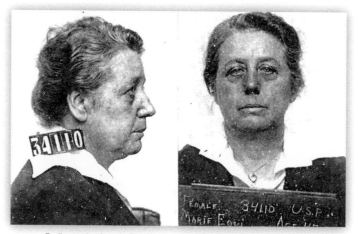

Equi's mugshot from the San Quentin Prison after being arrested for protesting.

The firebrand activist remained in the public eye, though she was slowed due to ill health and being a full-time mother. Her home became a center for the younger activists who sought her advice. Mary eventually went to college. She married in 1937 and named her daughter Harriet Marie after her own two mothers. After a series of illnesses and time in a nursing home resulting from a broken hip, Marie Equi died at age eighty in 1952. She was buried in Portland next to Harriet Speckart.

CHAPTER SIXTEEN

GLADYS BENTLEY

Blues-Singing Bulldagger

Like many young people eager to become show business stars, seventeen-year-old Gladys Alberta Bentley decided to try her luck in New York City. She arrived in the city sometime between 1923 and 1925. The timing was perfect. The Great War, today known as World War I, had ended in 1918. The industrial economy was booming and no one knew the Great Depression would begin in just a few years.

It was the Jazz Age, named for an exciting new form of music invented by African Americans such as Jelly Roll Morton and Louis Armstrong. This was also the time of Prohibition, when liquor was officially outlawed in the US but available in illegal bars called speakeasies. New York was a thriving international center for culture and entertainment. Harlem—the largest Black urban neighborhood in the north—was a hotbed of clubs, speakeasies, and nightclubs filled with the new music.

Bentley was one of the African American artists who were helping to create the Jazz Age. She was a singer who also played the piano, and even at a young age, she knew that she had talent. Bentley was drawn to Harlem as the perfect place for her to work and also because she had romantic relationships with women and thought Harlem would be an accepting place.

Bentley found part-time jobs as a pianist, and then got a break at Harry Hansberry's Clam House, one of Harlem's most noted clubs and speakeasies. The Clam House had a lot of queer customers and was located right in the center of Harlem nightlife, a stretch of 133rd Street between Seventh and Lenox Avenues known as "Jungle Alley."

Stories differ on how Bentley came to her famous look of dressing as a man. Some people claim that the Clam House was looking for a male piano player and Bentley began performing dressed as a man. Others claim that she already dressed in a "mannish" fashion and simply got the job because she was a great performer.

Dressing in clothing associated with the opposite sex was not as shocking in New York as it may have been other places. This was at the time when Julian Eltinge had his successful career in the theater. Same-sex attractions and breaking traditional gender norms were a largely accepted part of Harlem culture. Effeminate male performers (who dressed as men) were often called pansies, and "pansy performers" were an entertainment craze in America in the 1930s. (Bert Lahr as the Cowardly Lion, in the 1939 film *The Wizard of Oz*, is an example of a pansy performance.) Men who had sex with men, whether they identified as gay or not, might also be called "sissy men" or "freakish men." Masculine women, particularly masculine lesbians, were called "bulldaggers," which is the origin of the term "bulldyke." As a two-hundred-fifty-pound, well-built woman who dressed in men's clothing, Gladys Bentley was certainly a bulldagger.

Bentley found an audience, and a home, in Harlem's very openly queer night culture, which was wonderful as her life had not been easy before. She was born in Philadelphia in 1907. Her parents, George and Mary, were working people who wanted the best for their children and urged that their children act properly and look respectable. Bentley, although generally an obedient child, disliked wearing dresses and preferred her younger brother's clothing. She broke her school's dress code to do this and was ridiculed by teachers and other students. Later in life she wrote:

> Now, I tried to withstand my parents, but they got after me so often [about dressing in men's clothing] that we finally compromised, agreeing that I would wear middy blouses and skirts.

Bentley knew who she was and what she wanted from an early age, even though her ideas clashed with other people's notions of "respectability." She determined to use her vibrant singing and enormous skill at playing the piano to live life as she wished.

After building a strong following at Harlem nightspots, Bentley signed up with an agent and was given a contract to record eight songs. She was paid four hundred dollars, which would be just under six thousand today. That was a great deal of money for a young person in the entertainment industry at that time. Some of her songs she wrote herself; others were traditional blues numbers. All gave voice to the pain of women loving men, sometimes being hurt by them. As in many blues songs, the women

Gladys Bentley, the "Brown Bomber of Sophisticated Song."

in her songs were strong and open about their sexual desires and feelings.

Bentley came to life in her live performances. She wore a man's white tuxedo and a top hat and often had a chorus line of young men dressed as "pansies" or sometimes as women. In her songs—already sexually charged—she occasionally changed the pronouns to make them about same-sex relationships. Her audiences were ready for this, as there were existing queer blues songs such as "Sissy Man Blues" and "Two Old Maids in a Folding Bed."

Bentley became very famous in and outside Harlem. Noted Harlem Renaissance poet Langston Hughes, in *The Big Sea*, wrote:

Miss Bentley sat, and played a big piano all night long, literally all night, without stopping—singing songs like "The St. James Infirmary" from ten in the evening until dawn, with scarcely a break between the notes, sliding from one song to another, with a powerful and continuous underbeat of jungle rhythm.

Bentley's audience was also broader than lesbians and gay men. The Harlem newspaper the *Afro American* wrote in 1936:

> Prancing about in her cream-colored full dress suit, her hair closely chopped and slicked down into a pompadour, Miss Bentley (whom many mistake for a man) delivers her prize number "Nothing Now Perplexes Like the Sexes, Because When You See Them Switch, You Can't Tell Which Is Which."

Although Bentley never played on a Broadway stage, she was billed in Harlem as Broadway's Queen of Song and Jazz.

Misunderstood Gladys Alberta Bentley from Philadelphia was now famous and applauded not only for her talent and boldness but also for her frankness and for proudly displaying who she was. Other noted African American women performers had romantic relationships with women, including Alberta Hunter, Bessie Smith, and Ethel Waters, but none of them was as daring in public as Bentley. At the time, there were even widely believed rumors that Bentley had publicly married a woman in an unofficial ceremony, although there is no confirmed evidence that this happened.

As the Great Depression began affecting all of America, and Prohibition ended in 1933, the vibrant nightlife of Harlem also began changing. The excitement of the Roaring Twenties was over. New Yorkers, and most Americans, were now poorer. By the late 1930s Bentley's career needed a boost, and she went to the West Coast.

In Los Angeles, she played the noted gay club Joaquin's El Rancho, until the police stopped her from performing in men's clothing. They used the same law that would not allow Julian Eltinge to perform in dresses. By 1942 Bentley was appearing at San Francisco's famous lesbian bar Mona's 440 Club and was advertised as "The Brown Bomber of Sophisticated Song." All the entertainers at Mona's 440 Club dressed as men, many wearing tuxedos, and the bar was known for its happy embrace of sexual and gender difference. For example, singer and songwriter Kay Scott played there around the same time and was famous for singing these lines in the persona of a heterosexual man:

There goes my gal, she changed her name to Mike,
There's goes my gal, she turned into a dyke.
She cut her hair,
She's wearing shirts and ties,
She used to make men stare,
Now she gives the girls the eyes,
I just can't figure out how it all began,
There goes my gal, a lesbian.

Despite her popularity in San Francisco, Bentley's career began to decline. In 1945 she recorded some heterosexually themed blues songs with the Excelsior label, which specialized in African American artists and marketed to a multiracial audience. She moved back to New York and played clubs there as well as on the West Coast. She continued to make records into the 1950s.

In the August 1952 issue of the African American magazine *Ebony*, Bentley wrote an article, "I Am a Woman Again," in which she indicated she was no longer lesbian—although she never uses the word—and had undergone hormone treatment to become heterosexual. She even claimed to have gotten married to a man. This was untrue, although she did marry a man soon after the article was published.

So much of the article is blatantly untrue that it's difficult to find the few facts in the fiction. It does clearly show, however, that Bentley wanted to change her image. Later in life, Bentley settled in Los Angeles and lived with her mother, with whom she had so much trouble as a teenager. During this time Bentley had become religious and was very active in her church, where she trained to be an evangelical minister. Bentley died in her sleep in 1960 from complications of the flu. She was only fifty-two years old.

We don't know exactly why Bentley changed as she got older. Perhaps she felt pressure from the push for socially conservative attitudes in the 1950s. The law against cross-dressing in Los Angeles clubs is one example of that. On the other hand, this was also a time of tremendous growth, increasing visibility, and political awareness for the LGBTQ community. What we do know is that as an African American woman who had to deal with racism and prejudice against women, as well as homophobia, Bentley faced opposition her whole life. The more accepting culture of the 1920s, and of Harlem, allowed Gladys Bentley to become famous as the enormously talented person she was.

HARLEM: A SYMBOL OF FREEDOM

For about a hundred years, from the end of the Civil War to the end of World War II, the United States changed from a farm-based rural society to one where most people lived in cities. For LGBTQ people facing discrimination, urban life has many advantages. In small towns everybody knows you, knows your parents, knows if you're single or married, and knows your living arrangements. At that time, many people lived with their families or next door to them. In a big city it was, and still is, easier to be anonymous and lead a private life.

Cities allowed LGBTQ people a new measure of freedom. They could seek out and find one another in bars or clubs. They could also move to neighborhoods that were known to be more accepting of same-sex behavior and sexual choices. In Manhattan two of these neighborhoods were Greenwich Village, which was home to bohemians, artists, and political radicals, and Harlem.

The name "Harlem" dates back to the Dutch colonists who arrived in New York in the seventeenth century and called the area "Haarlem," after a city in the Netherlands. By the nineteenth century Harlem was home to many immigrant groups. By the

Harlem tenement neighborhood in the summer, 1930s.

early twentieth century it was quickly becoming home to African Americans who were migrating north after the Civil War. Though New York City was by no means free from racial abuse and segregation, many Americans still felt life was easier there. By the 1920s Harlem was a primarily African American neighborhood with its own stores, restaurants, bars, beauty shops, and apartment houses. African Americans held political office and ran their own businesses. At the same time Harlem became a symbol of and a center for African American intellectual and cultural life.

The neighborhood became a symbol of freedom and independence, and not just for African Americans. It also became known as a place where lesbians and gay men might feel safer, if not more welcomed. This might have been because it was filled with women and men who had traveled there to escape oppression and were therefore more tolerant. It was also because of the influence of the many musicians, artists, and other cultural leaders who lived there.

Crowds outside the Lafayette Theatre in Harlem at the opening of *Macbeth*, produced by the Federal Negro Theatre, 1936.

(continues on next page)

(continued from previous page)

Many of the leading Harlem writers and thinkers of this time were gay, lesbian, or bisexual. This group includes the poets Langston Hughes and Bruce Nugent; fiction writers Claude McKay, Wallace Thurman, and Alice Dunbar-Nelson; and playwright Angelina Weld Grimké. Along with other writers, artists, and performers, they were part of what is called the Harlem Renaissance, a movement of incredible artistic energy and political activism that celebrated African American life and culture.

The cultural energy and radicalism of Harlem didn't just come from writers and intellectuals. Blues singers in Harlem addressed sexuality with a frankness not found elsewhere. Ma Rainey, who got her start in the South, was famous for her "Prove It On Me Blues," in which she declared her bisexuality. Songs such as Bessie Jackson's "B. D. Woman Blues" ("B.D." was an abbreviation for "bulldagger") and Ma Rainey's "Sissy Blues," both from the 1920s, were other examples. Bisexual blues singer Bessie Smith was famous for her song of personal freedom, "Tain't Nobody's Biz-ness If I Do."

Harlem was also famous for its drag balls where women and men could dress and act as freely as they wanted. These events, called "costume balls," were held at Hamilton Lodge, the Rockland Palace, and even the staid Savoy Ballroom, and were attended by thousands of people. There were also speakeasies, jazz hangouts, and nightclubs that catered to an LGBTQ clientele.

There was homophobia in Harlem, just as there was in the rest of America. There was also a greater sense of tolerance and acceptance that allowed for more sexual and gender freedom.

CHAPTER SEVENTEEN

WORLD WAR II

The War That Started LGBTQ Politics

World War II profoundly changed American culture, especially the lives of LGBTQ people. While the conflict was immensely destructive and tragic, the war effort involved almost the entire population. Rules and codes of social and personal conduct that had existed before the war were put aside or overlooked. This had the effect of allowing people of all colors, genders, and sexualities to take on new roles. Women and men were expected to help with the war effort. Men usually joined the military. Because so many men were away training or overseas fighting, new opportunities opened on the home front for women. Breaking from traditional gender roles, women were allowed—even urged—to take on jobs, including industrial work, they had previously been denied. The image of the muscular, patriotic Rosie the Riveter—a character made famous by the iconic image of a woman welder with the slogan "We Can Do It!"—was a radical shift in how women were portrayed in the culture.

World War II began in Europe in September 1939. The United States did not enter until the Japanese attacked the Pearl Harbor military base in Hawaii in December 1941. By the end of the war, in 1945, more than sixteen million Americans had joined the armed forces. Ten million of those had been drafted. Millions of men from diverse backgrounds, races, and religions lived together in a completely new environment.

The majority of the men were white, but not all. Seven hundred thousand, or 4 percent of the military, were African American, and three hundred and fifty thousand, or 2 percent, were Mexican American. Chinese Americans, Native Americans, and Puerto Ricans joined in smaller numbers. Throughout the war the American armed forces were segregated. (This finally changed in 1948.) Only white men could become officers or fight in combat. African Americans and members of other minority racial groups worked as cooks, truck drivers, or warehouse workers.

The armed forces accepted men up to the age of thirty-eight, however the majority of the men in all branches were in their twenties. Thirty-five percent of the Navy during the war were teenagers. Young men, freed from the expectations of their parents or peers, were suddenly free to explore who they were. Many of these men, often in stressful, life-or-death situations, turned to fellow soldiers for emotional support or comfort.

Before the war only nurses were admitted into the military. Now women could enlist in separate women's branches of the services. Over 250,000 women signed up for the Women Auxiliary Army Corps (WAAC), the Women Accepted for Volunteer Emergency Service (WAVES), the Marines, and the SPARS, the female division of the Coast Guard.

Military service offered women the opportunities, status, and respect they were frequently denied in civilian life. Women performed numerous jobs, including nursing, weather forecasting, photography, and air traffic control.

Highly trained African American women workers building a warship during World War II, 1943.

Most vital was the work of radio and telephone operators and communications directors. They were viewed, by others and by themselves, as strong, competent, and skilled professionals. Historians, such as Lillian Faderman, surmise that many women in the armed services—single, with no children, and career oriented—were lesbians.

The war—in the trenches, on military bases, on battleships, or on the home front—turned life expectations upside down for everyone. People were away from home and family, meeting others they would not have met in their home town, being exposed to new ideas, and often forced—when facing the possibility of death—to think about who they really were. Some women and men knew they were homosexual before they entered the military; numerous others became aware of their sexuality during this time. Many service members were under twenty-one or a little older and ready to uncover new aspects of themselves. Some of these people found long- or short-term lovers during the war. Others may have waited until they reentered civilian life to act on their desires. Whatever their stories, World War II was a turning point for LGBTQ people and their community.

After the war many of the women and men who had discovered their homosexuality decided to actively pursue love lives and friendships with other LGBTQ people. Many did not move back to their small towns but went to cities where they found communities of other gay women and men. These are the beginnings of established LGBTQ neighborhoods. Being able to live in an actual *place* that welcomed them—the apartment buildings, stores, parks, cafes, bars, and streets of a neighborhood—was an important precursor to women and men discovering and building a social and a political community. These neighborhoods often sprang up where military ships docked: New York, San Francisco, Boston, San Diego, Baltimore, and Los Angeles. It was in these places that modern LGBTQ life in the United States began.

Here are two stories of a man and a woman who lived through the war and started a new chapter of LGBTQ American history.

JOSÉ SARRIA

In the 1950s José Sarria was famous as a drag performer at the noted Black Cat Cafe in San Francisco performing skits that dealt explicitly with themes of police entrapment and violence. He became so famous that, in 1961, he ran as an openly gay candidate—and won six thousand votes—for the San Francisco Board of Supervisors. He was the first openly gay candidate to run for office in the United States.

On December 9, 1941, two days after the attack on Pearl Harbor, Sarria was a just-under-five-feet tall, ninety-pound eighteen-year-old who wanted to join the armed services reserves. He was also gay and knew it. At the time, Sarria was a first-year college student and too young to enlist without his mother's permission, and she was against him joining up.

The Sarrias were a close-knit family. His mother, Maria Dolores Maldonado, was from an upper-class family in Bogota, Colombia. She had to flee the country for political reasons, and in San Francisco she met and married Julio Sarria. Julio soon deserted the family, and José was raised by his mother and godparents.

Behind his mother's back, Sarria convinced his godmother to sign the permission papers he needed to enlist. He was turned down by the marines (for being too short) and by the navy (he was not qualified to take the required math courses), however he got lucky when he went to the army. The major in charge of the recruitment center knew Sarria from the city's active gay social scene and, sympathetic to Sarria's desire to enlist, overlooked the height and weight requirements (as well as his homosexuality). The war effort needed so many men that throughout most of the war, enlistment centers would often overlook issues—such as being homosexual—that might otherwise exclude candidates.

Sarria was soon called up for active duty and was assigned to the Signal Corps, which is concerned with communications and "intelligence," the term used for information gathering. Because he spoke several languages he was assigned to the Intelligence School. The offer was withdrawn, however, after the army looked into Sarria's personal life. Later in life he was to say, with some irony: "I mean I had no lisp, but I wasn't the most masculine guy in town. . . . So I think that they figured that I was a little bit gay."

Remaining in the Signal Corps, Sarria was sent to Cooks and Bakers School, where he did very well. Men in the Signal Corps began to receive orders to go overseas, but Sarria, still a minor, could not be sent into battle. He was then assigned to the Army Specialist Training Program (ASTP) and would eventually be sent overseas as part of an infantry unit. Knowing that the infantry were the first men to go into battle—and had a high risk of being killed or wounded—Sarria managed to be assigned to the motor pool. There he met a young major named Theodore Mataxis, for whom he became an orderly and later a cook for him and his fellow officers.

It was already December 1944 when Sarria's unit shipped out of port from Boston and landed in Marseilles, France. The Allies had landed in Normandy in June of that year and were now advancing on Germany. After Marseilles, in southern France, the battalion moved north to Limburg, Germany, close to Frankfurt. By the end of the war, in the spring of 1945, when Germany surrendered, they were in Berlin.

Though the war was over, American and Allied forces continued to occupy Germany. Sarria was stationed in Berlin, where he organized and became supervisor of an officers' club in a stately old Berlin mansion. He spent the next two years there and was ultimately promoted to staff sergeant. Discharged in 1947, he returned home to San Francisco.

It was there he began his career as an entertainer and became a beloved community figure and spokesperson. After running for the San Francisco Board of Supervisors, he founded the Tavern Guild in 1962, a business association of gay bars and clubs that were being harassed by the police and city government. In 1963 he helped found the Society for Individual Rights, an early LGBTQ rights group.

José Sarria died on August 19, 2013, at the age of ninety, at his home in Los Ranchos de Albuquerque, New Mexico.

PAT BOND

Pat Childers was as patriotic as the next American. However, when she enlisted in the Women's Army Corps (WAC) in 1945—just as the war was ending—it wasn't really to support the war effort. Her real reason was to meet other lesbians.

Childers was an only child born into a Chicago family. Her parents divorced when she was young, and her mother remarried and moved the family to Iowa. Childers was smart, talented, and lonely. She read a lot and kept a diary. As a teen she had a crush on her female French teacher and then on a good friend, and after a while she realized that these were not school-girl crushes: she was a lesbian. Because she knew no other lesbians, she despaired of being all alone in the world. That was why, when she turned nineteen, she enlisted in the army.

She figured that among all the strong, butch-looking women in the service there must be some lesbians. Like a lot of women, gay or straight, she also knew that joining up was a way to be independent, to get out of the country, and to have adventures.

Childers found out that her hunch was correct. Later in life she told interviewers that many officers, and the majority of enlisted women, were also lesbians. It was against army regulations to be gay or lesbian at the time (and was for many years later). The army needed every person it could get, however, so that rule was ignored, as it had been for Jose Sarria. Women would often come to the enlistment center dressed in men's clothing, and as long as they said they had never loved a woman romantically, they were accepted.

After becoming a WAC, Childers's first assignment was in Hawaii where she cared for wounded soldiers who were returning from fighting in the South Pacific. Before she left, while stationed in San Francisco, she had married, perhaps as a cover, a gay man named Paul Bond. Now Pat Bond was "officially" heterosexual even though she was very much out as a lesbian in other parts of her life. In 1946 Bond and her WAC unit—who she claims were almost all lesbians—were sent to Tokyo, Japan.

Hundreds of thousands of gay men and lesbians had served and fought bravely in World War II. When the war was over, in 1945, the armed forces decided these soldiers, sailors, nurses, and others were no longer needed. The military began a purge to get rid of them. Many homosexuals were expelled and given dishonorable discharges, which made it almost impossible to find civilian employment. Bond's outfit saw over five hundred expulsions, and at least one woman committed suicide. Bond was safe because of her marriage, and after leaving the WACs, she moved to San Francisco.

Once in San Francisco, Bond quickly discovered a thriving lesbian and gay male community. She made friends, lived with other lesbians, and went to lesbian bars such as the previously mentioned Mona's 440 Club, which was one of the most popular. She also rediscovered a love of theater and earned bachelor's and master's degrees in theater arts from San Francisco State College (now San Francisco State University). She began to act in local theater productions and to write her own work.

By the later 1970s Bond was well-known in San Francisco as a great talker, personality, and performer. In 1978 she was featured, along with more than two dozen other LGBTQ people interviewed, in the documentary film *Word Is Out*. Bond wrote and performed a series of one-woman shows about her own life as well as lesbian women from throughout history, such as the American-born but Paris-based writers Gertrude Stein and her lover Alice B. Toklas. Bond also acted in films and television shows.

Bond was lucky to escape the antigay witch hunts in the armed forces; many women and men were not. These were a sign of a new backlash against the relative permissiveness of the war years.

CHAPTER EIGHTEEN

HARRY HAY

How His Society of Fools Started a Revolution

On November 11, 1950, five men sat quietly on a hill overlooking Silver Lake in Los Angeles. They did not realize it then, but this gathering was to be the beginning of the gay and lesbian rights movement in the United States. Out of that small meeting would grow the Mattachine (pronounced matt-a-sheen) Society, the first organization in the United States to fight for LGBTQ rights, becoming an openly gay political voice in national politics.

The men on that hill— Harry Hay, Rudi Gernreich, Bob Hull, Chuck Rowland, and Dale Jennings—had a complex series of relationships. Hay and Gernreich had been lovers for six months. Hull and Rowland had met a decade before and were lovers, roommates, and best friends. Although they lived together, they also dated other men. At that time Hull was having an affair with Jennings. In addition, Hay, Hull, and Rowland were, or had been, members of the American Communist Party. Many women and men had joined the party in the 1930s because of their support for the labor movement or to defend the Soviet Union, which during World War II was a US ally and at war with Germany.

There is little doubt that Harry Hay was the main organizer for the meeting, even though Hull and Roland had suggested it. Hay, who was still a member of the Community Party as an organizer, had been pondering an almost unimaginable concept for nearly two years. What if homosexuals—the word he used then—were to form a political organization to promote their basic human and civil rights? The belief that homosexuals are an oppressed minority may seem commonplace now, yet at the time it was revolutionary. So was the idea that, like other minorities, gay people shared a common identity, history, interests, and political goals. Hay—using Marxist thought and Communist Party language—called LGBTQ people a "social minority" or a "cultural minority." This was the first time anyone had stated it that way. Hay's political concept could be applied to both lesbian women and gay men, although Mattachine quickly evolved into an almost entirely gay male organization.

As Hay's thoughts had been evolving over the years, he had written up a statement, titled "The Call," which proposed an international organization of gay men. The proposed group would be "a service and welfare organization devoted to the protection and improvement of Society's Androgynous Minority." "Androgynous minority" was a coded term that referred to gay men.

Hay shared this document with a few other men, and Hull and Rowland responded enthusiastically. It was dangerous for the first five men to organize the group since there were actually laws against homosexuals congregating in public. These laws were usually used to arrest men who were gathering in parks or at bars looking to meet one another, but they could be used in any social situation, even private homes. Yet Hay and the other men began to do some very cautious outreach. After a few more

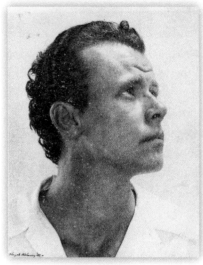
Harry Hay, 1933.

men joined, they chose the name Society of Fools. This was based on the belief, true or not, that in medieval times the king's "fool," or jester, was the only person allowed to tell the truth to the monarch. In April 1951, the Society of Fools voted to change the name to the Mattachine Society. This was the name of a medieval French all-male secret society who, because their identities were unknown, were able to challenge feudal power structures. This obscure name also served another function. No one would ever suspect it was a group of homosexual men with an explicitly political agenda.

The founding of the Mattachine Society might seem like a small act, but it changed history. Who was Harry Hay? How was he able to imagine and execute such a bold, radical idea in the conservative culture of the United States in the 1950s?

Hay's early life was filled with change and adventure. Although his parents were both Americans, he was born in 1912 in Sussex, a rural county in England. His father was a mining engineer and traveled for his work. When he was two, the family moved to Chile, but after his father sustained a severe injury in 1919, they moved to Los Angeles.

In the US, Hay was bullied by classmates for what they saw as his effeminate mannerisms. He was always attracted to other men, and at age nine was innocently experimenting with sex with a slightly older male friend. Even as a young boy Hay was a good student and an avid reader, and loved the theater. At age twelve, he discovered a book called *The Intermediate Sex*, by Edward Carpenter. That book, published in 1908, was one of the first works in English about same-sex desire. In this book Hay learned the concept of "homosexual"—Carpenter used the old-fashioned term "uranian"—and Hay knew it applied to him.

In his early teens Hay spent summers working on his cousin's cattle ranch in Nevada. While the other young men might be relishing the out-of-doors, Hay was making friends with the older ranch hands. Several of them were members of the Wobblies—the nickname for the radical workers' union the Industrial Workers of the World (IWW). This led Hay to study the theories of Karl Marx, the founder of modern communist thought. He also became very close to members of the Northern Paiute people and started a lifelong interest in Native American spirituality.

During his second summer in Nevada, Hay joined the Wobblies and received a union card. That fall, at age fourteen, he went to San Francisco. At the union hall he lied about his age to get a job on a cargo ship. After this adventure, he came home and after graduating high school attended Stanford University. Here he pursued his interests in theater, as well as progressive politics. He also actively pursued sexual relationships with men.

Hay's politics and personal life came together as he thought about the oppression of gay men. (One of his serious limitations is that he was never very interested in the lives of women.) Working in theater a few years later, he met and became involved with the actor Will Geer, who much later was well-known as a Hollywood actor, most famously as the grandfather on the TV show *The Waltons*. Geer was a Communist Party member, and Hay joined the party in 1938.

The Communist Party was radical in its thinking about workers and race. Its views on homosexuality were, unfortunately, no different than those of most of America. The party officially highly disapproved of homosexuality, which it called a symptom of "bourgeois decadence." They saw it as a harmful activity caused by a lack of moral and political dedication to Marxist ideals.

In 1939, on the advice of Communist Party members and his therapist, Hay married Anita Platky, a woman who shared his political commitments. In time they adopted two daughters, moved to New York, and then back to Los Angeles. Hay was involved in political organizing, theater, and teaching. Although married and a father, he was still having sex with men. Neither marriage nor heterosexual family life changed his sexual desires. In 1945 he became very ill with a series of physical ailments and anxiety disorders. Being in the closet literally made him sick.

Hay was married to Platky during the time he helped found Mattachine Society. He was also lovers with Rudi Gernreich. Finally, the underlying contradictions in their marriage proved too much. Hay and Platky divorced in 1951, and while Hay continued to support his family, Platky, understandably, felt angry and betrayed by him. Hay also told the Communist Party he was gay and offered to resign or to accept expulsion. This divorce was less acrimonious. The party did expel him as a security risk, not for being a homosexual. It also declared him to be a "Lifelong Friend of the People."

After his marriage ended, Hay devoted much of his time to Mattachine. There were many difficulties in organizing and running the organization. Because sexual acts between men, and between women, were illegal in all of the United States, people were very unwilling to come out. Just the rumor you might be gay or lesbian could get you fired from your job. If their sexuality was discovered, people were often disowned by their families. Being "out" took a great deal of courage and was often accompanied by hostility, pain, and very real danger of assault or arrest.

Because of these dangers, Mattachine needed to find ways to be open enough to get its message across and attract new members, while at the same time stay private enough to protect the members' identities. Hay's background in labor organizing and the Communist Party gave him the perfect plan of how to do this. He used the Communist Party model of "cells" to organize Mattachine. Members of one cell would not know the identity of members of any other cell, thus insuring a degree of privacy. He also drew upon organization models of older fraternal groups, such as the Freemasons, which built strong bonds among their members while keeping identities secret.

Over the years Mattachine published two magazines, *ONE* and the *Mattachine Review*. These were vital to men who were afraid or unable to come to meetings or who lived where joining Mattachine or even attending a Mattachine event was not possible. By the 1960s Mattachine had several chapters across the United States. Each of them functioned independently and in different ways, but they all provided a place for gay men to become involved in a wide range of political activities. Some chapters were open and bold enough to bring court cases to fight antigay discrimination.

Mattachine, like any organization, went through many changes, and Hay left it after a while as a new, more conservative, leadership took over. He remained involved in cultural ideas and politics until the end of his life. His relationship with Rudi Gernreich ended soon after Mattachine started, and he quickly entered into an eleven-year relationship with Jorn Kamgren, a Danish hat designer. The two opened a hat store in Los Angeles. Hay left Kamgren in 1962 and soon met John Burnside, with whom he would spend the rest of his life. In the late

"Homosexuals are different . . . but . . ." Mattachine Society poster declaring that the rights "of homosexuals are as precious as those of any other citizen," 1960.

1970s Hay and Burnside became involved in organizing a new group, and identity, for gay men: the Radical Faeries.

In forming this new group, Hay drew on upon his vast knowledge of Native American spirituality, European folklore, and psychology. Believing that gay men were spiritually and psychologically unique, Hay hoped his new group would help build their spiritual connections with each other. This was, in many ways, the ultimate expression of Hay's belief in building a larger community of loving friends. That community was one he sought to build throughout his life. Harry Hay died in 2002, at the age of ninety. John Burnside outlived him and died in 2008, at the age of ninety-one.

CHAPTER NINETEEN

PHYLLIS LYON
AND DEL MARTIN

Climbing the Ladder of Freedom and Justice

The story of Daughters of Bilitis—the first political and social organization for lesbians in America—begins as a love story.

The story starts after World War II. For many Americans it was a happy time. The war was over, and the US had defeated fascism. The economy was on the upswing, at least for the white middle class. (It is seldom noted that the 1950s, though a time of prosperity for some, also had a 22 percent poverty rate, the highest ever recorded in the US.) With the war over, the millions of men who had been in military service returned home, and they needed jobs. The millions of women who had gone to work in factories and offices during the war were expected to give up their jobs.

The radical social changes that occurred during the war gave way to more traditional trends. Women were now expected to resume traditional patterns: marry, raise children, and be homemakers. In this ideal, and false, picture-perfect version of life, they would move to the suburbs and live in a house with a white-picket fence. Some women actually lived that life, but certainly not all. Women at or below the poverty level could not move to the suburbs, and many women, particularly women of color, had to work to support their families. Lesbians were not going to marry the man of their dreams. They needed to find jobs to support themselves.

Neither Phyllis Lyon and Del Martin had worked during the war—they were too young—but they were now both women facing the problem of trying to find employment. They were also looking to figure out how to live productive, happy, and—if possible—somewhat open lives in the 1950s. That's what they had in common. Their backgrounds were quite different

Lyon was born in 1924 in Tulsa, Oklahoma. Her family moved frequently while she was growing up, and they finally settled in Northern California, the area she considered her home. Lyon's mother was a Southern belle, and by some accounts Phyllis took after her. She attended Sacramento High School and was popular, socially engaged, and energetic. Her friends said she was flirtatious and liked to dress up.

In 1946 Lyon graduated from the University of California, Berkeley, with a degree in journalism. For a few years after that she worked as a crime reporter for the *Chico Enterprise-Record* in a small town just north of Sacramento. She soon grew tired of small-town life, which had few social options for a young lesbian. In the late 1940s Lyon moved to Seattle, Washington, where she worked on the editorial board of *Pacific Builder and Engineer*.

Del Martin had a very different life journey before she met Lyon. She was born Dorothy Louise Taliaferro in 1921 in San Francisco. Taliaferro was an excellent student and the salutatorian of the first graduating class of San Francisco's George Washington High School. Like Lyon, she had an interest in journalism, a profession that was more open to women, including single women, at the time. She also attended the University of California, Berkeley, although did not know Lyon at the time. She later transferred to San Francisco State College.

While in college, at age nineteen, Taliaferro married James Martin and soon after had a daughter, Kendra. Many lesbians and gay men married during this time, because of social and family pressure or because life as part of a heterosexual couple seemed easier. The marriage lasted only four years. For several years after the divorce, Kendra lived with Dorothy, but when James Martin re-married, Kendra moved in with her father. Dorothy kept Martin's last name, which was common practice at the time for divorced women.

As a twenty-three-year-old, single, divorced woman and, for a while, full-time mother, Martin knew she had to start a new life. She moved to Seattle—a year or so after Lyon had moved there—and became the editor of *Daily Construction Reports*, a copublication of *Pacific Builder and Engineer*. Construction and engineering were traditionally male-dominated fields, even in their trade journals, but neither Lyon nor Martin were women to be daunted by convention.

The two women met through their work, and Lyon remembers being impressed by Martin because she was the first woman Lyon had ever seen carrying a briefcase. During her adult life, Martin favored tailored suits and shorter hair—the briefcase was a very fitting, and professional, complement to her look.

The two women became close friends—Lyon even threw a welcome-to-town party when Martin officially moved to Seattle—and they started a casual sexual relationship. After two years, they moved to a more serious relationship. By that time Martin had changed her first name from Dorothy to the more butch Del. She and Lyon moved in together and declared their commitment to each other on Valentine's Day, 1953.

By 1955 Lyon and Martin were living as a couple in San Francisco. Even then, it was a relatively gay-friendly town, with numerous bars and clubs run by and for women. Lyon and Martin did not know many other lesbians. At the time there was a newspaper campaign to "clean up" the city, and in particular lesbian bars because they catered to "sexually rebellious" teenage girls. The result was a series of police raids on both gay male and lesbian meeting places.

Phyllis Lyon (left) and Del Martin at a NOW conference, 1975.

Lyon and Martin decided there was now an urgent need to create new ways for lesbians to meet one another or merely make sexual contacts, and they envisioned a group to make that happen. As important, such a group could also help form a community where women could find friendship and companionship, share interests, and discuss their problems.

Lyon and Martin knew about the Mattachine Society and were critical of its almost entirely male focus. Mattachine members had never reached out to lesbians, and the issues it addressed, such as arrests for sexual solicitation in public places—which was rarely a concern for lesbians since they did not usually engage in this behavior—were mostly concerns of gay men. Yet, Lyon and Martin admired Hay's vision, which led them to start a similar group that would meet the needs and concerns of lesbians. Not surprisingly, the concerns of lesbians were often the concerns of women in general: finding good jobs and battling gender discrimination and sexual harassment in the workplace. They also included family law, divorce, and childcare, since many lesbians, like Martin, had married and had children before they came out.

In 1955 Lyon and Martin met with six other women and decided to start a social networking group called the Daughters of Bilitis. They choose the name carefully. As Harry Hay did with Mattachine, they wanted a name that would resonate with lesbians yet was invisible to heterosexuals. Many lesbians, at the time, knew of a volume of lesbian-themed poems titled *The Songs of Bilitis*. It had been written by a heterosexual French poet, Pierre Louÿs in 1894. Martin, Lyon, and the other women decided to call the new group *Daughters* of Bilitis because it echoed that most patriotic of American women's groups, Daughters of the American Revolution (DAR). The DAR was, and still is, a conservative organization of women who can trace their families back to the nation's earliest years.

Martin and Lyon, the unofficial leaders of the organization, began publishing a newsletter, the *Ladder*. Lyon was the first editor and Martin took over in 1962. Beginning as a stapled stack of typewritten and printed sheets, the *Ladder* soon evolved into a regular magazine with cover art and advertising. Its first issue was published in October 1956 and spoke to the needs and concerns of lesbians across America. There were articles explaining the scope and limits of antigay laws, interviews with psychiatrists about homosexuality, discussions about butch/femme roles, the possibility of same-sex marriage, what it meant to be a lesbian mother, and discussing lesbians and religion. There were also advice columns, notices about upcoming events, letters to the editor, and a long-running, comprehensive book review column, by librarian Barbara Grier, that alerted readers to new books with homosexual themes, many of which were not reviewed elsewhere.

The tone of the *Ladder*'s articles skated between serious and lighthearted: "Church Rules on Homosexuality" was in the same issue as "On Wearing Slacks—A New Twist on an Old Beef"; both appeared in the November 1957 issue. As important as these articles were, the cover art was more radical. The cover drawing for the October 1957 issue depicted a young woman removing a mask, with a tear running down its cheek, from her now smiling face. Its message was clear. Society wanted lesbians to remain invisible, keep quiet, remain in the shadows. Portraying an image, even a drawing, of a lesbian was bold, and by the mid-1960s the magazine was featuring photographs of actual lesbian women, which was unprecedented. It was no longer possible to think that lesbians were invisible; there was photographic proof.

Although it had only five hundred subscribers, the *Ladder* was read by many more, as copies were passed from hand to hand. Women who were afraid to subscribe themselves could still read the magazine. Soon after the founding of Daughters of Bilitis, women across the country started their own chapters. By 1961 there were chapters in Chicago, Cleveland, Denver, Detroit, Los Angeles, New York, New Orleans, Philadelphia, and San Diego. *The Ladder* and Daughters of Bilitis were a turning point in how lesbians lived their lives and thought of themselves. It was proof—even if you only heard of them and never went to a meeting—that there was a community of women who loved other women.

Lyon and Martin stayed with Daughters of Bilitis for many years and were also active in multiple community projects. In the later 1960s they were members of the National Organization for Women (NOW), and in 1972 they were early members of the LGBTQ political group the Alice B. Toklas Democratic Club, based in San Francisco. In 1977 Martin was the first open lesbian to be appointed to the San Francisco Commission on the Status of Women, and in 1995 US Senator Dianne Feinstein and Congresswoman Nancy Pelosi named Martin and Lyon delegates to the White House Conference on Aging.

In February 2004 San Francisco mayor Gavin Newsom challenged the state's marriage laws, and the city began issuing marriage licenses to same-sex couples. Over four thousand couples applied. Phyllis Lyon and Del

Martin—who had been together for fifty-two years—were first in line. A few months later the California Supreme Court ruled that these marriages were not legal. But, on June 16, 2008, when the California Supreme Court officially allowed same-sex marriage, they married again—the first in line and the only couple to be married by the mayor. Del Martin died on August 27, 2008, at age eighty-seven, survived by Phyllis Lyon, who was eighty-three at the time.

REVOLUTIONARY CHANGES

THE SEEDS OF PROTEST BEGIN TO BLOOM

1960–1977

CHAPTER TWENTY

PAULI MURRAY

"You must remember that truth is our only sword"

It took a lot of nerve to write the letter. After all, it accused President Franklin D. Roosevelt of overt racism, and it wasn't exactly polite. But Pauli Murray was upset and angry.

It was 1942, and Murray was a thirty-one-year-old law student at Howard University, a historically Black college. She'd been working day and night to help Odell Waller, a twenty-four-year-old African American sharecropper from Virginia. Waller had been accused of killing his white landowner and was convicted of murder by an all-white jury. He'd been sentenced to death.

Murray, working for the socialist Worker's Defense League (WDL), had campaigned with Waller's mother to build public support to save Waller from his death sentence. Sadly, the campaign failed and Waller was executed. To make matters worse, tensions around the case sparked a string of anti-Black incidents in Virginia, including lynchings and related violence.

Murray wrote her angry letter to Roosevelt because she felt the president had not done enough to help African Americans. She accused him of catering to the racism of Southern Democrats, even though, "black votes were among that large balance of power which swung you into office for two successive terms."

Knowing her letter stood little chance of reaching the president, she sent it to the First Lady. Eleanor Roosevelt was an outspoken, very public campaigner for civil rights. Murray asked Mrs. Roosevelt to pass the letter along to her husband, writing, "If some of our statements are bitter these days, you must remember that truth is our only sword."

Eleanor Roosevelt delivered the letter to her husband but also had harsh words for Murray: "For one who must really have a knowledge of the workings of our kind of government, your letter seems to me one of the most thoughtless I have ever read."

Murray quickly responded: "You have been totally frank with me, and I should like to be equally frank with you." Murray followed this with a long essay on political and social issues including international politics. In one section she compared American Jim Crow laws—which mandated racial segregation and other discriminatory practices—and racism to Hitler's racist practices. Roosevelt was so impressed she asked Murray to the White House. After that meeting the two women became close friends.

Pauli Murray's story is one of a woman's journey through a truly remarkable life. It is also the story of the African American civil rights struggle in this country, as well as the history of modern feminism and the struggle for women's equality under the law. Interwoven with that is an example of how one person, often publicly, navigated ideas about gender and sexuality in her life and her chosen communities.

Murray was born Anna Pauline Murray, on November 20, 1910, in Baltimore, Maryland. Her mother died when she was three, and her father, who had suffered emotional problems and was a patient in a segregated public mental hospital with an all-white staff, died after being beaten by an orderly. Pauline was raised by her aunt and grandparents in Durham, North Carolina. Her grandmother had been a slave, and her grandfather had fought with the Union army in the Civil War. Pauline was a very bright student who taught herself to read when she was five and excelled in school. After high school, she refused, on principle, to go to the segregated colleges in the South. Instead, she made arrangements to live with relatives in New York City. There she finished high school and then attended Hunter College, which at that time was an all-women's school and did not charge tuition.

As a youngster Murray was known for wearing pants rather than dresses and skirts. Her aunt Pauline referred to her as a "little boy-girl," and Murray sometimes called herself Pete or Dude. She began calling herself Pauli in 1934 when she published a short story with an ambiguously sexed narrator and wanted her authorship to be ambiguous as well. She used that name for the rest of her life.

In the relative freedom of the North, Murray began to think about her sexuality. At age nineteen she wrote in her journal that she found herself falling in love with members of her own sex, yet had no way of expressing it.

Murray resisted the label of "lesbian." She spoke with a psychiatrist and did her own research and decided she was a "pseudohermaphrodite." That was a term used in the 1940s to describe someone we might now call trans. Murray believed that even though she had been born with a woman's body, she was somehow biologically male. She was attracted to women and not interested in traditional female activities. She wanted to dress and present herself as a man, although she did not use male pronouns to describe herself in public.

Murray was married to a man in 1930, and the relationship was short lived—Murray was resistant to having heterosexual intercourse—although they remained legally married for eighteen years. She rarely spoke of this episode of her life. We know from her letters and journals that she had relationships with women, including her lover, Adelene McBean. We also know that she asked the photographer, socialite, and antiracism activist Nancy Cunard to take a photo of her as Pete, her "boy self."

In 1940 Murray and Mc-Bean went to visit Murray's family in North Carolina. Buses in the South then were segregated and African Americans were expected to sit in the back. On the way to Richmond, Virginia, the two women boarded a bus in which the seats in the back section were broken. They moved closer to the front. When the bus driver asked them to move, they refused and were arrested and sent to jail. That was fifteen years before Rosa

Pauli Murray as one of her "boy selves," 1935.

Parks's famous act of civil disobedience. The Workers Defense League, an advocacy group with whom Murray had worked, paid their fines, and the women were not charged with breaking segregation laws, only disorderly conduct, so the case never went to court.

In 1938 Murray applied to the University of North Carolina School of Law but was rejected because she was African American. In 1941 she entered law school at Howard University. However, there she faced discrimination as a woman. Teachers and her fellow male students were not shy about expressing their antagonism toward her for thinking a woman could become a lawyer. It was during this time that Murray coined the phrase "Jane Crow." If "Jim Crow" was the term used for the segregation laws and racist attitudes directed against African Americans, then "Jane Crow" referred to the specific oppression of Black women in America.

By this time, and especially after her work on the Odell Waller case, Murray was known as an expert organizer, civil rights activist, and a fighter for women's rights. Yet, despite being first in her graduating class at Howard, in 1944, she was unable to accept a fellowship for graduate work at Harvard Law School because it did not accept women to the school, although it did accept a limited number of African American men. After completing postgraduate work at the University of California, Berkeley, Murray was appointed the first Black deputy attorney general of California in 1946. In 1947 she was voted Woman of the Year by *Mademoiselle* magazine.

Throughout her life Murray demonstrated tremendous energy and drive pursuing equality and social justice.

In 1950 she published an important legal work, *States' Laws on Race and Color*. According to Supreme Court Justice Thurgood Marshall, Murray's book was the legal "bible of the civil rights movement" and was influential in helping him shape his arguments for *Brown v. Board of Education*, the landmark case that ended legal segregation in the nation's schools. In 1961 Murray was appointed by President John F. Kennedy to the Presidential Commission on the Status of Women. Betty Friedan, whose book *The Feminine Mystique* helped propel modern American feminism, was inspired by Murray and her work to cofound the National Organization for Women (NOW). Murray saw NOW as an NAACP (National Association for the Advancement of Colored People) for women and was on the board of directors. She left shortly after its founding because of the organization's lack of interest in women of color and issues of poverty.

Much of Murray's work was centered on discrimination against women—especially women of color. In 1963 she publicly criticized the groundbreaking March on Washington for Jobs and Freedom for not asking a woman to address the marchers. She then went back to law school, at Yale University, and graduated in 1965 with a doctor of law degree. It was her third law degree; she was the first African American to be awarded one at Yale.

During this time Murray also went through some major changes in her personal life. In 1956, two years after *Brown v. Board of Education* was argued and won, she took a job at a big New York law firm known for taking controversial, political cases. Murray celebrated her new position with an afternoon tea with Eleanor Roosevelt. There was something else to celebrate as well. At her new job, Murray met Irene "Renee" Barlow, the office manager, with whom she would become life partners. Murray was forty-six at the time, and Barlow was forty-two. Barlow had come to the United States from England at age six, and while very proper in her appearance, she was, at heart, a renegade. She and Murray connected immediately. Both were rebellious, both were women in a man's world and profession, and both were devout Episcopalians.

Murray and Barlow never lived together, but they vacationed together, shared a bank account, visited Eleanor Roosevelt together, and both were invited as a couple, to Eleanor Roosevelt's funeral, in 1962. They were together for seventeen years. Renee Barlow died of a brain tumor on February 21, 1973, at age fifty-nine. Murray was at her side for the month of her hospitalization.

In 1974 Murray's life took another surprising and groundbreaking turn. Her faith and spirituality had grown steadily over the years, due in part to her relationship with Barlow. At the age of sixty-four, after a lifetime of law and activism, Murray took up a new calling: the church. She entered the General Theological Seminary in New York and three years later became the first African American woman ordained as an Episcopal priest. She gave her first sermon in her family church in Durham and later continued her parish work in Washington, DC.

Murray died on July 1, 1985, at age seventy-four. Her ashes were interred along with those of Renee Barlow. In 2012 the General Convention of the Episcopal Church voted to honor Murray as one of its Holy Women, Holy Men, to be commemorated on the anniversary of her death.

Murray's life, concerns, and politics were at the epicenter of social justice movements of the twentieth century. Issues of race, gender, sexuality, and economic equality defined how she acted and the decisions she made. Feminists use the phrase "the personal is political" to define how lives and politics coincided. Murray's life is a perfect example of this.

CHAPTER TWENTY-ONE

BAYARD RUSTIN

A Life of Activism

Bayard Rustin's life story is full of surprising events and unconventional circumstances. It is also, in many ways, the story of the fight for freedom and justice in the United States. Despite setbacks and struggles, Rustin spent his entire adult life trying to make this country a better, safer, more accepting place in which all people could live.

The first surprise in Rustin's life was when he discovered that his older "sister" Florence was actually his mother. Julia and Janifer Rustin, the couple he thought were his parents, were in fact his grandparents. Florence, as a teenager, gave birth to Rustin in 1912, and everyone thought it best that he be raised by his grandparents. When he discovered the truth through town gossip, Julia confessed and told her son, "Florence is your mother but we're one big family and we are all mothers for everyone."

It was a loving, happy family. Julia and Janifer had eleven other children and lived in a large, spacious home in West Chester, Pennsylvania. They were well off, making their money with a catering business. They were also very connected to church communities and political activism, both of which were an inspiration to their grandson. Julia was raised as a Quaker, and both Rustin's maternal grandparents attended the liberal African Methodist Episcopal Church. Their church emphasized the importance of community service and solidarity.

Julia and Janifer were each aware of their own personal history and of the issues facing African Americans. Janifer's parents were slaves, and Julia was descended from the native Delaware tribe as well as free African Americans. Both were members of the NAACP, which at this time was not only fighting for legal reforms on issues of race but was also an organization through which intellectuals and activists such as W. E. B. Du Bois, Mary McLeod Bethune, and James Weldon Johnson could generate new ideas and strategies for making America a more just place for everyone. These leaders of the early civil rights movement stayed with the Rustins when they were in town. Religion and politics were always part of Bayard Rustin's life.

As was most of America, West Chester was racially segregated, and so was Rustin's high school. He thrived in school, played football, ran track, took the leads in the drama club's productions, and published poetry. He also loved music and sang in the church choir and in a gospel group. After graduating in 1932, he received a scholarship to Wilberforce University, a historically Black college in western Ohio. This was not a good fit, though, as Rustin, as a pacifist, disagreed with the school's mandatory student participation in required military training in a Reserve Officer Training Corps (ROTC) program, which prepared members for military service. After two years he transferred to the Quaker-founded Cheyney State Teachers College. However, he left that school after two years, unhappy.

Rustin knew he wanted to be an activist. At Wilberforce he led a student protest for better food. At Cheyney State Teachers College he became familiar with the American Friends Service Committee (AFSC), a Quaker social action organization. The AFSC was very active in the fight for civil rights, peace, and justice and in community organizing. Rustin would maintain an association with them for much of his life. He also became friends with the noted labor organizer A. Philip Randolph, who was to play an important part later in Rustin's life.

It was also around this time that Rustin came to understand that the closeness and affection he felt for men was sexual attraction. By 1937 he had moved to Harlem, with its very active gay social scene. He also became involved in the professional theater and politics. He sang at the famous left-wing Greenwich Village nightclub Café Society and became active in the Quaker community.

In 1941, after a series of jobs as an organizer, Rustin was hired at the Fellowship of Reconciliation (FOR), a pacifist organization founded on Christian principles. Here he participated in a number of projects, including strategizing ways to desegregate the armed forces, working to protect the property of the Japanese Americans sent to internment camps during World War II, and changing the policy of racial discrimination on interstate buses. He was also becoming increasingly committed to principles of pacifism and to the nonviolent philosophy and tactics of the Indian political leader Mahatma Gandhi. Rustin's work at FOR was so successful that he gained a reputation as an extraordinary political organizer.

In 1943, at a conference at Bryn Mawr College, Rustin met Davis Platt, eleven years younger and white, who was to become his lover. Platt came from a wealthy family and was distancing himself from them, fearing that they would discover he was gay. Platt was involved in the AFSC and had much in common with Rustin. Later in life Platt remembered his meeting with Rustin: "The moment our eyes met was electric. Maybe I fooled myself, but I think he really fell for me. And I certainly fell for him."

Rustin soon found his personal principles tested. In 1943, at the height of World War II, he was called by his draft board. Rustin responded, saying that, due to his pacifist ideals, he was unable to follow the order to report. He knew that this act would send him to prison. At this time, one in six federal prisoners were men, conscientious objectors, who were resisting the draft.

On March 9, 1944, Rustin arrived at the federal prison in Ashland, Kentucky. He knew that being a gay Black man in a segregated prison with white guards placed him in great danger. When he and Platt exchanged letters, Platt wrote as a woman so they would not be discovered to be lovers. In prison, Rustin taught classes and also organized against the system's racial segregation. Before, during, and after prison, Rustin was under great pressure from his superiors in FOR to abandon his homosexuality. He refused, and upon his release from prison in 1946, he moved in with Platt in an apartment in Harlem.

The two men were happy. Rustin was traveling the country on FOR business, while Platt, now a student, stayed in New York. Rustin was sexually active with other men, both on the road and in New York. For a while he and Platt had an open relationship, but eventually they separated. Rustin's habit of seeking hookups in public places, called cruising at the time, often got him into trouble with his superiors and the police. In 1953 he was arrested in Pasadena, California, for having sex with a man in a car and spent a short time in jail. He then went on a successful trip to Africa to expand a FOR program there, and on his return he was fired by the Fellowship of Reconciliation, as well as by the American Friends Service Committee. This was, in part, due to the homophobia in these organizations. They were also afraid that their work could be discredited due to Rustin's openness about his sexuality and the potential of negative publicity if he were to be arrested again.

That same year, 1953, Rustin was hired as executive secretary of the War Resister's League, a peace organization founded in 1923. He remained in that job for more than a decade. During that time, in 1956, Bayard Rustin was to meet the man who would have the most influence on his life and his career: the Reverend Dr. Martin Luther King Jr.

In December 1955 Rosa Parks, a member of the NAACP and a political organizer, was arrested in Montgomery, Alabama, for refusing to move to the back of a public bus. At that time buses were segregated, and Black people were legally required to sit in the back. Her refusal had been planned as a political action. This was the beginning of the Montgomery bus boycott, one of the turning points in the American civil rights movement. Rustin went to Montgomery to support the boycott and help train the community in nonviolent resistance, based on the principles of Gandhi. The atmosphere was tense; the homes of two organizers had already been firebombed.

The bus boycott was the first time the young Dr. King took a leading role in the civil rights movement. He soon

Activist Bayard Rustin speaking to a group of young people before a civil rights demonstration, 1965.

became known for his nonviolent resistance strategies, much of which he had learned from Rustin. The two became close allies. Rustin played an important role at a time of great crisis. He wrote protest songs, drafted speeches, and helped run meetings.

After Montgomery, Rustin and King continued to work together and cofounded the Southern Christian Leadership Conference (SCLC). Some civil rights leaders were uncomfortable with Rustin's sexuality. Dr. King ignored them and enlisted Rustin to organize the famous 1963 March on Washington for Jobs and Freedom. The leader of this march was Rustin's old colleague, A. Philip Randolph. Rustin and others worked tirelessly on the march, where King delivered his "I Have a Dream" speech. It was the crowning moment of Rustin's organizing career and the turning point in the American civil rights movement.

Rustin went on to help with many civil rights and labor battles. He founded and was the director of the A. Philip Randolph Institute, which helped build strong ties between the civil rights and American labor movements. He was also a regular columnist for the newspaper of the AFL-CIO, the nation's main union organization.

In April 1977, while crossing a street in Times Square, New York City, Rustin met Walter Naegle, who was twenty-seven years old. Naegle had worked in VISTA, a federal program founded in 1965 to help fight domestic poverty. The two men started talking and found they had many common interests, including folk music and protest movements. They become involved, and as their relationship blossomed, so did Rustin.

Rustin had never been comfortable speaking publicly about his sexuality or his relationships. For all of his activism, he had never taken a public position on the gay rights movement. Rustin was already publicly known to be gay because of his arrests, though he never formally came out as an LGBTQ activist. Now, with Naegle's support and encouragement, he began speaking out as a gay Black man. He became involved in LGBTQ politics and helped pass New York City's first LGBTQ antidiscrimination law.

Because same-sex marriage was not yet an option, Rustin and Naegle needed to find some way to form a legal relationship to secure inheritance rights and financial security after one of them died. In 1982, after five years together, Rustin adopted Naegle as his son. Rustin died, at age seventy-five, in 1987. Naegle is now the executive director of the Bayard Rustin Fund, which commemorates

Walter Naegle receives the Medal of Freedom from President Barack Obama on behalf of his partner, Bayard Rustin, during a ceremony at the White House, 2013.

Rustin's life, values, and legacy. On November 20, 2013, President Barack Obama presented Rustin with a posthumous Medal of Freedom for his work on the 1963 March on Washington for Jobs and Freedom. Walter Naegle accepted the award on Rustin's behalf.

CHAPTER TWENTY-TWO

CARL WITTMAN

Radical Movements, Political Organizing, and Country Dance

It was May 1969, the month before the Stonewall riots in New York. The idea of a gay revolution was already in the air on both the East and the West Coasts. LGBTQ activists looked at militant political movements such as the Black Power movement, radical feminism, and the Chicano rights movement (called El Movimiento) and wondered, When would the LGBTQ community have its own?

Carl Wittman was an East Coast antiwar activist who had been living in San Francisco for two years. A seasoned organizer and writer, Wittman knew it was time to put on paper the ideas that were swirling around the gay community. He sat down and, drawing upon all of his political experience, wrote "Refugees from Amerika: A Gay Manifesto," which would quickly become, and still is, the defining document for the gay liberation movement.

Wittman was twenty-six when he wrote the "Manifesto," and his life had already been full of formative personal and political experiences. Born in 1943 in Hackensack, New Jersey, Wittman, along with his parents and older sister, Joan, later moved to the suburb of Paramus. To their neighbors the Wittmans looked like a typical suburban family. And they were, except that Carl's parents, Walter and Jeanette, were long-time Communist Party members and political organizers. It was from them that Carl Wittman first learned about social justice and activism. These were lessons he carried with him his entire life.

Wittman was sexually active with boys and men beginning at age fourteen. He continued this through high school and college, although he never spoke about it or came out. After graduating high school in 1960, he enrolled in Swarthmore College. The school had a long Quaker tradition of political action, so it was a perfect fit.

Along with his studies and work on the college newspaper, the *Phoenix*, Wittman was involved in student activism. Most of this work related to protesting segregation and racial discrimination. He and other Swarthmore students were arrested protesting segregation policies in Chester, Pennsylvania, and in Cambridge, Maryland. Through these experiences, Wittman began to understand that ending racial discrimination was only part of fixing a much larger problem. He began to argue that it was necessary to build a movement that fought for political equality and social economic justice for all. In 1963, while still at Swarthmore, Wittman joined the recently formed Students for a Democratic Society (SDS). He became prominent in the organization and joined the national council. Later that year he and Tom Hayden, another SDS activist, wrote *An Interracial Movement of the Poor?* Here they argued that the injustice of racial discrimination would not be solved if issues of poverty and economic justice were not addressed as well.

After Swarthmore, Wittman worked on SDS organizing projects in Union City, New Jersey. The New Left (as this movement of young people was called) was not perfect. Most of the leaders were heterosexual men, and some promoted an institutional climate of misogyny (deep contempt for and prejudice against women) and homophobia. Feminists were just beginning their critique of sexism in American, and the concept of gay rights was just taking root in the American imagination. Faced with homophobia, Wittman left SDS but continued to be an activist.

In 1966 Wittman married his close friend, and a political colleague, Mimi Feingold. It wasn't unusual for gay men and lesbians in progressive groups to marry members of the other sex. This was partly because there was pressure to remain in the closet. These were not cold-hearted arrangements. The partners often loved one another, their intense shared experiences bringing them even closer.

Wittman and Feingold moved to San Francisco in 1967 and lived communally with other activists working to end the war in Vietnam and helping men to resist the draft. In 1968, when Wittman was called to report to the Oakland draft board, he made the political decision to declare his homosexuality. Under armed forces rules, this would automatically get him out of the draft.

To some, this decision might have seemed like an easy way to avoid service. (Occasionally, heterosexual men pretended to be gay in order to get out of the draft.) Wittman, however, was not merely trying to get out of the draft. He was making an open and courageous personal and political statement. He explained his action in his journal: "My being honest about my homosexuality was

as much a principle as refusing to fight their dirty wars."
As Wittman became more involved in the gay community,
he and Feingold drifted apart and had separated by 1969.

His essay, "Refugees from Amerika: A Gay Manifesto," was published by Red Butterfly, a radical gay male
collective in New York City and reprinted in numerous
gay and progressive magazines. Wittman's arguments in
"A Gay Manifesto" were simple but revolutionary. The
most important ideas were these: Being queer is not just
OK; it's good. In fact, it's great. It is important to come
out. It's important to work with a wide range of people
and groups on a wide range of political issues and never
compromise on your gay identity. It is important to speak
from your own experience. All people, gay or straight,
need to rethink their relationships and not unthinkingly
rely on traditional ideas such as marriage. Most important, he wrote that sexuality is one of the most important
aspects of our lives. By acknowledging this as important
in ourselves and others, we will be able to relate to one
another in more harmonious and constructive ways.

Wittman's manifesto was enormously influential. It
was the first published statement to bring together political concepts that had emerged from other movements and
reimagine them in the experiences of LGBTQ people.

Around this time, Wittman met and became lovers
with Stevens McClave. In 1971 they moved from San
Francisco to Wolf Creek, Oregon, with the plan of starting a gay male rural political community. A few years
later, Wittman met and entered a long-term relationship
with Allan Troxler, an artist who had been involved
with gay politics. Eventually, in 1974, they and others
began publishing *RFD: A Country Journal for Gay Men*

Allan Troxler (left) and Carl Wittman (right) with friends, 1975.

Everywhere, which explored all aspects of rural living. At heart, *RFD* promoted country living as a spiritual, back-to-the-earth alternative to urban life and sought to connect gay men to nature.

For Wittman, life at Wolf Creek increasingly revolved around environmental activism. The first Earth Day had been held in 1970, so environmental activism was a new movement. He also pursued his love of folk dancing. Folk dance, like folk music, was seen by some activists as a way to connect with a more communal and authentic culture while rejecting modern consumer society. Wittman researched, wrote about, and taught English and Scottish country dance. He developed new ways of thinking about and performing these dances that were non-gender-specific and more communal. Wittman believed that culture, art, and personal relationships should reflect your political principles just as much as your political activism. They were all connected and all demanded attention to social justice and equality.

After a decade at Wolf Creek, Wittman and Troxler moved to Durham, North Carolina, where they had friends and family. Wittman continued to take on organizing projects, including the first Gay and Lesbian Pride March; helped to cofound the Durham Lesbian and Gay Health Project; and worked on community-based environmental issues.

Wittman was diagnosed with HIV-AIDS in the mid-1980s when there was no effective medical treatment available. As he became increasingly ill and realized he had few, if any, acceptable options, he took his own life with a painless lethal drug and died at home. Allan Troxler, his family, and friends were there with him. As he had done all of his life, Carl Wittman made an informed decision according to his sense of ethics and acted on it with dignity and grace. The impact of Wittman's "Refugees from Amerika: A Gay Manifesto" was tremendous. His experience in the civil rights movement, SDS, and the peace movement allowed him to articulate the essence of the radical potential of gay liberation.

CHAPTER TWENTY-THREE

RITA MAE BROWN

The Lavender Menace Writes
Her Way to Freedom

It was the covert action that changed the course of the gay liberation movement, as well as feminism. And they did it all with T-shirts.

It was 1970. The women's movement, which had started in 1963 with the publication of Betty Friedan's book *The Feminine Mystique*, was in full swing. The National Organization for Women (NOW) had been founded in 1966. In just four years it was making progress changing laws and changing minds. NOW, however, had a big problem. It was an organization for women, but not all women. It was very uncomfortable with—in fact, it did all it could to avoid—women who were openly lesbian. Friedan, NOW's founder and director, thought the presence of open lesbians in the organization would give feminism a bad reputation. Lesbians were considered by many in society to be social outcasts, mentally ill, even criminals and Friedan did not want the women's movement to be associated with them. She went so far as to call lesbians the Lavender Menace.

On May 1, 1970, NOW was hosting the Second Congress to Unite Women. The event was being held at a middle school in Greenwich Village, New York. There were over three hundred women in the school auditorium waiting to hear speakers and start discussions. Just as the first speaker approached the podium, the entire room went dark. A minute later the lights flashed back on and suddenly there were seventeen women, including Rita Mae Brown, standing around the room wearing T-shirts that boldly proclaimed "LAVENDER MENACE." Many held signs that read "Take a Lesbian to Lunch!" or "Superdyke Loves You!" At that moment American feminism was put on notice that lesbians were feminists, and they were not going away. And they had a really great sense of humor.

How did the Lavender Menace action—which was called a "zap," in the political lingo of the time—happen? Who was behind it? The story sounds like one of those fairy tales in which children are switched at birth.

Rita Mae Brown (right) during the "zap" at the Second Congress to Unite Women wearing a Lavender Menace T-shirt, 1970.

It begins in Hanover, a small town in Pennsylvania, population just over thirteen thousand. Brown was born there, in 1944, to an unwed teenage mother. Her father was married to someone else. (Later in life, Brown ironically explained, "Let's say I had illegitimate parents.") Unable to raise her baby, Brown's mother brought her to an orphanage. The infant was quickly rescued by her cousin, Julie Brown, and her husband, Ralph. They raised little Rita Mae as their own child.

Brown grew up in York, Pennsylvania, and then Fort Lauderdale, Florida. Even as a child she was a bright, unruly, opinionated, and driven person who knew her mind and who she was. Her first try at college, on scholarship, was at the segregated University of Florida at Gainesville. Her stay there ended after Brown angered the administration with her civil rights work and her open lesbianism. Both behaviors were completely unacceptable to the authorities. She transferred to another college in Florida, then decided to hitchhike to New York to explore better educational opportunities. She was accepted to New York University (NYU) on a scholarship in 1964, but had no money for a dorm room. Homeless for part of this time, she did her class work in a library as she worked toward her bachelor's degree in classics and English. She graduated in 1969.

While a student, Brown was a powerhouse of political organizing. She helped organize New York's first women's center and worked on other feminist projects. At NYU she was one of the cofounders of the Student Homophile League, one of the first LGBTQ student groups in the country. In 1968 she joined NOW but ultimately left (or was asked to leave) because of the group's refusal to deal with lesbianism. She then joined the Redstockings, a radical feminist group of mostly heterosexual women, and challenged them on their resistance to dealing with the oppression of lesbians.

In 1969, after the Stonewall rebellion, Brown joined the Gay Liberation Front (GLF). There she found the same resistance—this time from gay men—to lesbian issues that she had found in the women's movement. She wasn't alone. Some lesbian activists decided to stay in GLF and work to change it. Many others, including Brown, decided that they needed to strike out on their own to make their voices heard.

That was when Brown had the idea for the Lavender Menace zap at the NOW meeting. Bringing together lesbians she knew from GLF, Brown proposed writing their own manifesto. Their statement would explain why lesbian issues were vital to any discussion of both feminism and gay liberation. A group of about twenty women—who called themselves Radicalesbians—wrote the short, hard-hitting declaration titled "The Woman Identified Woman." They argued that lesbian identity—because it revolved only around women—was at the center of feminism. When the activist "lavender menaces" took over the NOW meeting, they passed out copies of "The Woman Identified Woman" to all the women assembled.

Some of the heterosexual women felt their meeting had been hijacked. They got angry and left. Amazingly, many others stayed and took part in discussions about the importance of including lesbianism and lesbian sexuality in feminist discussions. "The Woman Identified Woman" played as decisive a role as Carl Wittman's "Refugees from Amerika: A Gay Manifesto" did. It is still read and taught in courses about LGBTQ history.

Brown continued writing political essays and also began to write fiction. In 1973, after moving to Los Angeles, Brown published the semiautobiographical *Rubyfruit Jungle*. This was one of the first post-Stonewall LGBTQ coming-of-age novels, a critical success that wound up selling over a million copies.

Published by Daughters, Inc., a small feminist press, *Rubyfruit Jungle* told the story of Molly Bolt, a refugee from the South, and her adventures in New York City. Molly gets into scrapes, has love affairs, and finally becomes a filmmaker. The book is filled with politics, humor, and explicit lesbian sex scenes, which were shocking at the time. It became a model and inspiration for many lesbian-themed novels that followed.

Brown went on to write for film and television and may be best-known as the author of many bestselling mystery novels featuring the feline detective Sneaky Pie Brown, a cunning cat who, because she knows humans so well, is great at solving crimes.

Brown stopped being actively involved in the LGBTQ rights movement in the 1970s. However, she continues to speak out on political topics, including feminism, LGBTQ rights, AIDS, environmental issues, human rights, and animal rights.

In "The Woman Identified Woman," Brown and her coauthors caught a truth at exactly the right moment. Lesbians were women but often had different concerns than heterosexual women. They were homosexuals—a

word Brown would have used about herself growing up—
but, as women, had very different concerns than gay men.
"LGBTQ" is a great acronym, however, it is important
to remember that each of those letters represents a group
that has specific, individual experiences that need to be
articulated. Working together—as the Lavender Menace
knew—is important. Being able to say who you are and
what you need is equally important.

CHAPTER TWENTY-FOUR

GLORIA ANZALDÚA

A Life Between Borders

Our social order is built, in part, by putting people into neat categories. This person is male and that person is female. This person is white and that person is Black. We are meant to believe there are clear lines or borders between these categories and you have to be one or the other. From that belief comes the idea that if you do not fall neatly into a category, then you and maybe your entire life is, somehow, less real. Gloria Anzaldúa worked her entire life to argue that there is a vibrant existence that crosses the borders between the supposedly fixed categories of people. She lived the same way, crossing borders, mixing categories, and she made everyone's lives richer.

Anzaldúa's life began on a border. She was born on September 26, 1942, in the small town of Raymondville, Texas, just a forty-five-minute drive from the Mexican border. The town is known for its onion farms, a crop that is harvested by migrant workers, many from across the border. It is also a town with a long history of racial tensions and violence between the US-born and English-speaking farm owners and any farmworkers who dared form a labor union.

Anzaldúa's parents were Urbano Anzaldúa and Amalia Garcia Anzaldúa. Their families had been farmers in the area for six generations. Decades earlier, there had been many Chicano farmers around Raymondville, including Anzaldúa's grandparents. Some owned their own land, while others held land communally. In the 1930s, several summers of drought had caused the crops to fail, and cattle died of hoof-and-mouth disease. Anzaldúa's grandmother was unable to pay her property taxes and lost the land. Many other Chicano landowners found themselves in

Gloria Anzaldúa, 1980.

the same predicament, forced to sell to large agribusiness companies. In one generation they went from being land-owners to sharecroppers.

Sharecroppers farm land owned by someone else. Historically, they would owe a share of their crop to the landowner at harvest time. The more modern version of sharecropping meant that Anzaldúa's parents would borrow money from the landowner to buy seeds and other materials. At the end of the season they had to repay the loan, and then owed the company 40 percent of the profits, no matter how much they made.

One year, the Anzaldúas left Texas and worked on a farm in Arkansas. Unfortunately the earnings there were even worse. They then moved back to Texas, to the town of Hargill, not far from Raymondville. Anzaldúa grew up on three different company-owned farms there, including a chicken farm, where she and her siblings had to clean, weigh, and package eggs.

Group of children posing under sign that reads "U.S. Department of Agriculture Farm Security Administration Farm Workers Community," 1941.

Anzaldúa was the oldest of four children, and they all worked from an early age to support the family. Schools were segregated in Texas at this time, and Anzaldúa went to one for Hispanic students. She grew up speaking Spanish at home, the language her family had always spoken. In school the teachers demanded the students speak English at all times and harshly scolded them if they didn't. Even when she was in school, Anzaldúa never stopped working on the farm. Then, in June 1957, when she was fourteen, her father died, and she needed to work even more to support her family.

Despite these problems Anzaldúa thrived in school, even though her teachers assumed Hispanic students were less intelligent. She always wanted to be a writer, and after graduating high school in 1962, she enrolled in Texas

Woman's University. The university was far from home and ultimately she had to leave school to go back and work on the farm. Later, in 1965, she returned to college, this time at Pan American University, which was closer to home. She worked during the days and at night took classes in English and education.

Growing up near the border, Anzaldúa understood that her identity was complicated. She was both Chicano and American, and her Mexican heritage was also a mixture of different cultures, including Spanish and Indian. Anzaldúa did not see this as a problem but something of which she could be proud. She also knew that she lived on the borders of sexuality and gender. She was attracted to women and identified as a lesbian but was also sometimes attracted to men.

Anzaldúa came to believe that neither she—nor anyone —could be put into a neat category. Everyone is a mixture in their personality, in their heritage, and in their culture. To express this, Anzaldúa took the Spanish word *mestizaje*, originally meaning a mixture of races, and applied it in a broader way. In her writing, *mestizaje* means to live without binaries, to stop thinking of the world as being neatly divided into two halves. To fully express this, Anzaldúa began writing in a mixture of formal and colloquial Spanish and English, or

A sign in a small town in Texas, 1941.

what is sometimes called Spanglish, and in other languages. In all, she identified eight languages that she used.

These ideas about borders—the places where two identities or cultures meet, almost always with friction since one is usually more powerful than the other—informed Anzaldúa's thinking and writing.

Anzaldúa believed that this kind of mixture, living on the borders between categories, created great energy and creative opportunity. She would pursue this idea throughout her life. After earning a master's degree in 1972 from the University of Texas at Austin, she moved to Indiana. There she worked in schools with the families of migrant farmers. She tried to apply the lessons she had learned growing up on the border.

The work was rewarding for her, although it was also difficult and emotionally draining. After two years she returned to the University of Texas at Austin to begin a PhD program in comparative literature. During this time she became involved in feminist and lesbian politics, as well as with a broad range of Chicano political groups. The scope of these groups was not large enough for Anzaldúa's ideas. She wanted to create identities that went beyond those categories. She eventually left the program to teach and write.

In 1981, along with Cherríe Moraga, she edited *This Bridge Called My Back: Writings by Radical Women of Color*. The book completely transformed the discussions about race in the women's movement. *This Bridge Called My Back* was a collection of essays, literary criticism, poems, memoir, and reflection that gave voice to a full range of experiences of women of color. It was a demand that white women of all sexualities hear the voices of their sisters. The book existed on the uncomfortable borders of discussions of race and feminism, ethnicity and sexuality.

After *This Bridge*, Anzaldúa felt she had more to say and more work to do to explain her ideas. Over the next few years she moved about the United States, from San Francisco to New York, from Cambridge, Massachusetts, and New Haven, Connecticut, to Brooklyn, New York, finally settling in Northern California. She supported herself with part-time jobs, some teaching, and speaking engagements, and she often lived hand-to-mouth on food stamps and with help from friends.

In 1987 Anzaldúa published *Borderlands/La Frontera: The New Mestiza*. This collection of essays, autobiography, poems, myths, history, and fiction transformed readers' thinking about politics, identity, and history. The work was written in the mixture of the eight languages she had identified earlier and had a tremendous impact on the feminist and the LGBTQ movements. So much thinking in these movements was based on simple binaries—women and men; gay and straight—that Anzaldúa's insistence that life was more complicated, that change and tension happened on borders, pushed many people to think more deeply about their own lives.

Anzaldúa went back to school—this time to the University of California at Santa Cruz—for her PhD. She published another anthology, and in the 1990s published two bilingual books for children featuring the fictional character Prietita. She explored ideas about friendships and undocumented workers in *Friends from the Other Side/Amigos del otro lado* in 1993. Four years later *Prietita and the Ghost Woman/Prietita y la llorona* drew upon the Mexican legend of La Llorona, a weeping ghost—a mother looking for her dead children—and made it into a feminist tale of a young girl growing up and being helped by La Llorona.

In 1992 Anzaldúa was diagnosed with type-1 diabetes and struggled with health problems. Despite her fame as a writer, thinker, and teacher, she also had money problems. She won multiple awards for her groundbreaking work and published another anthology—a sequel to *This Bridge Called My Back*—and continued working on her PhD. She died, at age sixty-one, on May 15, 2004, of diabetes-related health problems, months before submitting her doctoral dissertation. She was awarded her doctorate posthumously.

Like so many other brave queer thinkers, Gloria Anzaldúa demanded that her communities take risks, think harder, and try to imagine worlds that did not yet exist. She demonstrated that the only way to move forward was to think outside of what we accept to be reality, at least for the present.

HOLLY WOODLAWN: ANY GENDER IS FABULOUS AS LONG AS IT HAS STYLE

The rumors started buzzing in December 1970. Movie critics began discussing the favorite films of the year and who might be up for an Oscar. Surely Holly Woodlawn, the star of Paul Morrissey's underground film *Trash*, would be nominated for Best Actress. Or would it be Best Actor? Woodlawn's knockout performance did not answer the question. Was Woodlawn's character a woman? A male drag queen? A transgender woman? Whatever the category, Woodlawn's was the best performance of the year.

In spite of that, Woodlawn was not nominated in any category. Hollywood was not ready. Yet, the fact that this was even considered a possibility proved that the culture, and the United States, was changing. The movement for gay liberation was just over a year old and was already prompting debates and discussions across America. Some discussions were about the lives of gay men and lesbians. Other discussions were about how sexuality was connected to, and different from, gender. The LGBTQ community had always promoted the freedom for people to express their gender as they saw fit. Cross-dressing for men and women, for fun and to express identity, was a vital aspect of gay male and lesbian culture for centuries. Holly Woodlawn brought that into the open.

Holly Woodlawn was born October 26, 1946, in Juana Díaz, Puerto Rico, and was named Haroldo Santiago Franceschi Rodriguez Danhakl—although she would use female pronouns later in life. Her mother was Aminta Rodriguez and her father, an American soldier Aminta had met at a dance and, after a short romance, married. Her father, homesick for mainland America, left shortly after. Aminta moved to New York to find better job opportunities when Woodlawn was two years old. There she met Joseph Ajzenberg, a Jewish refugee from Poland who had fled the Nazis just years before and worked as a resort waiter. They fell in love and married and eventually moved to Miami, where the jobs were plentiful and living more relaxed.

In Miami, the Ajzenbergs found a comfortable life. And Woodlawn, who identified as part of the gay male community, found the gay male beach, where she made friends. Coming out at fourteen Woodlawn knew she was a gay. She also knew she wanted to move to back to New York to have a life of her own. Two years later, she had enough money for a bus part-way there. She traveled with a friend and hitch-hiked the rest of the way to Manhattan. In the early 1960s in New York, living on close to nothing and working part-time jobs was tough. Woodlawn quickly made friends

(continues on next page)

(continued from previous page)

in Greenwich Village and gradually began using make-up and dressing in women's clothing. Sometimes she passed as a woman, other times as a gay man in drag.

She soon became friends with Candy Darling and Jackie Curtis, two up-and-coming performers. They were part of the new avant-garde, mostly queer, theater and art scene that revolved around artist Andy Warhol and playwrights such as Charles Ludlam. Haroldo had started using the name Holly and now added Woodlawn—and thus a new persona was born. After appearing in *Heaven Grand in Amber Orbit*, a play by Jackie Curtis—a raucous comedy in which Woodlawn played Cuckoo the Bird Girl—she, through self-promotion, nerve, and talent, landed the starring role in the 1970 film *Trash*.

The movie made Woodlawn a star, but stars can fade. Throughout the 1970s and 1980s, except for some small films and cabaret acts, her career dwindled. In 2000—thirty years after *Trash* and twenty years after the publication of a 1991 memoir, *A Low Life in High Heels*—Woodlawn was back in the spotlight with a hit cabaret act. Audiences loved her, and she appeared on television shows such as *Transparent* in 2014. Later in her life, when the word was available to her, she identified as transgender. Woodlawn died in 2015 of cancer of the brain and liver. In her final gift to her community she left her estate to endow the Holly Woodlawn Memorial Fund for Transgender Youth at the Los Angeles LGBT Center.

BACKLASH

YEARS OF STRUGGLE AND RESISTANCE

1977–1990

SYLVESTER AND ANITA BRYANT

Marching to Two Very Different Drummers

Our lives and our history are informed by music. A song or melody can remind us in an instant of a happy or a sad moment in our lives. Couples talk about "our song," which reminds them of when they met and fell in love. Even history has a soundtrack. Baby boomers remember the 1960s through the soundtrack of the Beatles, the Rolling Stones, and Aretha Franklin.

The 1970s was a time when there were two different soundtracks running in the background of Americans' lives. These two playlists reflected parts of American culture and politics that were in direct opposition to one another. In 1977 these two cultural soundtracks—and the viewpoints they represented—clashed and sparked a heated debate across the United States, a debate that is, in many ways, still going on today.

The first soundtrack was the new sound of disco music. Disco—dance music with a strong syncopated bassline beat that became popular in LGBTQ, Latinx, and African American clubs—is not often thought of as political, but for many LGBTQ people, disco represented a new freedom to be open about your sexuality and proud of who you are. One of the most famous disco performers was an openly gay, flamboyant, androgynous African American known as Sylvester. Sylvester James Jr. lived in San Francisco and during his short career was known as the "Queen of Disco."

Disco diva Sylvester (right) at a Halloween party in the Castro district of San Francisco, 1976.

Disco arrived in the years after the Stonewall riots when there was a sudden burst of open LGBTQ culture. A growing number of people felt comfortable enough to come out of the closet. LGBTQ issues were discussed positively in newspapers and on television. More books on LGBTQ issues were published, and gay characters began appearing in Hollywood films and sometimes even on television. LGBTQ Pride marches were becoming larger and larger, and many cities were passing legislation that outlawed discrimination of LGBTQ people in employment and housing. It was in the context of this new, if still cautious, liberation that many LGBTQ people embraced the freedom to dance and enjoy themselves to disco music.

The second soundtrack of the 1970s was very different. In many ways it was a backlash not just against gay liberation but all the cultural shifts that had shaken the country during the 1960s. Rock and roll was associated with hippies and protestors. Disco was associated with gay people and sexual freedom. Older or conservative

Americans still enjoyed the types of popular music that had been in the mainstream in the 1950s. These were popular ballads, Broadway show tunes, and old-style country songs, as well as songs with religious or patriotic themes.

Many conservatives not only enjoyed the older styles of music but believed that rock and roll and disco had led to the destruction of what they called the American Way of Life and "family values." They thought the new music was part of a "sexual revolution," responsible for higher rates of divorce, teenage pregnancy, drug addiction, and the growing presence of LGBTQ people in society. This was very similar to what some conservatives said twenty years later when they claimed that rap music was leading American youth into violence and crime.

Anita Bryant was a mainstream pop singer who lived in Miami, Florida, and was a paid spokesperson for the orange juice industry, often appearing in TV commercials. Starting in 1969 she took on another role—as a leader of the cultural backlash against gay liberation and what she saw as the growing sinfulness of American culture.

These two performers, Sylvester and Anita Bryant, stood on opposite sides of a great cultural divide that was separating Americans. It was a divide that began in the 1960s and continues, in many ways, today. The two singers were polar opposites, yet they shared two important qualities: both saw themselves as activists for their communities and both led lives that were centered on their churches.

Bryant was born on March 25, 1940, in Barnsdall, Oklahoma. Her parents divorced when she was very young, and she and her sister went to live with their grandparents. Encouraged by her grandfather, Bryant began singing Christian hymns at the age of two and was soon singing in church.

Sylvester was born on September 6, 1947, in the Watts section of Los Angeles. Like Bryant, his parents also divorced when he was young. His mother, Letha, attended a Pentecostal church in South Los Angeles, and it was there that Sylvester learned to love gospel music. He began singing at age three and as a child joined the church choir.

Bryant grew up deeply committed to her religion and often claimed that singing was not just a job but an expression of her faith. By the time she was in her twenties she had a growing career and two gold records. In 1969 she became the spokesperson for the Florida Citrus Commission, the orange juice industry.

Sylvester's path was very different. He was effeminate in his manner and even as a child knew he was gay. Other members of his church disapproved of his affect and gossiped that he was having an affair with the church organist. At the age of thirteen he left the church to get away from its judgment and prejudice. At fifteen he left home, staying with friends or his grandmother. He often dressed in women's clothing and slowly developed a unique look that was neither recognizably male nor female. For his high school graduation photo he wore a chiffon dress and a beehive hairdo.

After high school Sylvester moved to San Francisco— then a center of gay culture—where he joined the gay theatrical troupe the Cockettes. This rag-tag group—who made their costumes from items they found in thrift stores and the trash—did satiric and campy parodies of culture and was becoming nationally famous. One of Sylvester's early performances was praised in *Rolling Stone* magazine. Starting in 1972 he began making records with different bands, and then in 1977 he released his first solo album, followed by a second one year later.

Meanwhile, Bryant was making a name for herself, along with her singing, as a conservative activist. In 1969 she appeared at an event called Rally for Decency at the Orange Bowl stadium in Miami. This was billed as a "protest" against the overly sexual behavior of rock musicians. Bryant began to speak out against gay liberation and any form of acceptance for LGBTQ people.

Bryant became nationally famous with her antigay speeches in 1977. In that year the Miami-Dade County Human Rights Commission passed a law that made it illegal for the county government to discriminate against lesbians and gay men. This meant that public employees, including public school teachers, could not be fired simply for being LGBTQ. Bryant was an angry opponent of this new law. Like many conservatives, she believed that gay and lesbian teachers would "turn" their students gay or, worse, sexually abuse them.

She said: "[What] these people really want, hidden behind obscure legal phrases, is the legal right to propose to our children that theirs is an acceptable alternate way of life. [. . .] I will lead such a crusade to stop it as this country has not seen before."

Bryant started a campaign called Save Our Children to repeal Dade County's new law. Save Our Children was the most prominent example of the national debate in states about gay rights and the new, open presence of LGBTQ people in society. Conservatives across the country rallied to Bryant's cause and used the slogan "Save Our Children" to organize their own local groups. Early

Gay activists demonstrate against Anita Bryant, 1977.

in 1978, a California state senator named John Briggs introduced a ballot measure, Proposition 6, also known as the Briggs Initiative. It called for a state-wide referendum that would ban lesbian and gay male teachers, and anyone who supported gay rights, from all public schools.

In response, the LGBTQ community across America mobilized. Since Bryant was the spokesperson for the orange juice industry, many activists called for a national boycott of orange juice. There were marches and rallies against Bryant's campaign and in support of LGBTQ rights in many cities. Gay and lesbian bars across the country—where Sylvester's music was often played—raised money for this political fight. Some bars banned the traditional drink the screwdriver (made with orange juice) and instead served the "Anita Bryant," made with apple juice. The national backlash was so strong that Bryant lost her job as the spokesperson for the citrus commission.

Bryant had started a national movement, and at the same time, Sylvester's career exploded. He played gay bars in San Francisco and began changing his image from the androgynous glam-rock persona to one more traditionally masculine. His 1977 solo album, *Sylvester*, was a hit, and his next two albums did very well, and he became a leading figure in disco. Five of his songs went gold—which means that they sold over five hundred thousand copies. Disco, by this time, was becoming increasingly popular even outside the LGBTQ community, one of the places where it had first surfaced. This was a moment in which a trend in the gay community influenced the larger popular culture. It was so popular that the 1977 film *Saturday Night Fever*, with John Travolta, popularized the phase "disco fever" to the entire country. Sylvester, even with his less androgynous look—although he was still identifiable as a gay man—was a part of this. Although he had not attended church for years, he began going to the Love Center Church in East Oakland where music—a contemporary version of traditional gospel—was a central part of worship and where everyone was welcome.

As much as Americans loved disco, which had its roots in LGBTQ culture, they were also fearful of granting LGBTQ people full legal rights. Part of this was because of the great progress the queer movement had made during the 1970s. State- and county-level legal reforms were passed, and as important, the number of LGBTQ people who were coming out made homosexuality more visible and more discussed, and this allowed more people to come out safely if they chose to. This visibility, however, caused a backlash. John Briggs called San Francisco "the moral garbage dump of homosexuality in this country."

This was a culture war as well as a political one. Anita Bryant was successful in helping to repeal, by a two-to-one margin, the Miami-Dade County law in 1977. (The Briggs Initiative failed by a sixty-forty margin.) Bryant won that battle, but she lost the war. Her campaign, as well as the Briggs Initiative, ignited a larger, stronger national gay rights movement. Personally, Bryant's life was in tatters. Her antigay, conservative positions became punch lines to jokes about her in the national media, her career suffered, and she eventually declared bankruptcy. She later began her own evangelical ministry.

By coincidence, as the first wave of conservative backlash against gay rights (there would be others in the future) began to fizzle, so did the craze for disco music. By 1981 Sylvester's career began to fade. While he still released records and made personal appearances, he was not the national star he was a few years before. Tragically, it was at this time that the HIV-AIDS epidemic started. Sylvester lost many friends to the disease, including his lover, Rick Cranmer. During these years Sylvester performed at many HIV-AIDS benefits and volunteered to care for patients on the HIV-AIDS ward at San Francisco General Hospital.

By the end of 1987 it became clear that Sylvester, too, was infected with HIV, and his health declined. He attended the 1988 San Francisco Gay Pride March in a wheelchair. That year, the annual Castro Street Fair was dedicated to him. He was too sick to attend, but the crowd in the street outside his apartment shouted his name loudly so that he could hear it. Sylvester died on December 16, 1988. In his will he stipulated that his funeral take place at the Love Center Church, and he bequeathed the royalties from his songs to the AIDS

Emergency Fund and Project Open Hand, both HIV-AIDS foundations in San Francisco.

Although in some ways they could not have been further apart in their politics and their lives, Anita Bryant and Sylvester were both, in a sense, religious in their music. She sang to praise God as she understood him. Sylvester's church was the gay bar and disco music the hymns he sang to celebrate the joy of love and being alive.

HIV-AIDS

Probably very few people saw the headline of a short article, tucked away on page 20, in the holiday weekend edition of the July 3, 1981, *New York Times*: "RARE CANCER SEEN IN 41 HOMOSEXUALS: Outbreak Occurs Among Men in New York and California – 8 Died Inside 2 Years."

However, it did not go unnoticed by gay men and those who cared about them. This was the first time anyone in the United States had heard about the condition that would eventually be called HIV-AIDS. The article reported on a medical study explaining that some gay men were being diagnosed with, and dying from, a rare form of cancer. Doctors did not know what was causing this cancer—called Kaposi sarcoma—to appear, nor did they have any idea why it was manifesting itself in groups of gay men. Gradually it became clear to researchers that this cancer, as well as many other rare diseases and infections, was attacking people whose immune system was severely compromised. But the research was in a losing race with the devastation that this mysterious immune deficiency was causing. In 1981, of the 152 reported cases in the United States, 128 people had died.

Scientists and researchers were doing their best, even though President Ronald Reagan's conservative administration had drastically cut the budgets for the National Institutes of Health and the Centers for Disease Control. By 1985 they discovered that what would eventually be called HIV (the human immunodeficiency virus) was responsible for the immune suppression. By the end of that year, 37,061 similar cases had been reported in the United States and 16,301 people had died. Because many of the cases reported were gay men, AIDS became commonly referred to as a "gay disease." The first name researchers gave it was gay-related immune deficiency (GRID).

Although identifying the virus was a huge step, researchers could not design drugs that would be effective against it. Some, such as AZT, introduced in the later 1980s, had a limited effectiveness and often did more harm than good. Unfortunately, because many gay men were infected—and because HIV-AIDS was seen by many as a "gay disease"—many people with AIDS faced discrimination. They were fired from their jobs, evicted from their apartments, denied insurance, and even turned away from hospitals.

In the next few years researchers discovered that HIV was a retrovirus. This is a type of virus that infects the DNA of the host so that it is very difficult to eradicate. They also discovered that the virus was primarily in blood, semen, and mothers' milk. It became clear that there were only a few ways of transferring the virus: through vaginal or anal intercourse, through contaminated blood (especially in blood transfusions or sharing contaminated needles), and by breastfeeding. But most important, it was clear that only women and men who were HIV positive—meaning that their bodies contained the virus—could transmit it to another person, if the virus entered the other person's blood. This mean that, even though many gay men were infected, this was not a "gay disease." It was not a disease connected to an identity—how people thought of and labeled themselves—but one that was transmitted through an activity. Rather than saying that gay men were a prime population to contract HIV, educators began saying that it was men who had sex with men (MSM) who were at risk.

(continues on next page)

(continued from previous page)

The epidemic continued to grow. By 1993, 399,250 cases were reported in the US and 194,334 people had died. It soon became clear that HIV-AIDS affected many populations, not just gay men. And technically HIV-AIDS was not even a disease but a condition that allowed an infected person to catch what were called "opportunistic infections." Although HIV-AIDS was first identified in the US, it was now understood to be a global pandemic. The majority of cases were caused by the transmission of the virus during heterosexual sex.

Because HIV-AIDS affected so many gay men in the 1980s and 1990s, the LGBTQ community quickly and rapidly organized to help those who were afflicted with it. The first organizations were formed simply to help people who were sick and needed care. Soon organizations began doing education, forming support groups, and helping with basic services such as bringing food to people who were ill, taking them to doctor's visits, and even helping walk their dogs. LGBTQ nonprofit legal groups quickly formed HIV-AIDS projects to help seriously ill men make out wills and, even more important, to help fight the discrimination people with AIDS faced.

In March 1987 women and men, LGBTQ and some heterosexuals, founded ACT UP in New York City. ACT UP was an acronym for AIDS Coalition to Unleash Power. Individual chapters of ACT UP quickly formed in US and European cities. ACT UP members held large public demonstrations to demand more money for research, an end to discrimination, and changes in a broad range of public policies that would help people dealing with HIV-AIDS.

Because of the vast amount of organizing in the LGBTQ community, including ACT UP, people living with AIDS now had a better life. In 1997 new antiviral drugs did not destroy HIV, but they did help stop its replication so that HIV-AIDS became a manageable condition. The LGBTQ political and social organizing that helped change the political, scientific, and social culture that produced these drugs helped everyone with HIV-AIDS worldwide.

AIDS is still with us today. In 2017 a United Nations report stated that there were estimated to be 36.9 million people around the world living with HIV-AIDS. In the US there are approximately a thousand new transmissions a week, many of them between men who have sex with men. HIV-AIDS is a very serious problem but much less so now because of the courage and energy of LGBTQ people who began fighting against it in the early years of the epidemic.

CHAPTER TWENTY-SIX

ROBERT HILLSBOROUGH AND HARVEY MILK

Struggle and Violence, Grief and Rage

This is a story about violence and two men who were murdered because they were openly gay. One man was a famous activist at the time of his death and became even more famous afterwards. The other was just an everyday working person who was happily open about his sexuality. They both lived in San Francisco, considered by many to be one of the most welcoming places for LGBTQ people. Yet for these men, and for so many others, there was no refuge from antigay violence. This is not just a story about violence and tragedy—it's also a story of community action and resistance.

Robert Hillsborough was a professional gardener who worked for the city and liked to plant brightly colored hyacinths in the pattern of rainbow flags. In 1977 he was thirty-three years old and had moved to San Francisco a few years earlier looking for community and a boyfriend. On the evening of June 21, 1977, Hillsborough went out for an evening of disco dancing with his boyfriend, Jerry Taylor. For all we know, they danced to Sylvester's music. Afterwards, they stopped for a late-night snack at Whiz Burgers, a popular local drive-in restaurant. Sitting in their car in the parking lot, the two men kissed.

Four young men saw them kissing, and one of them, John Cordova, walked over and punched Hillsborough in the face through the open car window. Hillsborough sped out of the parking lot, and the men followed them in their own car. Hillsborough and Taylor drove to their apartment. As they tried to get inside their pursuers caught up and assaulted them. Taylor managed to run away. Hillsborough was brutally stabbed by Cordova, while his friend Thomas Spooner watched, screaming, "Faggot! Faggot!" Taylor fled to a friend's apartment and called the police, but it was too late. Hillsborough was stabbed fifteen times in the face and torso, and died hours later. He was the nineteenth gay man murdered in San Francisco in as many months.

The following Saturday, June 25, was San Francisco's Gay Freedom Day March. The city was already very tense. Just three weeks earlier, Anita Bryant's Save Our Children referendum had passed by a two-to-one margin in Miami-Dade County, Florida. Only a week later, California state representative John Briggs introduced Proposition 6, which would have banned gay men and lesbian women from teaching in California's public schools. The LGBTQ community was under physical and political attack.

San Francisco city officials were afraid that Hillsborough's murder would spark more violence, that either the parade would be attacked or that the LGBTQ community would react in anger and strike out. But the community remained strong. Mayor George Moscone ordered the city's flags to be flown at half-staff and offered a five-thousand-dollar reward for information leading to the arrest of Hillsborough's murderers. He blamed Hillsborough's murder on the atmosphere of hate promoted by

Anita Bryant and John Briggs. Moscone said that Briggs "will have to live with his conscience."

That year, the Gay Freedom Day Parade became both a memorial for Robert Hillsborough and a political protest. Thirty thousand people marched and many of them left flowers in Hillsborough's honor at the door to city hall. Thousands more carried signs opposing Proposition 6.

One of the people who was prominent in the news that day was Harvey Milk, a forty-seven-year-old former New Yorker who had moved to San Francisco in 1972. Milk owned a camera shop on Castro Street, in the center of San Francisco's main LGBTQ neighborhood. He was a community leader and nicknamed "the mayor of Castro Street." In 1976 Milk had run for the state assembly and lost, but now he was running for the city's board of supervisors. Before this, the supervisors were elected city-wide. A new plan, however, carved the city up into districts. This meant that for the first time the gay community had a chance to elect its own representative.

Harvey Milk at the opening of his campaign for city supervisor, 1975.

In November 1977 Harvey Milk won the election. He was the first openly gay politician to win an election in California, and the most prominent openly gay politician in the country at that time. His term

Crowd gathered outside San Francisco City Hall after the murders of Milk and Mayor George Moscone, 1978.

began in January 1978, just months after the murder of Robert Hillsborough and in the face of the upcoming Proposition 6 vote. Milk's election and his support from other politicians, including San Francisco mayor George Moscone, offered hope to the LGBTQ community and its supporters. On November 7, 1978, Proposition 6 was defeated at the polls. It even lost in Briggs's own conservative Orange County. It was a moment of joy and celebration that would be short-lived. Later that month, on November 27, a man named Dan White walked into San Francisco City Hall and shot and killed Harvey Milk and Mayor Moscone.

Dan White was a conservative ex-policeman who had been elected to the board of supervisors along with Milk and resigned after a disagreement over his salary. He attempted, but failed, to regain his position. After the murders, White turned himself in to the Northern Police Station, where he had once worked, and confessed with these words: "I just shot him."

San Francisco's LGBTQ community, and the city itself, was shocked and grief-stricken. The night of the murder, forty thousand people marched in the streets of San Francisco in honor of Harvey Milk and George Moscone. (Dianne Feinstein, also a city supervisor, became mayor and spoke eloquently about her late colleagues and the LGBTQ community. She is now a US senator from California.) There was a growing sense of rage and helplessness on the streets. The question many people asked was "Can gay people just be murdered? Will the police and courts act to protect us?"

The trial of the men who had murdered Robert Hillsborough was still in progress. Ultimately, the trial and verdict, which was announced after the Milk and Moscone murders, were disappointing to the gay community, who felt that justice had not been served. John Cordova, who stabbed Hillsborough, had been convicted of second-degree murder and sentenced to ten years in prison. Charges were dropped against Thomas Spooner, Cordova's friend who stood cheering him on. Hillsborough's parents had tried to sue Anita Bryant for $5 million. They charged that she had run a "campaign of hate, bigotry, ignorance, fear, intimidation and prejudice" that had set the stage for their son's murder. The suit was thrown out of court. Now the people of San Francisco and across the country waited to see if justice would be done when Dan White came to trial.

White was charged with first-degree murder, but there was a great deal of sympathy for him in the city. Some police wore "Free Dan White" T-shirts, and several jury members cried as his taped confession was played for them. White's lawyers argued that White was depressed and not in his right mind at the time of the murders because of his diet of sugary snacks and soft drinks. This explanation became known as "the Twinkie defense," and it became the punch line of bitter jokes even as it outraged many people.

On May 21, 1979, White was convicted of voluntary manslaughter and given the lightest possible sentence: seven years in prison. It seemed as if the worst fears of the LGBTQ community were coming true. LGBTQ people could be murdered and the government would not protect them or give them justice. That night the grief of the community turned to rage as a scheduled peaceful march in the Castro turned into a riot. Over 1,500 people attacked, overturned, and burned police cars and disabled trolley cars. The San Francisco police retaliated by attacking gay people and gay bars in the Castro while screaming homophobic insults and slurs. By the end of the evening San Francisco, which many had imagined as a gay paradise, was consumed by violence.

The next night, which would have been Harvey Milk's forty-ninth birthday, twenty thousand LGBTQ people gathered at City Hall Plaza to celebrate his life. They were angry, peaceful, and determined that the deaths of Robert Hillsborough and Harvey Milk would not be forgotten.

The assassination of Harvey Milk is now a touchstone in LGBTQ history. There are organizations and schools named after him, as well as an Academy Award–winning documentary, a Hollywood movie, an opera, and choral music. It is a wonderful thing that he is remembered. It is important, however, not to forget that his death occurred in the context of social changes and upheavals that we are still experiencing today. Anita Bryant's Save Our Children campaign and Proposition 6 were part of the emergence of a larger conservative movement that argued against legal equality for LGBTQ people, the rights of women, and a whole range of personal freedoms. While Bryant's campaign language might not be acceptable today—and it was unacceptable to many back then—many of its sentiments are with us still.

CHAPTER TWENTY-SEVEN

ESSEX HEMPHILL

The Power of Blackness

I t was an act of incredible bravery, one of many that occurred in a short life.

In November 1983, *Essence*, a popular, mainstream lifestyle magazine for African American women, published a groundbreaking essay in their monthly column "Say, Brother." The piece opened with the sentence, "I am a homosexual," and the author was Essex Hemphill, a twenty-six-year-old African American poet, essayist, and performer.

Throughout the 1970s, LGBTQ people and issues had gained increasing coverage in the press. For a number of reasons, the African American media was slower to embrace the discussion. Given that, Hemphill's essay was startling to many *Essence* readers. He began simply and honestly:

> I am a homosexual. I love myself as a black man
> and a homosexual. I have known since I was five
> that I would love men, but I did not know then that
> "brother," "lover," "friend" would take on more
> intimate and dangerous meanings. I did not know a
> dual oppression, a dual mockery, would be practiced
> against me.

Essex Hemphill, 1991.

Hemphill was not just daring in his openness about his personal life. He was daring in the way he criticized the African American community for many members' refusal to deal honestly and openly with homosexuality. He was also outspoken in criticizing the gay community and movement for its racism. His essay was more amazing since it came in the early years of the HIV-AIDS epidemic, when both gay men and people of color were being affected by, and blamed for, AIDS.

What gave Essex Hemphill the courage to challenge two communities he loved?

Hemphill was born April 16, 1957, the second of five children, to his parents, Warren and Mantalene. He did not have an easy childhood. His parents' marriage was troubled, often violent, and ended in divorce. Before the divorce, his family had moved from Chicago to Washington, DC. His summers were spent in Columbia, South Carolina, with his maternal grandmother, whom everyone called Miss Emily and whom Hemphill adored. His mother, who was very religious, held the family together after the divorce.

Hemphill's friends in high school included many athletes, although Hemphill himself was not interested in sports. When other boys hung out after school, Hemphill often went home and wrote poetry. There was another huge difference: Hemphill knew he was gay and attracted to men, and he had to keep his desires and true nature a secret.

In 1971, when the LGBTQ rights movement was only a few years old, and Hemphill was fourteen, he was already having a sexual relationship with an older white man. At the same time he also began dating young women, in whom he had no sexual interest, so his friends and family would think he was heterosexual. Much of his poetry at this time was about his confused feelings of desire.

In 1975 Hemphill graduated high school and, eager to leave home, enrolled at the University of Maryland. There he met Wayson Jones, who was African American and gay. Hemphill was not out yet, but Jones had already come out to his friends and family. When Hemphill left school after only a year, he stayed in touch with Jones. Knowing another African American man who was out gave Hemphill both courage and the knowledge that being honest about your sexuality was possible and good. Jones and Hemphill would meet later in life and work together on various projects, including theatrical performance pieces and literary publications that promoted African American LGBTQ culture.

During this time, African American lesbians and gay men began organizing. Many felt excluded from LGBTQ organizations, which they felt, with much justification, did not take issues of race seriously. They also felt excluded as gay people from many African American political groups. In 1978 some African American lesbians and gay men started the National Coalition of Black Gays (which became in 1984 the National Coalition of Black Lesbians and Gays). This group worked with other national LGBTQ groups to articulate the specific needs of lesbians and gay men of color. Many lesbian and gay male African American writers and artists, including Hemphill, were also beginning to meet and form creative communities.

These years were chaotic, exciting, and fruitful for Hemphill. He had a series of part-time jobs as he feverishly worked with colleagues on publications, theater performances, spoken-word pieces, and music, as well as writing his own poetry, fiction, and essays. In 1978 he helped cofound, with two lesbian friends, the *Nethula Journal of Contemporary Literature*. He and Larry Duckett cofounded Cinque, a theater troupe that later included Wayson Jones. Cinque blended choral recitation, jazz, and spoken-word poetry. The excitement and professionalism of Cinque established it as a center of LGBTQ African American arts circles.

Due to his output and originality, Hemphill began receiving wider recognition. In 1982 he self-published two poetry chapbooks, *Diamonds Was in the Kitty* and *Some of the People We Love Are Terrorists*. His works were praised for their honesty and ability to speak the truth of the experience of an African American gay man.

Artists, and certainly poets, rarely make a living from their art, and Hemphill was no exception. In the mid-1980s he worked for the Potomac Electric Power Company as a graphic artist but, encountering racism, soon quit. Over the next few years Hemphill struggled with jobs while working on his writing. He gave readings and published his own work. In 1985 he released the book *Earth Life* and, a year later, *Conditions*. In 1986 he was included in the prestigious anthology *Gay and*

Lesbian Poetry in Our Time and contributed to *In the Life: A Black Gay Anthology*, a groundbreaking collection of writings by African American gay male writers, edited by Hemphill's close friend Joseph Beam. In 1987 Hemphill was invited to give a series of readings in London and other cities. These readings—mostly to people of color—were a huge success.

Beginning in 1981, when the first cases of AIDS surfaced, HIV seemed to be centered in the gay male community and especially urban communities of men of color. It took years for the virus to be identified, and there was a great deal of fear and misunderstanding about why people were dying and how the disease was spread. In those early years, some people thought it was a disease that only gay men could get. Black gay men, racially stereotyped as IV-drug users, were often accused of spreading it. Some people, despite all available medical evidence to the contrary, feared that HIV could be caught like the flu, just by being near someone who had it. There was no effective treatment at the time, and people with the disease were often shunned. This made it harder for people to admit they had it, and seek treatment. These problems were compounded by the fact that the administration of President Ronald Reagan was reticent, because of homophobia, to adequately fund its own health agencies to do research or look for a cure.

In 1986 HIV was finally identified, yet it still aroused fear and misunderstanding. Then, in March 1987, a group of lesbians and gay men in New York City founded ACT UP, an HIV-AIDS organization, with the mission of fighting for the rights of HIV-AIDS patients, raising awareness about the true nature of the disease, and

ACT UP New York poster demanding a national plan for the AIDS crisis, early 1990s.

demanding action by the government to end discrimination and find treatment and a cure. ACT UP quickly became known for its militant, highly visible protests and direct action.

It was in that atmosphere that Hemphill discovered that he was HIV positive, meaning that he had contracted the virus. It's unclear when he knew or when he began to show symptoms. In late 1986 he excused himself from performing at the first National Black AIDS Conference because of "circumstances related to my health."

Hemphill was outspoken as an African American, gay male poet and activist. He was also outspoken about the impact of HIV on his community. He did not, however, see himself as an AIDS activist and was slow to identify himself as a person with HIV-AIDS. Even when his close friend Joseph Beam died, in December 1988, Hemphill was reluctant to speak about his own health.

He did, however, keep on writing. He became well-known as a writer and public speaker. Isaac Julien, a noted British filmmaker and artist, asked Hemphill to be in *Looking for Langston*, a 1989 film he was making about Langston Hughes, a famous gay African American poet of the Harlem Renaissance. That same year Hemphill and his work were prominently featured in *Tongues Untied*, Marlon Riggs's groundbreaking documentary about the complexities of race and gender identity of African American gay men. Then, in 1994, Hemphill appeared in Riggs's film *Black Is . . . Black Ain't*.

The next years were both rewarding and difficult for Hemphill. His fame mounted as he gained success with his writing, but he was also becoming increasingly ill. He began working on a novel, and his collection of poetry and essays, *Ceremonies*, was released, to acclaim, by a major New York publishing company. He was invited as a visiting scholar to the Getty Center for the History of Art and the Humanities in Santa Monica, California, where he worked on numerous ongoing projects. It was at the Getty Center that his health began to seriously decline. Yet he struggled to keep working up until his death on November 4, 1995.

In a letter to his close friend, writer and activist Barbara Smith, on December 8, 1993, Hemphill wrote, "I just remember to say 'thank you' for every day I am able to have. I don't really desire too many things other than the chance to keep creating."

Many writers have published much more than Essex Hemphill—everything he published might be contained in one lengthy anthology—but few have had the tremendous impact he had on people's lives and on the LGBTQ movement. Hemphill was uncompromising, insisting that the, at that time, mostly white LGBTQ movement listen to the voices and concerns of lesbians and gay men of color. He was equally demanding of the African American community, that they hear and accept the LGBTQ people who were their family, neighbors, and fellow church members. He understood the power of his sexuality and Blackness and what it meant to him and how it had to be acknowledged by others.

CHAPTER TWENTY-EIGHT

KIYOSHI KUROMIYA

Man of Many Movements

Kiyoshi Kuromiya was an American who was born in a US government internment/prison camp. His parents, both native-born American citizens, had been sent to the camp in the months after the Japanese attack on the Pearl Harbor military base in Hawaii, in 1941. Their only crime was that they were Japanese American. From the moment of his birth, in 1943, Kuromiya was considered a dangerous outsider in his own country.

Kuromiya's father, Hiroshi, was a produce buyer, and his mother, Amiko, an orthopedic instrument trainer. Both were born in California. After they married they lived in Glendale and, like any young couple, were planning on starting a family. On December 7, 1941, the Japanese air force attack on Pearl Harbor set off a wave of anti-Japanese feeling in California and across the US. In February 1942, just two months after Pearl Harbor, President Franklin Roosevelt signed an executive order to "relocate" all American citizens and residents of Japanese ancestry living on the West Coast to government "internment camps." Over 120,000 people were forced to leave their homes with almost no notice. The sudden move compelled many of them to sell their belongings and businesses, often at a loss.

Winter at the Manzanar internment camp in California, 1940s.

The government claimed the reason for the relocation was to prevent Japanese Americans from helping a possible invasion of the US West Coast by the Japanese armed forces. There was absolutely no military basis for the order, and there was no similar order rounding up German Americans or Italian Americans, descendants of the other two countries the US was fighting. Racism and racial fear were clearly behind the action.

Amiko was pregnant when the family was sent to the camp, and Kiyoshi—who was given the name Steven—was born in the Heart Mountain Relocation Center, Wyoming, on May 9, 1943. His sister, Marijane, was born there as well. Later, after the war, a third sibling, Larry, joined the family.

When the war ended and they were released from the camp, the Kuromiyas moved to Monrovia, California, where Steven grew up. (He began using his Japanese name when he went to college.) He was physically mature for his age and also sexually active with older boys. At the age of eleven he was arrested for having sex in a park and placed in a juvenile detention hall for three days.

Kuromiya was one of only a handful of Asian American students in his high school. Despite his early run-in with the law, he excelled in his classes and graduated with honors. In 1961 he was accepted to the University of Pennsylvania, in Philadelphia, where he planned to study architecture. He loved architecture. For him, it was not simply a feat of engineering and design skills but an art in the sense that it combined form, aesthetics, grace, and emotion. Kuromiya had a similar attitude about politics later in his life—that it was not simply a matter of getting a law passed or helping people but, rather, a complex intellectual engagement that combined skill, thought, and art to produce a new beautiful design for society and people's lives.

At U Penn, Kuromiya, now known as Kiyoshi, was not yet out to his friends as gay. But he immediately became involved with the political movements growing on American campuses. He was a member of Students for a Democratic Society, a radical group that was against the war in Vietnam and domestic social inequalities, and the Student Nonviolent Coordinating Committee, a civil rights organization. In 1962 Kuromiya, with members of the Congress of Racial Equality, participated in a campaign to desegregate restaurants and other public facilities along Route 40 in Aberdeen, Maryland, which was the road most commonly used by diplomats traveling between their Washington, DC, embassies and the United Nations in New York. The next year Kuromiya was at the March on Washington, where Dr. Martin Luther King Jr.

spoke. He met Dr. King at that time and become more involved with the civil rights movement. In 1965, while marching on the state capitol building in Montgomery, Alabama, with African American students on a voter registration drive, Kuromiya was badly beaten by police and had to be hospitalized. During this time he became close to Dr. King and his family. After Dr. King was assassinated, in 1968, Kuromiya cared for the King children the entire week of the civil rights leader's funeral services.

Kuromiya viewed the protests against the Vietnam War and in support of the civil rights movement as part of the same struggle for human liberation and equality. This was also how he viewed the struggle for LGBTQ rights. In 1965 he made the decision to come out and help form a new group called the East Coast Homophile Organization (ECHO). "Homophile"—meaning loving the same—was a word used before people regularly said "gay" or "lesbian." On July 4, 1965, Kuromiya and eleven other men and women of ECHO marched in front of Independence Hall in Philadelphia—the birthplace of American freedom, where the US Constitution was signed—and peacefully marched holding signs proclaiming "Homosexuals Should Be Judged as Individuals" and "Homosexual Citizens Want: Equality of Job Employment." They named the protest the Annual Reminder.

This brave action occurred four years before the Stonewall riots and at the beginning of the modern movement for gay and lesbian liberation. ECHO returned to Independence Hall every year until 1969, when Pride parades began to be held across the country. In 1969 the name "the Annual Reminder" was changed to Christopher Street Liberation Day.

The 1960s and 1970s were a whirlwind of activity for Kuromiya. He continued his antiwar work, and in October 1967, he, along with one hundred thousand other people from across the nation, descended on Washington, DC, to participate in one of the largest protests against the war in Vietnam. One of the highlights of that weekend was when Kuromiya, activist Abbie Hoffman, and openly gay poet Allen Ginsberg, and others took part in a symbolic protest on Saturday, October 21, 1967. The antiwar activists said they were going to use their positive powers of peace, as well as an ancient Aramaic exorcism rite, to both drive the demons from and levitate the Pentagon to stop the war. It was an exciting, theatrical protest and spoke to Kuromiya's ideas about politics as art.

After Stonewall, Kuromiya helped start a chapter of the Gay Liberation Front in Philadelphia. He was often one of the few people of color in the group and was pleased that this new wave of the gay rights movement was better at welcoming people of all races and backgrounds. In 1970 he spoke as a representative of the Gay Liberation Front to a gathering of activists called the Revolutionary People's Constitutional Convention, in Philadelphia. Around this time Kuromiya became friends with Huey Newton, the head of the Black Panther Party. Kuromiya's activism brought him under the notice of the FBI. During the time the FBI routinely conducted surveillance on any group they considered radical. This included many civil rights, feminist, and gay liberation groups. From 1960 to 1972 the FBI monitored Kuromiya's political activities and personal relationships.

Kuromiya's interests spread beyond politics. His study of architecture led him to the work of the visionary architect and inventor Buckminster Fuller. Fuller—the grand-nephew of transcendentalist Margaret Fuller—believed that people could, through technology and imagination, solve all the problems of society. Fuller was one of the first theorists to talk about building sustainable economies—meaning an economy that can support humans and not hurt the environment—and societies.

Kuromiya traveled with Fuller for speaking tours and research, and he collaborated with Fuller on six books, from 1978 to 1983, the year of Fuller's death.

Soon after, Kuromiya's life took yet another turn. He was diagnosed with AIDS and joined the growing movement to demand fair treatment for HIV-positive people and government action to find a cure. In 1988, using the ideas he had learned from Buckminster Fuller, Kuromiya started the Critical Path AIDS Project. Based in Philadelphia, this project was aimed at bringing together all the available information about HIV, treatment, and support. It was one of the first to use the newly emerging technology of the internet, and it constructed a database that brought together a wide range of the latest facts, studies, and analysis to provide people with vital information. The use of the internet for political purposes was revolutionary at the time.

Kuromiya help found ACT UP in Philadelphia in 1987 and worked in numerous HIV-AIDS related organizations. In 1996 he joined a lawsuit challenging the federal Communications Decency Act (CDA), which attempted to control pornography on the internet but at the same time also made it illegal to post sexually explicit safe-sex information—ways to avoid HIV transmission while engaging in sexual activity—to teenagers. Three years later

Activist Kiyoshi Kuromiya.

Kuromiya led another lawsuit that challenged laws prohibiting the use of medical marijuana, which was emerging as an important substance to help people deal with the physical pain of many of the symptoms associated with HIV-AIDS.

After a lifetime of being an outlaw, resisting authority, and making the world a better place for LGBTQ people, Kiyoshi Kuromiya died of complications from HIV-AIDS on May 10, 2000, at the age of fifty-seven.

In many ways Kiyoshi Kuromiya embodied the spirit of the gay liberation movement. He understood how connected all progressive political movements could be. When he was profiled in *Life* magazine, in October 18, 1968, in an article titled "The Defiant Voices of S.D.S," he said: "I was in the South during the spring and summer of 1965. . . . We marched and I was clubbed down and hospitalized. When you get treated this way, you suddenly know what it is like to be a black in Mississippi or a peasant in Vietnam." Kuromiya's understanding and energy was as expansive as his political vision was limitless.

CHAPTER TWENTY-NINE

FELIX GONZALEZ-TORRES

Art in the Face of Death

Imagine entering the Museum of Modern Art in New York City in 1991. You are there to see an interactive artwork called *Untitled (Placebo)*. The artwork is simple: Mounds of hard candy called Fruit Flashers, wrapped in bright, multicolored cellophane foil, are piled on either side of a walkway. The piles are equal to the weight of a human being. Visitors are encouraged to take a candy and during the day the piles slowly shrink. (At night the candies are replaced.)

Now realize that the candies are meant to represent the artist's lover, a man named Ross Laycock, who had died of AIDS. The candies disappear just as Laycock disappeared. Suddenly the piles of candy become a moving tribute to a loved one and a striking visual representation of the loss caused by the AIDS epidemic.

That artwork was the creation of Felix Gonzalez-Torres, an openly gay, Cuban American artist, who was to die of AIDS himself just a few years later, in 1996. Although he was just thirty-eight at the time of his death, Gonzalez-Torres left behind an important body of work and a lifetime of activism. In his short life, Gonzalez-Torres was hardly ever in one place for a long time, and this constant movement helped shape his ideas about art. It also shaped the ways his art responded to his life experiences and the HIV-AIDS epidemic.

Gonzalez-Torres was born in Guáimaro, Cuba, on November 26, 1957, the third of four children. It was a time of revolution and great change in Cuba as Fidel Castro led a revolt against the US-backed dictator, Fulgencio Batista. Castro went on to set up a communist dictatorship backed by the Soviet Union. Like many people, Gonzalez-Torres's parents first supported Castro and the new government, but eventually became disillusioned with it.

Gonzalez-Torres never spoke or wrote much about his early life. Maybe this was because life for the family in Cuba at this time was stressful and he did not want to remember it. In an interview he claimed that his favorite toys as a child were "Minnie and Mickey; after that, the Flintstones, and Pee-Wee Herman. I hate Barbies." In one brief biographical note for a museum he wrote, "In 1964 Dad bought me a set of watercolors." He was seven at the time and we can presume that this set of watercolors started him on his journey as an artist.

In 1970, when he was thirteen, his parents sent him and his sister Gloria to Madrid, Spain, with the hope that they would be better off out of Cuba. Shortly after, though, the two siblings moved to Puerto Rico to live with an uncle. Gonzalez-Torres went to high school there and then studied art at the University of Puerto Rico. He was also intrigued with contemporary critical theory—which is a way of understanding the world as being continuously constructed and reconstructed by humans—which he claims was very influential for his art. During these years he became part of the artistic community in San Juan, Puerto Rico.

Gonzalez-Torres moved to New York City in 1979, and his parents and remaining siblings fled Cuba for Miami in 1981. In New York, Gonzalez-Torres became part of the LGBTQ community, yet everyday life was a struggle. He lived hand-to-mouth working as a waiter and performing other low-paying jobs to make money while he continued his studies. He attended the Pratt Institute and received his bachelor in fine arts degree in photography in 1983, the same year he met Ross Laycock, a Canadian living in New York. In the summer of 1985 they traveled to Europe together. They spent a year in Venice, where Gonzalez-Torres studied painting and architecture.

In 1987, back in New York and more secure in his artistic vision, Gonzalez-Torres became part of Group Material. This was a collective of New York artists and activists who decided to work and create art together in community settings. Their mission was to use art as an activist weapon while helping younger people enter the field.

Group Material was a perfect working environment for Gonzalez-Torres. During this time he began putting everyday objects into his art—string, wrapped candies, children's puzzles, stacks of paper, photographs of ordinary things such as unmade beds—and using these simple objects to see the world in a new way. His vision—or theory—of this work was to take things we see in daily life and to place them in different surroundings or place them next to one another in unexpected ways so that we see them in new ways and have a different understanding of our world.

In 1988 Gonzalez-Torres's mother died of leukemia, the first of many deaths he would experience in the next few years. Ross Laycock was diagnosed with HIV-AIDS that same year. This was a time of activism and struggle for the LGBTQ community. Following on the heels of Anita Bryant and her anti-LGBTQ crusade, the election of Ronald Reagan in 1980 brought a new wave of conservatism to the United States. Politicians spoke of the wishes of a "moral majority," which too often represented and enacted a bigoted, antigay backlash.

Another social policy of this conservatism was the move to cut back on government spending on federal healthcare programs, food programs for the needy, arts and humanities support, and medical research. Not only was funding for HIV-AIDS research reduced but funding for the National Endowment for the Arts was restricted, and the US Congress passed a ruling that works featuring positive images of gay sex could not be funded by the federal government.

Gonzalez-Torres and many other LGBTQ artists spoke out against these policies both with protest and with the creation of political art. The arts collective Group Material was an important part of this movement. In his work with them, Gonzalez-Torres expressed themes of love and loss, sickness and rejuvenation, gender and sexuality.

After struggling with HIV-AIDS for many years, Ross Laycock died in 1991 at his home in Toronto. He and Gonzalez-Torres had been together for seven happy years. There were more deaths to come in Gonzalez-Torres's life. His father died three weeks after Laycock did, and many other friends were becoming ill, some dying of HIV-AIDS. Gonzalez-Torres was himself HIV-positive though not yet sick.

Turning his grief and anger into art, Gonzalez-Torres continued to work and became increasingly well-known and respected. Many of his works had to do with loss, most notably a billboard that only contained the phrase "It's Just a Matter of Time." With this simple statement, Gonzalez-Torres was asking the viewer to think about what comes next: after AIDS; after a conservative government; after a relationship ends with the death of a partner. So, it's only a matter of time, but until what?

In the last years of his life Gonzalez-Torres had exhibits in major museums and galleries around the world. In his art, he brought his private grief into public view. This was his way of proclaiming his belief in the goodness of his sexuality and his love for men. When interviewers asked about what his art meant, he often answered: "I'm still proposing the radical idea of trying to make this a better place for everyone."

He stated in an interview before he died, "When people ask me, 'Who is your public?' I say honestly, without skipping a beat, 'Ross.' The public was Ross. The rest of the people just come to the work." Ross Laycock, the man he had loved so deeply, inspired him in life and in death.

Felix Gonzalez-Torres lived at a time when the world was experiencing huge loss and grief. Gonzalez-Torres took this grief and turned it into art. This was his way of building community with others—of reaching out to them with some form of comfort—during a terrible time.

MOVING CLOSER TO LIBERATION

THE FUTURE IS IN SIGHT

1990–PRESENT

CHAPTER THIRTY

JAMIE NABOZNY

Gay Teen Hero

By the late twentieth century there had been so many changes in the United States that made the lives of LGBTQ people better. Some states—though not a majority—had passed laws protecting LGBTQ people in employment and housing. Many cities and counties had as well. Companies in the private sector were not only implementing antidiscrimination measures but, in some cases, were actively trying to hire LGBTQ people. Increasingly, more schools across the nation—those in more liberal states and cities—established gay-straight alliances (GSAs), which allowed LGBTQ youth a voice and a visibility they were previously denied. Gay male, lesbian, and bisexual people were represented in films and some television shows. (The next few decades would bring visibility to transgender characters.) HIV-AIDS was still a major problem in the gay male community, but by the mid-1990s, new drugs, as well as education about the disease, was making the epidemic manageable. By the early 1990s the idea of marriage equality was being discussed, and some lawyers were thinking of ways to make it a reality.

As wonderful as all of this was, LGBTQ people still faced many problems. In many cities and states in the United States you could be fired from your job, evicted from your apartment, or even denied service in a restaurant because you were LGBTQ. Many states still had laws that criminalized same-sex activity. People with HIV were marginalized in many ways. Lesbian women and gay men were not allowed to serve openly in the military. Most strikingly, violence against LGBTQ people was still very much a reality. Some studies—using FBI statistics of hate crimes against LGBTQ people—show that homophobic and gender-based violence has been increasing since 2015. This may have been due to higher levels of reporting or because LGBTQ people had a new level of visibility they never had before. Violence could happen anywhere—in public, in private, and even at school in the form of taunting, harassment, bullying, or overt unwanted physical contact. This is what happened to Jamie Nabozny and this is the story of how he fought back.

Jamie Nabozny was born in 1979 in Ashland, Wisconsin, a small town of just over eight thousand people and a port on Lake Superior. His parents, Bob and Carol, both from Ashland, never graduated high school and did not have much money. Their marriage was difficult, since both struggled with alcohol. They divorced and then remarried each other—twice. Being local people, they sent their son, Jamie, to the same local public school they had attended.

Nabozny turned thirteen in 1992 and was in the seventh grade when bullying started in earnest. Students called him "faggot" and "queer," and he was even pushed into a bathroom stall and hit. The bullying became so bad that his parents sent him to be homeschooled by his aunt and uncle. This was a relief for Nabozny, until he told his aunt that he was gay, and she insisted that he pray every night to become heterosexual. Nabozny was so upset that he ran back to his parents' home. His aunt, worried about him, called the police and told them that her nephew was gay. The police then told his parents.

Nabozny's mother was kind and sympathetic, but his father was angry. With few other choices for his education, they sent him back to middle school, where the bullying continued. It went from verbal taunting to physical harassment, and some of the bullies even pretended to rape him during a class when the teacher was out of the room. He ran to Principal Mary Podlesny's office, crying and with his shirt ripped, but she would not speak to him because he did not have an appointment.

Bob and Carol Nabozny complained to Podlesny, who did nothing. Despite all evidence she refused to believe that Nabozny was being bullied or assaulted. She also told Nabozny that if he was going to be openly gay at school, he should expect this because "boys will be boys." A few days later, depressed and angry, Nabozny took every pill in his parents' bathroom and was found unconscious on the floor later that day. He was taken to the hospital and had his stomach pumped.

Nabozny did not go back to middle school for that semester. When he started Ashland High School, the bullying started again in the first weeks. The high school principal did nothing after Nabozny was attacked and urinated on by some male students. Depressed and in despair, Nabozny attempted suicide again. He went to live with another aunt and uncle, but unfortunately they were not sympathetic and even refused to celebrate his fifteenth birthday.

Furious at being treated this way, fifteen-year-old Jamie Nabozny bravely fled their home and hitchhiked, two hundred miles, to Minneapolis, where he lived on the streets. His parents panicked and put out "missing child" alert posters. He was eventually found and brought home. There were few educational options open to Nabozny. His parents did not have high school diplomas and were not legally allowed to homeschool him. They could not afford a private school. Nabozny's only choice was to return to Ashland High. There the bullying became even worse. Even after a school counselor took his side, the principal, William Davis, and the assistant principal refused to stop the violence or even punish the boys torturing Nabozny. In eleventh grade a gang of boys beat and kicked Nabozny so badly he needed abdominal surgery.

In December 1992, in the middle of his senior year, Nabozny decided this abuse had to stop. He was just seventeen, penniless, and determined, no matter what, to make his life better. Nabozny cashed a few phony checks in Ashland and got on the next bus to Minneapolis, where he might be homeless but felt safer than at school.

Luckily for Nabozny, he was taken in by a gay couple. With his biological parents' permission, he became their foster child. Jamie Nabozny was now finally safe. He was still hurting. His foster parents sent him to a doctor and a therapist, and he was diagnosed with PTSD (post-traumatic stress disorder) and depression. Once Nabozny began to heal, he continued his education and received his GED, a high school equivalency diploma. Eventually he enrolled in the University of Minnesota.

Getting the education that he deserved, and had been denied him, was not enough for Nabozny. He knew that what happened to him was happening to other gay youths. He was right. A National Gay and Lesbian Taskforce Study found that 45 percent of gay male and 20 percent of lesbian students suffered some form of verbal or physical abuse in school. Nabozny felt that it was time to confront this systemic problem that was destroying the lives of LGBTQ young people. He decided to go to court.

First Nabozny hired a local lawyer, who brought a harassment case against the Ashland school system and against Principals Podlesny and Davis. The Ashland school system's district lawyer argued that since the principals did not participate in, advocate, or authorize the harassment, they were not guilty. A Wisconsin district court judge agreed and decided against Nabozny.

Nabozny would not be stopped. He went to Lambda Legal, a national organization that fought for LGBTQ rights. His lawyer, Patricia Logue, a lesbian, realized that the case was not just about Jamie Nabozny but about all LGBTQ youth not provided with sufficient protection from violence at school. The case was called *Nabozny v. Podlesny*, since Principal Mary Podlesny was named in the suit.

When Logue took the case to the US Court of Appeals, she sued under a federal law, Section 1983, also known as the Ku Klux Klan Act. This was a series of laws passed by Congress in the 1870s to protect African American citizens from violence and harassment by white supremacist groups such as the Ku Klux Klan. Logue argued that LGBTQ people were guaranteed equal rights under the Constitution and that Jamie Nabozny had been denied those rights. The appeals court agreed that Nabozny had the right to sue and that the case could go before a jury.

In November 1996 Logue stood before jurors from a conservative, rural region of Wisconsin. The jurors were not unlike the people who went to Ashland High School, their parents, or their siblings. It was unclear what they

Jamie Nabozny (right) and his family, 2018.

would decide. Yet it took these twelve women and men just under four hours to decide that Jamie Nabozny had been denied his constitutional rights. The school district eventually settled for a payment of $900,000 plus $62,000 to cover Nabozny's medical costs. More important, the case became the basis for other court rulings that protected the rights of LGBTQ people. Thanks to the persistence and bravery of Jamie Nabozny, as well as the legal arguments of Patricia Logue, *Nabozny v. Podlesny* has ensured that LGBTQ people are now more fully protected as American citizens.

Jamie Nabozny went from being a bullied gay kid in his middle school to a hero for the LGBTQ movement. His courage in fighting back to be accepted and respected as a gay American brought him to the US Court of Appeals, and the decision made life safer for other LGBTQ teens in schools.

JACK BAKER AND MICHAEL MCCONNELL

It Started in a Barber Shop

The right of same-sex couples to legally marry seemed, to some people, to appear very suddenly. It was fiercely debated in the early years of the twenty-first century and then, in 2015, thanks to a US Supreme Court decision, it became the law of the land. This great victory, however, had its roots in the struggles of a gay couple that occurred many decades before.

Two gay men, Jack Baker and Michael McConnell, fought for their right to be married starting in 1970. They managed to become legally married in 1972, and though their case did not change the law, their example pointed the way forward for others.

Their story starts even earlier, in Norman, Oklahoma. In 1957 McConnell was fourteen years old and often helped out in his father's barbershop. Standing around the shop and helping to sweep up, he realized that he was sexually attracted to the male customers. And McConnell realized he was interested in more than just sex—he wanted to find a man to share his life with and "live happily ever after."

Just nine years later, in 1966, McConnell was studying at the University of Oklahoma. There he met Jack Baker at a friend's Halloween party for gay men. Baker was his age, a veteran of the US Air Force, and had just started working as an engineer.

They came from very different backgrounds. McConnell was raised in a stable, happy family with several siblings. His entire family accepted his sexuality. Baker, on the other hand, was orphaned at the age of five and spent his early years in a Catholic orphanage. The only family he saw was his grandmother and an older sister.

Over the next few years the two men dated, fell in love, and moved in together. Like many young couples, they wanted to get married. They had what is called an "open relationship," meaning they could date other people if they chose but were also deeply committed to one another and planned to make a home and a life together. For them, this meant having a legal marriage that was recognized by the government and their community.

In the early 1970s hardly anyone, even activists in the LGBTQ community, seriously thought that same-sex couples would ever have the right to legally marry. This was a battle that, it was thought, would be impossible to win. In addition, the post-Stonewall LGBTQ movement had many other important fights: police harassment, violence against LGBTQ people, laws that made homosexual sexual activity illegal, and job and housing discrimination. Same-sex marriage, what we now call marriage equality, just wasn't on most people's radar.

McConnell and Baker weren't concerned about all that. They went on planning their lives together.

McConnell got his master's degree in library science and became a librarian. Baker decided to go to law school at the University of Minnesota, in part so he could figure out a way for him and his lover to get married under United States law.

Activism wasn't new for Baker. In 1969 he was voted president of Fight Repression of Erotic Expression (FREE), an LGBTQ political group at the University of Minnesota. At the time, it was only the second gay rights support group established on a college campus (the first was the Student Homophile League at Columbia University founded in 1966) in the United States. In his first year at law school, Baker began doing research on Minnesota marriage laws. He found that same-sex marriages were not specifically prohibited by Minnesota law. (Marriage is regulated by state, not federal, laws.) The laws just assumed that any couple who wanted to marry would be heterosexual. Baker understood the fundamental legal principle that anything not specifically prohibited by law is legally permitted. Since Minnesota law did not mention same-sex marriage, then, he reasoned, same-sex marriage was legal in that state.

On May 18, 1970, McConnell and Baker applied for a marriage license in Hennepin County, Minnesota. They were promptly denied the license by Gerald Nelson, the court clerk. The couple went to district court to get a judge to order the clerk to issue the license, but in November 1970 they were denied again. They then appealed that court's decision to the Minnesota Supreme Court in *Baker v. Nelson*. This time their case began to get news coverage. The local and national press wanted to know

Michael McConnell (left) and Jack Baker (right) receiving their marriage certificate, 1972.

more about Jack Baker, Michael McConnell, and this new idea—gay marriage.

The couple gave interviews and were featured in national publications including *Life* and *Look* magazines. In *Look*, the article about them was titled "The Homosexual Couple" and pictured McConnell and Baker shaving together, lounging with friends, and chatting with a priest at the University of Minnesota's Catholic Center. Over six million copies of *Look* were published each week, which meant that six million homes in America had photos of a happy, loving gay male couple on their coffee tables. This was an amazing gift to young LGBTQ people, most probably closeted, living in their parents' homes. McConnell and Baker also appeared on many national television and radio talk and news shows.

Despite the publicity, Jack Baker and Michael McConnell knew it was unlikely they would win their case in court. Rather than be discouraged, like all good political activists, they had highly inventive, alternate plans to attain their goals.

On August 1971, after their appeal to the district court was denied, Michael McConnell legally adopted Jack Baker, a legal orphan, in Hennepin County court. This achieved two aims. First, it connected them legally— as father and son, not husband and husband—which gave them some of the same legal rights as married couples. For example, they could visit each other in the hospital if one of them got sick. Second, the adoption was an important part of their secret plan. In it Jack changed his name to the gender neutral Pat Lyn, although everyone still called him Jack.

Later that month, McConnell and Baker moved in with a friend in Blue Earth County, Minnesota, which was one hundred miles away from Hennepin County. There McConnell applied for a marriage license for himself and Pat Lyn McConnell. The county clerk just assumed that Pat Lyn McConnell was a woman. He even joked that he had seen many couples with the same last name apply for licenses. Without a second thought he granted them the license. On September 3, 1971, Jack Baker and Michael McConnell, wearing matching white bell-bottom pants suits, were officially married. The wedding took place in a Victorian mansion, and their three-tier wedding cake was topped by figures of two grooms.

The ceremony was performed by the Reverend Roger Lynn, a Methodist minister who was sympathetic to the new gay rights movement. Lynn arrived at this position through a personal experience. A good friend in high school, with whom he had been in the church choir, was gay and so harassed later in life that he committed suicide.

Lynn believed that "we should be judged by who we don't love rather than by who we love." He had no problem marrying two men in a deeply loving relationship.

Meanwhile, *Baker v. Nelson*, the legal case of the first license, proceeded through the court system. On October 15, 1971, two months after Baker and McConnell were legally married in Blue Earth County, the Minnesota Supreme Court decided against them declaring, "The institution of marriage as a union of man and woman, uniquely involving the procreation or rearing of children within a family, is as old as the book of Genesis." Determined to win, McConnell and Baker, with the help of the Minnesota Civil Liberties Union, appealed *Baker v. Nelson* to the US Supreme Court, but in October 1972, the court dismissed the case, saying it was not a federal issue, since marriage was regulated by the states.

Baker and McConnell were upset their case was not heard by the Supreme Court. The good news was that the court did not rule against them. Since the marriage had never been annulled or revoked, it was technically valid, making McConnell and Baker the first same-sex couple to be legally married in the United States. Ever since, the two have lived together, had wonderful careers, grown older, retired, and have pretty much lived happily ever after.

Happily ever after is great. However, it is not the same as, or even close to, complete equality under the law as mandated by the US Constitution. Michael McConnell and Jack Baker managed to find a way—through adoption—to establish a legal connection to one another and surreptitiously obtained a marriage license. This was not a sustained legal advance for LGBTQ people to have equality under the law and to be full citizens.

If the United States government has decided, as most governments have, that it is in its interest to regulate marriage by issuing licenses—which is, in essence, a legal contract—then this option should be open to all adults who decide to partake in it. The couple's race, sex, or gender should not matter. Nor should what they may do sexually in their relationship. There should be one standard for marriage for everyone. The Declaration of Independence speaks of a fundamental right to the pursuit of happiness. If, for some people, this entails a legal marriage, then it must be available to everyone. The battle for marriage equality was a major fight for the LGBTQ rights movement.

MARRIAGE EQUALITY AND THE COURTS

The story of Jack Baker and Michael McConnell demonstrates that the fight for marriage equality was being waged long before it became a broad-based campaign and legal demand. Beginning in the late 1980s the LGBTQ rights movement began to systematically discuss and make plans to fight for marriage equality under the law. The first major victory was a 1991 decision by the Hawaii Supreme Court—*Baehr v. Lewin*. This ruling found that prohibiting marriage between same-sex couples was unconstitutional in the state of Hawaii, because the state constitution mandated equal treatment under the law for all people.

Baehr v. Lewin was the first in a series of legal fights in many states for the right of same-sex couples to marry. Some of the cases resulted in the compromise position of a legal "civil union," which was a legal marriage in many respects without using the word. Most LGBTQ people rejected this "compromise" as a form of separate but equal, which was as unacceptable as the segregated schools outlawed by *Brown v. Board of Education*.

After the Hawaii Supreme Court decision, opponents of marriage equality fought back and in 1998 pressed for a state constitutional amendment to allow the legislature to define marriage as between "one man and one woman." Similar battles took place in many other states. Then, on November 18, 2003, the Massachusetts' Supreme Judicial Court ruled that banning same-sex marriage was unconstitutional and discriminatory. Allowing time for appeals, the court ruled that same-sex couples could begin getting legally married in Massachusetts on May 17, 2004. There was, of course, a backlash. In February 2004 President George W. Bush called for a constitutional amendment "defining and protecting marriage as a union of a man and woman as husband and wife." Multiple states followed suit by amending their own constitutions. On a wave of court cases, election campaigns, and activism, eventually thirty-six states followed Massachusetts' lead. This led to a hodgepodge of laws and rulings in which some states allowed same-sex marriage, others had civil unions but no marriage, and still others continued to ban marriage equality.

Finally, the issue was decided by the US Supreme Court. In *United States v. Windsor* (2013), the court ruled that a federal law defining marriage as only between a man and a woman was unconstitutional. Two years later, in *Obergefell v. Hodges* (2015), the court ruled that same-sex couples are guaranteed the right to marry by the US Constitution. Since then marriage equality has been accepted as the law by state governments across the United States.

SYLVIA RIVERA

A Life in the Streets and a Guiding STAR

Gender identity is more complex than a simple binary choice of male or female. Jemima Wilkinson refused any gender designation, took the name Publick Universal Friend, refused the pronouns of "he" and "she," and preached to thousands of people in the late eighteenth century. Albert Cashier, who was assigned female at birth, understood himself to be a man and fought as a man in the Civil War. Julian Eltinge cross-dressed on stage and played women's roles to such acclaim that he had a Broadway theater named after him.

Today, increasing numbers of people understand that the two categories of male and female do not capture all the complexity of human biology, identity, or imagination. People who fall outside traditional binary roles still face a difficult struggle for acceptance. Even activists in the LGBTQ movement have not always been accepting of gender-variant people. There have been activists, even leaders of the gay rights movements, who felt that LGBTQ people should present themselves in the most socially acceptable ways. They lacked the vision to see that to be truly successful and liberating, the LGBTQ movement needed to include everyone. It also needed to address the broader social, economic, and political problems that many LGBTQ people faced. Often they were not receptive to the specific needs of people of color, poor people, or gender-variant people. They avoided or excluded people who were too "angry" or "militant," and people who, by conservative standards, "did not look right," because they were deemed to have a bad image for the movement.

Some LGBTQ people have had to fight their own movement for acceptance and representation. Sylvia Rivera was such a fighter. She learned to fight, literally, on the streets and grew up to fight for the rights of many LGBTQ people, especially youth, who did not have a voice.

Sylvia Rivera had a hard life, yet she transformed herself into someone who was a model of fabulousness and militancy. She was a political visionary and a founder of Street Transvestite Action Revolutionaries (STAR) in 1970, the first transgender political group in the United States. In the fifty years of her life Rivera struggled with numerous, often life-threatening, problems while at the same time always working to make the world a better place.

Rivera was born Rey Jose Christian Rivera Mendoza in 1951 to Carmen and Jose Rivera in Spanish Harlem (or East Harlem), a racially mixed, working-class neighborhood on the Upper East Side of New York City. To the large numbers of Spanish-speaking people who lived there, it was also known as El Barrio. Her parents' marriage was violent and her family life was unstable. Rivera's father left when she was two, and her mother remarried and gave birth to Rivera's sister, Sonia.

Struggling with depression, her mother committed suicide at twenty-two by swallowing rat poison. She urged Rivera to do the same; fortunately, the child refused.

Neither of Carmen's husbands demonstrated any interest in raising their children. So, when they were young, Rivera and her sister were taken in by their maternal grandmother, whom they called Viejita or "little old one." They lived in Jersey City—just across the river from New York City—and struggled to make ends meet. Soon after, Sonia's biological father took her to live with him in Puerto Rico, and the two half-siblings rarely saw one another again. Viejita and Rivera moved back to New York City, to the Lower East Side, and life was still difficult for them. Viejita was depressed, working all the time, and she often sent Rivera to live for short periods of time with friends.

Life with Viejita was stressful for Rivera, in part, because her grandmother was embarrassed by Rivera's increasing identification as a woman. Rivera began wearing makeup to school in the fourth grade and liked to dress in skintight clothes. Her grandmother was fearful that Rivera would grow up to be a *maricón*, a Spanish slur for a gay man. Even at this young age Rivera was engaging in sexual behavior with her older male cousin, a married neighbor, and a male teacher at school.

After being bullied at school by students who called her "faggot," Rivera dropped out of school and began to frequent New York's Forty-Second Street, which is in the Times Square area, where many gay men and trans women hung out and traded sex for money. For many of them, living on the street and "hustling"—the term used for male-male prostitution at the time—was the only way they could survive. Rivera was not yet twelve years old.

Viejita discovered Rivera's life outside of the home and bitterly fought with her about it. In despair, Rivera

Sylvia Rivera (left) and Marsha P. Johnson (to her left) sharing an umbrella at a New York city hall rally for gay rights, April 1973.

attempted suicide and was committed by Viejita to a mental hospital. Upon release, Rivera ran away, back to Forty-Second Street, where she found a community of gay men—some dressing in drag, some passing as women, some presenting as men—who accepted and protected her. They even had a "christening" for her when she began using the name Sylvia Lee Rivera.

During this time Rivera met two people who were to become very important in her life. The first was a man, who is usually referred to as Gary, although that is not his actual name. He and Sylvia fell in love. They lived together, making money as sex workers, sometimes addicted to drugs. They remained a couple for seven years. Around this time Rivera also met her lifelong friend and political comrade Marsha P. Johnson. (Johnson would often quip that the "P" stood for "pay it no mind.")

Johnson was born in Elizabeth, New Jersey, in 1945, as Malcolm Michaels Jr. After graduating high school, Johnson moved to Greenwich Village, sometimes dressing as a woman. She referred to herself as a drag queen, worked part-time jobs, engaged in survival sex, and mostly lived on the streets. Johnson was raised Roman Catholic, and in spite of the church's intolerance for LGBTQ people, she always remained religious.

Life on the street was hard, and Johnson dealt with a series of mental health problems that occasionally lead to her being institutionalized. When she and Rivera met, in 1962, Johnson, who was six years older, took Rivera under her care and protected her as much as she was able. Even though Rivera and Gary lived in a relatively safe, twenty-five-dollars-a-week hotel room, Rivera still faced hardships and was assaulted, robbed, and arrested numerous times.

In the mid-1960s Rivera began hormone treatment thinking that she wanted to undergo some form of body transformation. After a few treatments, she decided that this was not a route she wanted to pursue. She told friends, "I just want to be me. I want to be Sylvia Rivera. I like pretending. I like to have the role. I like to dress up and pretend, and let the world think about what I am. Is he or isn't he? That's what I enjoy."

Rivera's life was a hard one. There were part-time jobs but never enough money, passing bad checks to get by, and too many drugs, many of them addictive. However, she and Gary managed to live full lives, have friends, and make a life together. Rivera, however, learned on the streets to be a realist, and she knew that being gay, and certainly being effeminate, placed a person on the social and political fringes of society. When the Stonewall riots began in the early morning hours of June 28, 1969, Sylvia understood their importance.

Sylvia Rivera claims to have been fighting with the police on Christopher Street, where the Stonewall Inn was located. Not everyone agrees with this. Marsha P. Johnson said that Rivera had fallen asleep in Bryant Park, behind the New York Public Library on Forty-Second Street, and missed the event. Other people involved do not remember seeing her there. Even if she were not there, Rivera embraced the rebellion and was energized by it. She felt it was now time for those people not fully accepted by more "mainstream" gay men and lesbians— the drag queens, street youth, effeminate men, and butch dykes—to fight for recognition and acceptance. She and Marsha P. Johnson then decided to start STAR, Street Transvestite Action Revolutionaries.

For large parts of their teen and adult lives, Rivera and Johnson lived on the streets of New York. Being openly gay men who dressed in women's clothing—they called themselves "transvestites"; today we commonly refer to them as "transgender"—they faced enormous job and housing discrimination. There was constant harassment from police and from strangers on the street. Because they made their money as sex workers, they were always in danger of being arrested. Although they frequently dressed as women, they were biological men and, if arrested, they would be placed in a men's jail, where they were at high risk of physical and sexual assault.

Rivera and Johnson were not alone. New York in the early 1970s, especially in the summer, had a very large population, numbering in the thousands, of young people living on the streets. Many were gay and had been thrown out of their homes by their parents. Some ran away from home and to Greenwich Village because they heard that there were others like them in that part of New York City. Some had drug problems; some didn't. Almost none of them worked because they were too young, had no job history, lacked proper identification, or had to make sure their few belongings (kept in paper bags or shopping carts) were not stolen. There were only a few shelters for these young people—often run by churches that condemned homosexuality—and there was no place to go for safety, a bed for the night, a free meal, or just to sit quietly without fear of being arrested.

Rivera and Johnson knew from experience that people in that situation could not expect help from those in power. In November 1970 Rivera and Johnson rented a long-neglected, physically unsafe four-room apartment on the Lower East Side to be the first STAR House. It was less a homeless shelter than a drop-in center. Drug use was rampant, as were fights among visitors. Though Rivera and Johnson saw themselves as protective parents—they called the younger cross-dressers their "children"—they could, at times, barely manage their own lives, never mind the others'. Despite these problems, STAR House offered some safety in an urban environment that had none. Although the rent was only $200 a month, some of which was obtained through fund-raisers, panhandling, and sex work, because of mismanagement, theft, and lack of funds, STAR House was evicted in July 1971.

STAR continued to function as an organization. They held meetings, joined protest marches with other LGBTQ groups, and were highly visible in the annual Gay Pride marches. They also supported other radical groups, including the Black Panthers and the Young Lords, both of which were grassroots political groups that worked to empower African American and Latinx people, and took on issues related to homelessness, prison reform, and street violence. At the 1973 New York Gay Pride Rally, officially called Christopher Street Liberation Day, Rivera gave an impassioned speech about the lives of trans people.

Rivera and Johnson knew that effective political change came by working in alliance with other groups. Unfortunately, other LGBTQ rights groups did not want to be associated with STAR. While respected by some at a distance, STAR never received the support it needed from the larger movement and quickly disappeared. Rivera and Johnson continued to be vibrant figures in the movement over the next two decades, demanding that the lives of all trans people be taken seriously, even when many people resisted. Rivera famously said later in life: "When things started getting more mainstream, it was like, 'We don't need you no more.'" And, she added, "Hell hath no fury like a drag queen scorned."

Ultimately Rivera and Johnson succeeded. Although STAR burned brightly for a short time only to be extinguished, the idea of STAR was the start of the organized transgender movement we have today.

Marsha P. Johnson died in 1992. She was found floating in New York City's Hudson River, possibly the victim of violence. Rivera died of liver cancer at age fifty in 2002. After her death, a street in Greenwich Village was named after her, and activists founded the Sylvia Rivera Law Project, a nonprofit legal group that fights for the rights of transgender people.

The work that was started by Sylvia Rivera and Marsha P. Johnson in 1970 is more vital today than ever before. More and more youth are coming out as transgender. Many of these young people—especially youth of color—face enormous problems with homelessness, police violence, and harassment at home and at school, as well as social and economic discrimination. In numerous ways, life for many young transgender people today is not much better than it was for Sylvia Rivera and Marsha P. Johnson. Many groups—including the Sylvia Rivera Law Project—have taken up the fight for the legal rights of transgender people. All national LGBTQ groups, such as Lambda Legal, the Human Rights Campaign, and the National LGBTQ Task Force, under pressure from trans people and their allies, have, over the years, begun to include transgender rights in their agendas. Rivera's "Hell hath no fury like a drag queen scorned" has paved the way for many changes today.

COMING OUT OR STAYING IN

New Queer Ways of Living in the World

Coming out is usually a private moment. You come out to your friends or family, or someone comes out to you, while sitting at the kitchen table or over a cup of coffee. It might even be by text because it's just too complicated to say in person.

Now imagine coming out in a much more public way—like on the cover of *Time* magazine. This is what air force sergeant Leonard Matlovich did on September 8, 1975.

Leonard Matlovich was a decorated air force serviceman. During the war in Vietnam he was awarded the Bronze Star, a Purple Heart, and an Air Force Commendation Medal. The son of an air force sergeant, Matlovich was born in 1943 and grew up on military bases. He joined the air force in 1963, and a decade later—after ten years of service in the air force—came out to himself and had sex with a man for the first time. He knew that sex between men was prohibited by US military law, and so he concealed his sex life from his commanding officer.

A year later, knowing nothing about the gay liberation movement, he read an article about Washington, DC–based activist Frank Kameny, who had helped some servicemen bring lawsuits to challenge the military's rules.

Matlovich contacted Kameny. Working with a lawyer from the American Civil Liberties Union, Kameny helped Matlovich bring a discrimination lawsuit against the armed forces. The plan was to generate publicity, come out to his superiors, and see what happened. Matlovich presented his commanding officer with a letter stating that he was a gay man and then told the press. The story was in the *New York Times* on May 26, 1975, and on the cover of *Time* on September 8 of that year.

Matlovich's mother was distraught when he told her and believed that her son's sexuality was God's punishment on her for something *she* had done. His father found out from a news story on television and cried for two hours. He quickly rallied to his son's defense, though, and, aware that homophobic backlash was inevitable, proclaimed: "If he can take it, I can take it."

Matlovich's case went before a discharge board, which ruled that, because of his service record, Matlovich be given an Honorable Discharge in October 1975. Matlovich sued the air force for reinstatement, and his case went to court. It was a long battle of decisions and appeals, most in Matlovich's favor. But after five years Matlovich decided to settle out of court, and the air force offered him a settlement of $160,000 (worth nearly $500,000 today), which he accepted. After his return to civilian life Leonard Matlovich worked as an LGBTQ activist and then an HIV-AIDS activist, until he died of HIV-related causes in 1988. Matlovich's gravestone, at his request, does not give his name. It simply reads: A Gay Vietnam Veteran. Under that are the words "When I was in the military they gave me a medal for killing two men and a discharge for loving one."

The singular message of the Stonewall riots and the gay liberation movement was to come out. For many LGBTQ people, *the* major political and personal issue they faced was being open about their identity with family, friends, colleagues, classmates, neighbors, and teachers. The high-spirited, positive energy of the movement allowed and encouraged people to be open about their sexual desires and to feel emotionally and socially liberated. It was never easy, though, and the people who did come out, like Leonard Matlovich, were brave, often facing serious consequences.

Many LGBTQ activists, in the early days of the gay liberation movement, hoped that coming out would become easier for everyone, but that is not how life and history works. They had hoped that Leonard Matlovich being on the cover of *Time* would have broken old ways of thinking and set a new standard. That is not what happened. Over the years, whenever a celebrity would come out, it continued to be big news. It seemed, again and again, that mainstream, nongay America was constantly surprised that there were many LGBTQ Americans.

■ ■ ■

In 1981, a few years after the Matlovich *Time* cover, tennis champion Martina Navratilova made national headlines when the press reported that she was bisexual. Born in 1956 in Prague, Czechoslovakia (she became a US citizen in 1981), Navratilova was chosen by *Tennis* magazine as the greatest woman player during the years 1975 to 2005. She is now considered to be one of the greatest, if not the greatest, female tennis players of all time.

Like Leonard Matlovich, Navratilova knew that the stakes of coming out were high. Professional sports were, and still are, notoriously homophobic. In 1981, just after she obtained her US citizenship, Navratilova mentioned to a reporter that she was having an affair with the novelist and lesbian activist Rita Mae Brown. Navratilova requested that the reporter keep the information quiet—that it was "off the record"—until she was ready to come out publicly. But the reporter did not honor her request, and Navratilova was outed before she had planned to do so.

In the next two years, she, and her story, were on the cover of *People, Newsweek,* and *Sports Illustrated.* Coming out did not hurt Navratilova's career as a champion player, but did lose her major endorsement revenue. She rose to even greater heights as a tennis player in the next two decades, reaching the Wimbledon final nine consecutive times between 1982 to 1990.

■　■　■

In 1988 the Human Rights Campaign Fund (now known simply as the Human Rights Campaign) instituted National Coming Out Day. This was to commemorate the March on Washington for Lesbian and Gay Rights, held the previous year, in which half a million people participated in a protest demanding equal rights. The day has been celebrated on October 11 every year since. In the spirit of the gay liberation movement, National Coming Out Day urged LGBTQ people, if it wasn't too dangerous for them personally, to come out to their family, friends, and communities.

Even with this progress, Americans were still completely surprised in 1997 when actor and comedian Ellen DeGeneres decided to address—on national television—rumors of her lesbianism through her TV show.

After a successful, nearly two-decades-long career as a stand-up comic, film, and TV actor, DeGeneres got her own TV sitcom, *Ellen*, playing Ellen Morgan, a fictionalized version of herself. During its third season, tabloid newspapers had begun hinting that DeGeneres was a lesbian. On the April 30, 1997, episode of the show, her character Ellen Morgan came out. As a build-up to the episode, and to reinforce her own coming out, DeGeneres appeared on the April 14 cover of *Time* magazine with the headline "Yep, I'm Gay," and made an appearance on the *Oprah* show.

The coming out episode of *Ellen* was a sensation. People sponsored "Ellen Coming Out House Parties" and watched with their friends. A few advertisers withdrew their sponsorship of the show, and some conservative groups attacked DeGeneres, the show, and ABC, the television network it appeared on. The episode had a huge audience of forty-two million viewers. It now appeared that "coming out" was routinely national news.

Yet, in spite of all this—Ellen DeGeneres's public coming out took place over two decades ago—when celebrities come out, it is still news. George Hosato Takei—who played Hikaru Sulu, helmsman for the USS *Enterprise* in the original *Star Trek* series as well as in many of the subsequent films—came out to the press in 2000, at the age of sixty-eight. He spoke about his relationship with his partner (now husband) of eighteen years. Even through Takei had never really hidden his sexuality—he

Laverne Cox at the trans march in San Francisco, June 2015.

was a member of several LGBTQ groups—this became a national news story.

Notable people coming out has become a regular news item, in each case getting national publicity. These days almost all Americans know about famous LGBTQ people: actors Cynthia Nixon of *Sex and the City*, Jim Parsons of *The Big Bang Theory*, Laverne Cox of *Orange Is the New Black*; singers Melissa Etheridge, k. d. lang, Elton John, and Frank Ocean; Apple's CEO Tim Cook; the television commentators Robin Roberts, Rachel Maddow, and Anderson Cooper; and model and activist Jazz Jennings. Yet, somehow, more than half a century after Stonewall, the mere fact that someone is *not* heterosexual is still fascinating to many heterosexual Americans.

The reality is, many young people still face serious obstacles in coming out. According to a national study by the Human Rights Campaign, four in ten LGBTQ youth feel they live in a community that does not accept them. LGBTQ youth are twice as likely as other young people to be the target of physical assaults. Twenty-sex percent of LGBTQ youth say that their biggest problems are not being accepted by their families, being bullied at school, and fear of being outed against their will.

Despite these problems, all studies show that people today—and especially younger people—are coming out more frequently and at earlier ages. A 2017 Gallup study showed that the number of Americans who identify as LGBTQ is now at 4.1 percent, up from 3.5 percent in 2012. Millennials—those born between 1980 and 1998—are coming out at increasingly higher rates than any other group: 7.3 percent of this group identifies as LGBTQ as opposed to 5.8 percent in 2012.

Jazz Jennings at New York City Pride, 2016.

The Gallup study notes, "Millennials are more than twice as likely as any other generation to identify as LGBT. In 2012, they accounted for 43% of LGBT-identified adults. As a result of their disproportionate increases in identification since then, they now account for 58%. Millennials comprise 32% of the general adult population." The study also noted that the highest coming out rates—for all ages—were in the African American, Asian American, and Hispanic communities.

These numbers show the strength and growth of the LGBTQ community. But they do not tell us the complexity of what it means to come out now. Today there are many more ways for people, especially younger people, to come out. Rather than coming out as gay, lesbian, or bisexual, many younger people are claiming an identity as queer—meaning that they reject the old categories of sexual identity. They may have sexual lives that resemble traditional ideas of gay, lesbian, or bisexual, but they don't fit into those categories. Those labels don't accurately describe who they are.

Other people may call themselves "sexually fluid," or "pansexual"— meaning that they experience their sexuality as open and shifting. They may be attracted to men and then to women, or to both at one time, and this may change day by day or year to year. "Sexual fluidity," or "pansexuality," is a term that is increasingly used. Actors such as Cara Delevingne, Lily-Rose Depp, and Kristen Stewart describe themselves as sexually fluid. This makes a great deal of sense. Human knowledge—from our own experience as well as scientific studies—tells us that sexuality is not stable. Sexuality changes over time, depending on our current situation and current relationships. Our sexual desires—who we find attractive, what we want to do sexually, what turns us on—may be different at thirteen than at twenty-five.

Coming out now also entails, for many people, a description of their gender identity. We know that throughout history, categories of male and female have not fit everyone. These categories were so strictly defined that people were forced to choose one or the other, even if they felt they didn't fit into either. Today, our discussions of gender are far more complex. People can describe themselves as transgender, as nonbinary, gender queer or gender fluid. For many people, finding a way to describe their gender is as important as coming out about their sexuality.

Our ideas about relationships are also changing. Some people, queer and not queer, define themselves as polyamorous. They reject the traditional idea of two people becoming a monogamous couple (for a short- or long-term relationship) and are looking at relationships that are nonmonogamous, or perhaps include not just two but three or more people. Often, people involved in these relationships refer to themselves as being involved in consensual, ethical, and responsible nonmonogamy. These ideas about relationships are not new. People throughout history have always found ways to construct healthy, meaningful relationships that were outside the norm, but the discussion of these relationships has moved into the mainstream in ways that never happened before.

These days, if an individual feels it is safe to do so, it is possible—and emotionally, psychologically, and sexually healthy—to come out in many ways about your sexuality, gender, and relationships. That these choices are now possible is a result of the progress that LGBTQ people have made in helping shape this country since American was founded. Lesbian, gay, bisexual, and transgender people—through activism or just living their lives—have always provided creative, alternative models of how humans might form their relationships and communities.

JASON COLLINS

It was maybe the best-kept secret in sports, the tightest door on the most secure closet. The door was so tight that even the man in the closet was, at times, unsure that it was even true. He did not even tell his little brother—well, his twin brother who was eight minutes younger than he was—one of the most important things about himself: he was gay.

When in April 2013, basketball superstar Jason Collins came out as a gay man, his friends, his fans, the sports

(continues on next page)

(continued from previous page)

world, and the media were shocked. All it took was a few modest words delivered in a *Sports Illustrated* cover story:

> I'm a 34-year-old NBA center. I'm black. And I'm gay.
>
> I didn't set out to be the first openly gay athlete playing in a major American team sport. But since I am, I'm happy to start the conversation. I wish I wasn't the kid in the classroom raising his hand and saying, "I'm different." If I had my way, someone else would have already done this. Nobody has, which is why I'm raising my hand.

Such carefree words—perfect language for a positive coming out story—don't reflect the reality, that Collins struggled for years. Born in 1978, in the Northridge neighborhood of Los Angeles, he excelled in basketball. He and his twin brother, Jarron, who also became a professional player, were on the team at the prestigious Harvard-Westlake School and both continued to play at Stanford University. After graduating in 2001, Collins played for the New Jersey Nets of the NBA and soon became the starting center, helping to take the team to the NBA finals in 2003. From 2008 to 2013 Collins played with a number of teams. It was after that season, when Collins became a free agent, that he decided it was time to publicly come out.

As it is for many people, Collins's decision came after years of thought, first trying to understand who he was and then trying to figure out the right thing to do. Collins knew he was attracted to men in high school but had never acted on it. He knew gay people, including his uncle Mark, who lived in New York and was openly gay and in a long-term relationship. Social pressure, especially in the world of professional sports, made coming out very difficult for Collins.

He dated women and was even engaged for nine years, but by 2011, when he turned thirty-three, he felt it was time to accept himself and be honest about who he really was. He first came out to his aunt Teri, a superior court judge in

San Francisco, and was surprised to hear that she'd always thought he was gay. As he wrote in *Sports Illustrated*: "The relief I felt was a sweet release. Imagine you're in the oven, baking. Some of us know and accept our sexuality right away and some need more time to cook. I should know—I baked for 33 years."

When Collins wrote this piece, hardly anyone—and certainly not his teammates—knew he was gay. "I've been asked how other players will respond to my announcement," he wrote. "The simple answer is, I have no idea. I'm a pragmatist. I hope for the best, but plan for the worst."

There were some people who criticized Collins—despite his being a practicing Christian who grew up helping his parents teach Sunday school—because their individual religious beliefs condemned homosexuality. Many others, however, were completely supportive. Former First Lady Michelle Obama tweeted, "So proud of you, Jason Collins! This is a huge step forward for our country. We've got your back!" Former president Bill Clinton declared, "I'm proud to call Jason Collins a friend." Even athletes from other sports spoke out in support, including the entire Red Sox baseball team, which tweeted, "We salute you, @jasoncollins34 for your courage and leadership. Any time you want to throw out a first pitch at Fenway Park, let us know."

After coming out, Collins played for the Nets again and became the first openly gay player in the NBA. He was accepted by his teammates, who were more worried about the distracting attention of the media on the issue than Collins's personal life, and his fans were completely supportive. He received very warm applause when he played his first post–coming out game in Los Angeles and

Jason Collins, 2014.

(continues on next page)

(continued from previous page)

received a standing ovation at his first home game in Brooklyn, where the Nets now played.

Professional sports is one of the most difficult environments in which to come out. Cultural ideas about masculinity and femininity often dictate how athletes are supposed to behave. Heterosexuality is always presumed. Collins's actions are a benchmark of how far we have come as a society. In his coming out story Collins said, "I'm learning to embrace the puzzle that is me." In many ways, that is true of America as well.

CHAPTER THIRTY-FOUR

YOUNG PEOPLE TODAY
The Future of Queer History

A lot of people reflect on their time in high school, both the wonderful moments and the horrible ones. Few do it in a witness stand in a federal courtroom. That is what Aidan DeStefano, eighteen years old and a recent graduate of Boyertown Area Senior High School in Pennsylvania, did as a witness in a case before a federal appeals court in Philadelphia in April 2017. In many ways, his is a great American story of personal bravery, social progress, the power of understanding, and the dedicated activism of youth to change the course of history.

In 2016 the Boyertown Area Board of Education enacted a trans-friendly policy that allowed students to use the restroom or locker room that matched their gender identity, no matter what gender they had been assigned at birth. This policy was enacted, in part, because of DeStefano's unrelenting activism as a student and member of the school's gay-straight alliance. In 2017 this policy was challenged by four nontransgender students and their parents, who claimed that the students' right to privacy was being violated. Historically, the legal concept of a "right to privacy" has focused on protecting an individual's personal information or life from government or media intrusion. It has often been framed as "the right to be let alone." The idea that non-trans students were having their privacy intruded upon in a restroom or locker room had no legal precedent and did not make much legal sense.

The Boyertown school policy was defended in court by the ACLU and supported by pro-trans sentiment in the high school. The federal appeals court was divided and reached no decision. They sent the case back to a lower court, the Third US Circuit Court of Appeals, to let them review it again.

DeStefano was a popular student at Boyertown who transitioned from female to male in the eleventh grade. At first some students objected to him using the men's room, but their attitudes changed. DeStefano was not harassed, shamed, or bullied. He was a prize athlete, first on the women's track and cross-country teams and then on the *men's* track and cross-country teams. He was also nominated to homecoming court.

We think about history as something that has happened in the past. We make distinctions such as "ancient history" or "recent past," reinforcing the idea that history is what already happened. History is being made today. It is all around us—in the media, online, on blogs, in tweets, in our lives. In the opening pages of this book James Baldwin was quoted, making the point that "the great force of history comes from the fact that we carry it within us, are unconsciously controlled by it in many ways, and history is literally *present* in all that we do. It could scarcely be otherwise, since it is to history that we owe our frames of reference, our identities, and our aspirations." We are all part of history. Most important, young LGBTQ people are the future of history.

One of the most amazing aspects of Aidan DeStefano's story is that it could not have happened even a few years earlier. At any time in the past, it would have been astonishing—impossible—to have transgender students accepted in high schools, playing on sports teams of *both* genders, and testifying in a federal appeals court to *defend* an in-place pro-trans policy. DeStefano's story shows how far LGBTQ people have come and that our fight for political equality has put us at the forefront of changing how Americans live—in other words: making history.

Young people have always been leaders in American political movements. Your voices have been part of the labor movement, the women's movement, and the civil rights movement. This was true of many people in the early struggles for LGBTQ rights in the 1950s and 1960s. It is especially true of the post-Stonewall gay liberation movement, which was propelled forward by the energy and actions of people just like you, in their late teens and early twenties, such as Rita Mae Brown and Carl Wittman. In the early days of the gay liberation movement, numerous gay youth groups formed across the country. The members were often inspired by their involvement with other political issues and groups: the civil rights movement, the Black Power movement, feminism, protests against the war in Vietnam, political action to decriminalize the use of some drugs, and a vast network of counter-culture people often referred to, in the most general terms, as "hippies."

Throughout American history we have seen young LGBTQ people changing the world. Publick Universal Friend renounced gender and became a preacher at age twenty-four. Albert Cashier was a teen when he moved

Pride parade in San Francisco, 2012.

to the United States from Ireland, and nineteen when he joined the Union army to fight against slavery. Charlotte Cushman was eighteen when she first went on the stage to support her family. Gladys Bentley was sixteen when she moved to New York from Philadelphia in 1923 and began a singing and performing career—getting four hundred dollars for her first recording. Bayard Rustin was in high school when, inspired by his religious beliefs, he began his career of peace work and early civil rights organizing. Sylvia Rivera was nineteen when she and Marsha P. Johnson started Street Transvestite Action Revolutionaries (STAR) in 1970.

We now live in an age of incredible transition, debate, and even upheaval about issues that affect us individually, in our culture, and for our common future. LGBTQ activism, often led by young people like you, touches on key issues facing our society. Fighting for gender-neutral bathrooms raises the issue of new definitions of gender. Demanding service for gay couples from small businesses asks, Is discrimination okay, even when it's in the name of "religious freedom"? Does a private company have the right to discriminate on the basis of sexual orientation? Can private adoption agencies deny their services to same-sex couples?

Today's activists talk about "intersectionality," meaning that the struggles for equality and justice for all groups are interconnected. This is not a new idea. In the late 1960s the Gay Liberation Front also believed all oppressions were interconnected. Today young LGBTQ activists are involved in many political issues, such as #BlackLivesMatter, the #MeToo movement, and the #NeverAgain gun control movement. They are involved in these movements because the social issues they address are integral to their lives. This includes the fight against racism, to end poverty, to end unjust wars, to protect women's reproductive rights, and to protect the environment.

In the past twenty years the growth of new technologies has radically altered how we relate to one another, see the world, share information, and see ourselves. Who would have thought, a decade ago, that the selfie would become a major marker of identity? Mobile phones made personal communication much easier by moving it out of the home, and more sophisticated phones allow us to record and send videos and photos. Most striking, people can now record and document public and private

instances of violence and injustice, making it harder
to deny that these events took place and easier to seek
justice.

What does this mean for LGBTQ life? Now it is
possible for LGBTQ people to come out on Instagram to
people they do not even know (and not be out to their
families). Some celebrities—such as hip-hop star iLove-
Makonnen—have even come out on Twitter. LGBTQ
people—like heterosexuals—can meet one another
through online dating apps, thus creating "virtual" gay
bars. In the past you had to live in cities where such gathering places existed. Now people interested in connecting
with other LGBTQ people, including finding real-world
gay bars, community centers, or gay-friendly restaurants,
can more easily and safely do so.

Gone are the days when we had to pass printed
newsletters secretly from hand to hand. It is now possible
for young queer people—or anyone—who have questions to anonymously research anything on the internet
and protect their privacy if they feel at risk at home or at
school. People who are seeking basic medical facts about
sexual health, sexually transmitted illnesses (STIs), and
HIV-related topics can do so without having to have a
face-to-face encounter with a medical professional, which
may be uncomfortable or potentially dangerous for them.
Young trans people have access to a huge amount of
information that may be life-saving for them. Everyone,
queer and not, can find out about LGBTQ history and
learn about how LGBTQ people have shaped the world.

Most important, political activists can use social
media and a whole host of other new technologies to

do political organizing. It is now possible to announce a demonstration on Twitter or Facebook and reach thousands of people. In the past activists had to rely on telephone calls, paper flyers, and word of mouth.

Imagine what Stonewall world have been like if Twitter existed? Imagine how many people ACT UP would have been able to get to a demonstration if they had had Facebook? Think about how many more people would have had access to HIV-AIDS and safe-sex information if social media existed in the 1980s.

LGBTQ activists fifty years ago could never have envisioned the enormous changes that have occurred since then: the advent of marriage equality; openly queer people in state legislatures, Congress, and the armed forces; proclamations for LGBTQ Pride Month (held in June in honor of the Stonewall riots) coming from federal agencies and the military; more and more openly gay athletes on professional and Olympic teams; openly LGBTQ characters on prime-time television shows and even the Disney Channel; lesbian and gay male couples appearing in mainstream advertising; gay-straight alliances in many US high schools; Queer Prom nights; Gay Days at amusement parks; gay men and lesbians thanking their spouses and partners at the Academy Awards ceremony.

This is a world that is radically different from 1999, never mind 1969.

The "future of queer history" sounds contradictory, but it is not. Since before this country was founded, there have been people who refused to conform to gender and sexual norms living in and creating America. Often, because they lived outside certain cultural traditions, they led the way for new ways of seeing the world, new ways of seeing America. Sometimes they were persecuted for this; sometimes they were praised. Often, people in the mainstream realized only after the fact the vision and new values queer people brought to American culture. Those people did that in the past. That is American history. Now you, your friends, your classmates, your communities, and your colleagues are the ones who will make those changes, have those visions, and create a new future for America, a new America.

ASEXUAL/ASEXUALITY   "Asexuality" is a relatively recent
term used by those who, for some period in their lives, do
not experience sexual desire. Some individuals adopt this
as a sexual orientation—similar to heterosexuality, bisexuality, or homosexuality—but for many others, asexuality
is a temporary feeling.

BERDACHE (TWO-SPIRIT)   When Europeans came to North
America they found, in many indigenous cultures, a wide
range of sexual and gender behaviors they found unacceptable. These included men and women not conforming
to expected gender roles. Each native culture had specific
words for these identities. French missionaries, however,
labeled them *all* as *berdache*, a French word meaning
"sodomite" (see *sodomy*). In recent decades many Native
Americans have used the term "two-spirit" to describe
nonbinary or gender-variant people.

BINARY   "Binary" means something, including an idea,
having two parts. Recently activists have applied this to
gender and sexuality. They argue that people traditionally
have incorrectly understood gender and sexuality—male
and female; heterosexual and homosexual—as binary sys-
tems. We now understand that both gender and sexuality
are far more complex than just two possibilities. Today
some people choose to label their gender identity as

"nonbinary," in resistance to the traditional, and limiting, binary system of gender.

BISEXUAL   Women and men who are sexually and romantically attracted to both, or various, genders often call themselves "bisexual." Many psychological and sociological studies, including the famous Kinsey Reports, demonstrate that a majority of people are, to some degree, attracted to people of various genders.

CISGENDER   This is a relatively new word in the English language. It describes a person whose gender identity aligns with their biological sexual organs. In many ways it is the opposite of "transgender." Both words come from Latin roots—"transgender," from the prefix *trans* (which means "across from"), and "cisgender," from the prefix *cis* meaning "on this side of."

CROSS-DRESSING   "Cross-dressing" is a general term to describe a cisgender woman or man who dresses in the garments usually associated with the other gender. It can be used to describe actors in theatrical productions or women and men who dress up for a special occasion, such as a party. See also *transvestite*, a similar but different term.

DYKE/BULLDAGGER   Usually meaning a butch, or masculine-appearing, lesbian. No one is quite sure how this term originated. People in 1920s Harlem, within and outside the LGBTQ community, used the term "bulldyke" (or "bulldagger") probably as an insult. In the 1950s "bulldyke" was used; "bulldagger" had fallen into disuse, and the term was widely used as a slur. After Stonewall and the advent of lesbian-feminism, many women appropriated "dyke" as a positive label or identity that meant they were strong and determined.

FAG/FAGGOT   In colloquial English, since the early twentieth century, these are terms for a gay man. It is unclear how this began. In sixteenth-century England, it was an abusive term for a troublesome woman; later it meant a younger boy in an all-male British boarding school. Overwhelmingly derogatory, since Stonewall it has been used by some gay men as a positive term. See also *dyke* and *queer*.

FEMINISM   Feminism is the belief in and practice of women's equality, in all aspects of thought, psychology, politics, economics, and life. Much of the thinking in the gay liberation and LGBTQ rights movements is indebted to feminist theory. Almost all lesbians see themselves as feminists.

GAY   In traditional English usage this word meant "cheerful" or "happy." By the seventeenth century it had acquired sexual connotations. Since the early twentieth century it describes people sexually and romantically attracted to the same gender. After Stonewall, "gay" replaced the more medical "homosexual." Globally, it is commonly used as a general cultural term (i.e., "gay bar"), but lesbian, trans, and bisexual people may prefer to use those terms that refer specifically to them.

GENDER/GENDER IDENTITY   "Sex" and "gender" are often confused. "Sex" is an identity assigned, usually at birth and by others, most often based on our genitalia. "Gender" is how we perceive ourselves—as a man, a woman, a nonbinary person—as our identity. An easy way to remember the difference is this phrase: "sex is what is between our legs; gender is what is between our ears."

HERMAPHRODITE (SEE ALSO INTERSEX)   We see this term in older medical and literary texts. It is no longer used medically. It describes a person with some mixture of both male and female primary and secondary sexual characteristics. The word comes from the name Hermaphroditus, who, according to Greek mythology, was the son of Hermes and Aphrodite, and was both male and female.

HETEROSEXUAL/HETEROSEXUALITY   From the Greek and Latin prefix *hetero* meaning "other." This term describes sexual and romantic attraction to what is traditionally described as the "opposite sex" from oneself—male or female. Though people have always been involved in opposite-sex relationships, the word describing those relationships was only coined in 1892 as the alternative to "homosexual," which was first used in 1868. Even after 1892 the word "heterosexual" was not in common use for decades.

HOMOPHOBIA   "Homophobia" describes a dislike or even hatred of LGBTQ people. It comes from the Latin suffix *phobia* meaning "fear of" (for example, "claustro*phobia*" is a fear of enclosed places). The term was invented in the late 1960s by George Weinberg, a heterosexual, pro-gay therapist, to describe his patients' unease about LGBTQ people and issues. Similarly, "transphobia" is a dislike or fear of trans people.

HOMOSEXUAL/HOMOSEXUALITY   From the Latin prefix *homo* meaning "the same," "homosexuality" describes sexual and romantic attraction to the same sex or gender. It was coined in 1868 by the German writer Karl-Maria Kertbeny. The word "homosexual" was intended to replace the insulting slur of "sodomite."

INTERSECTIONAL   This word is commonly used to describe the multiple identities a person may have, each of which is important. An African American lesbian with a disability deals with four distinct identities, each with its own strengths and struggles. All people have multiple identities that make up who they are. "Intersectional" is also a political term to describe groups with different political interests that find ways to work together for a common cause.

INTERSEX   This is the medical term, first coined in 1917, that replaced the word "hermaphrodite." "Intersex" reflects a better scientific understanding of the complexity of the human body and of gender. It describes people who have any mixture—genital, hormonal, chromosomal, or reproductive—of male and female sexual characteristics.

LESBIAN   This word describes a woman who is attracted romantically and sexually to other women. In late-sixth- and early-seventh-century Greece, the poet Sappho, who lived on the Greek Isle of Lesbos, wrote love poems to women. In the nineteenth-century, women who loved women were often called "sapphists." The word "lesbian" became commonly used in the early twentieth century. After Stonewall the word became a way for women to identify as both queer and a woman.

LGBTQ An acronym for lesbian, gay, bisexual, transgender, and queer. Any attempt to encapsulate a complex community must fall short. It does not include groups— such as the intersexed or those who identify as nonbinary or gender queer—who see themselves as part of a larger community. Often "queer" is used to include everyone. This also has limitations, though, as some people do not like the word since it has been used as a slur. But it is more commonly used now in a positive way than ever before.

QUEEN Beginning in the 1920s, this word became a catch-all term for gay men. Often used affectionately, sometimes mockingly, it is still used today. It is often adapted by adding a word before (for example, "opera queen"). The term "drag queen" was used in the 1950s to describe men who cross-dressed as entertainers or just for fun.

QUEER In the English language of the sixteenth century, "queer" meant "odd," "quaint," or "strange." In the late nineteenth century, it was used as a slur against LGBTQ people. During the twentieth century, some gay people began to use it defiantly and even affectionately, although it is still used as an insult in the mainstream culture. In the 1980s, some LGBTQ people began using the word proudly, although some older women and men, remembering the slurs of their youth, did not like this. As mentioned, the word is commonly used now.

SODOMY   This word has biblical roots and comes from the story of Sodom and Gomorrah in the Old Testament, which has been wrongly interpreted to condemn homosexual sexual activity. From the Middle Ages onward, it has been used legally to describe any number of sexual acts that did not lead to procreation. Many countries have had or still do have "sodomy laws" that punish these behaviors. In the past "sodomy" was commonly used to refer to anal sex, and men who had anal sex were called "sodomites," though this term is rarely used today.

TRANSGENDER   Commonly used now, this word was coined in 1965 to replace "transsexual." It was originally used to discuss people who were having sex-reassignment surgery. (Both words come from the Latin root *trans*, meaning "across.") The meaning of "transgender" has broadened to include all people who feel they do not fit into the socially prescribed—and limiting—concepts of gender.

TRANSSEXUAL   This word was first used in 1949 to describe people who wanted to undergo sex-reassignment surgery, a process that surgically alters primary and secondary sexual characteristics to conform with a person's perceived gender. Because it was specific to the surgical aspect of transitioning, many people who are transitioning today prefer the word "transgender," which includes a broader range of people, including those who do not have sex-reassignment surgery. "Transsexual" is still used today but in very specific, limited ways.

TRANSVESTITE "Transvestite"—literally, "cross-dressing" from the Latin, *trans*, meaning "across," and *vesti*, meaning "clothing"—was used to describe a person, usually male, who cross-dressed, most likely for his own pleasure and sometimes for sexual excitement but not for entertainment purposes. First used in the early twentieth century, it gained popularity and was used medically and colloquially in and outside the LGBTQ community. Today the terms "cross-dresser" and "drag queen," if speaking about a performer, are more commonly used.

This bibliography lists chapter by chapter many of the books that were used to write *A Queer History of the United States for Young People.*

Prologue

James Baldwin, "The White Man's Guilt," in *The Price of the Ticket: Collected Nonfiction, 1948–1985* (New York: St. Martin's Press, 1985).

David Carter, *Stonewall: The Riots That Sparked a Revolution* (New York: St. Martin's Press, 2004).

Martin Duberman, *Stonewall* (New York: Dutton, 1993).

Donn Teal, *The Gay Militants* (New York: Stein and Day, 1971).

Introduction: Before We Start

Alfred C. Kinsey, *Sexual Behavior in the Human Male* (Philadelphia: W. B. Saunders, 1948).

Alfred C. Kinsey, *Sexual Behavior in the Human Female* (Philadelphia: W. B. Saunders, 1953).

R. I. Moore, *The Formation of a Persecuting Society: Power and Deviance in Western Europe, 950–1250* (Oxford, UK: Blackwell, 1987).

SIDEBAR: *Christine Jorgensen*

Christine Jorgensen, *Christine Jorgensen: A Personal Autobiography* (New York: Paul S. Eriksson, 1967).

Chapter One: Native Peoples

Ramon A. Gutierrez, *When Jesus Came, the Corn Mothers Went Away: Marriage, Sexuality, and Power in New Mexico, 1500–1846* (Stanford, CA: Stanford University Press, 1991).

Will Roscoe, *Changing Ones: Third and Fourth Genders in Native North America* (New York: Palgrave Macmillan, 2000).

Howard Zinn, *A People's History of the United States* (New York: Harper & Row, 1980).

SIDEBAR: *European Missionaries*
Jonathan Katz, *Gay American History: Lesbians and Gay Men in the U.S.A.: A Documentary History* (New York: Crowell, 1976).

Chapter Two: Thomas Morton
John Dempsey, *Thomas Morton, "The May Lord of Merrymount": The Life and Renaissance of an Early American Poet* (Stoneham, MA: privately published, 1999).
Thomas A. Foster, *Sex and the Eighteenth-Century Man: Massachusetts and the History of Sexuality in America* (Boston: Beacon Press, 2006).
Richard Godbeer, *Sexual Revolution in Early America* (Baltimore: Johns Hopkins University Press, 2002).

Chapter Three: Jemima Wilkinson
Susan Juster, "Neither Male nor Female: Jemima Wilkinson and the Politics of Gender in Post-Revolutionary America," in *Possible Pasts: Becoming Colonial in Early America*, ed. Robert Blair St. George (Ithaca, NY: Cornell University Press, 2000).
Paul Benjamin Moyer, *The Public Universal Friend: Jemima Wilkinson and Religious Enthusiasm in Revolutionary America* (Ithaca, NY: Cornell University Press, 2015).

Chapter Four: Deborah Sampson
Daniel A. Cohen, *The Female Marine and Related Works: Narratives of Cross-Dressing and Urban Vice in America's Early Republic* (Amherst: University of Massachusetts Press, 1997).
Sandra M. Gustafson, "The Genders of Nationalism: Patriotic Violence, Patriotic Sentiment in the Performance of Deborah Sampson Gannett," in St. George, *Possible Pasts*.
Herman Mann, *The Female Review: Life of Deborah Sampson, the Female Soldier in the War of the Revolution* (1797) (n.p.: Forgotten Books, 2017).

Chapter Five: Nineteenth-Century Romantic Friendships

Nancy F. Cott, *The Bonds of Womanhood: "Woman's Sphere" in New England, 1780–1835* (New Haven, CT: Yale University Press, 1977).

Richard Godbeer, *The Overflowing of Friendship: Love Between Men and the Creation of the American Republic* (Baltimore: Johns Hopkins University Press, 2009).

Chapter Six: The Mystery of Emily Dickinson

Blanche Wiesen Cook, "'Women Alone Stir My Imagination': Lesbianism and the Cultural Tradition," in *Signs* 4, no. 4, The Labor of Women: Work and Family (Summer 1979): 718–39.

The Letters of Emily Dickinson, ed. Thomas Johnson and Theodora Weld (Cambridge, MA: Harvard University Press, 1914).

The Poems of Emily Dickinson, ed. Thomas Johnson and Theodora Weld (Cambridge, MA: Harvard University Press, 1914).

Rebecca Patterson, *The Riddle of Emily Dickinson* (Boston: Houghton Mifflin, 1951).

Chapter Seven: Julia Ward Howe, Samuel Gridley Howe, and Charles Sumner

Elaine Showalter, *The Civil Wars of Julia Ward Howe: A Biography* (New York: Simon & Schuster, 2016).

Gary Williams, *Hungry Heart: The Literary Emergence of Julia Ward Howe* (Amherst: University of Massachusetts Press, 1999).

Chapter Eight: The Amazing Life of Albert D. J. Cashier

DeAnne Blanton, *They Fought Like Demons: Women Soldiers in the American Civil War* (Baton Rouge: Louisiana State University Press, 2002).

Chapter Nine: Charlotte Cushman

Faye E. Dudden, *Women in the American Theatre: Actresses and Audiences, 1790–1870* (New Haven, CT: Yale University Press, 1994).

Joseph Leach, *Bright Particular Star: The Life and Times of Charlotte Cushman* (New Haven, CT: Yale University Press, 1970).

Lisa Merrill, *When Romeo Was a Woman: Charlotte Cushman and Her Circle of Female Spectators* (Ann Arbor: University of Michigan Press, 1999).

Martha Vicinus, *Intimate Friends: Women Who Loved Women, 1778–1928* (Chicago: University of Chicago Press, 2006).

Chapter Ten: Walt Whitman

Nicholas Marshall, "The Civil War Death Toll, Reconsidered," *New York Times*, April 15, 2014.

Gary Schmidgall, *Walt Whitman: A Gay Life* (New York: Dutton, 1997).

Charley Shively, *Calamus Lovers: Walt Whitman's Working-Class Camerados* (San Francisco: Gay Sunshine Press, 1987).

Walt Whitman, *The Complete Poems* (New York: Penguin, 2004).

Walt Whitman, *Walt Whitman: Poetry and Prose*, ed. Justin Kaplan (New York: Library of America, 1982).

SIDEBAR: *Sex Between Men in the Navy*

B. R. Burg, *An American Seafarer in the Age of Sail: The Erotic Diaries of Philip C. Van Buskirk, 1851–1870* (New Haven, CT: Yale University Press, 1994).

Charles Warren Stoddard, *Cruising the South Seas: Stories, 1843–1909* (San Francisco: Gay Sunshine Press, 1987).

Chapter Eleven: Rebecca Primus and Addie Brown

Farah Jasmine Griffin, ed., *Beloved Sisters and Loving Friends: Letters from Rebecca Primus of Royal Oak, Maryland and Addie Brown of Hartford, Connecticut, 1854–1868* (New York: Alfred A. Knopf, 1999).

SIDEBAR: *Social Purity and the Battle over Who Is an American*

Timothy J. Gilfoyle, *City of Eros: New York City, Prostitution, and the Commercialization of Sex, 1790–1920* (New York: W. W. Norton, 1992).

Beryl Satter, *Each Mind a Kingdom: American Women, Sexual Purity, and the New Thought Movement, 1875–1920* (Berkeley: University of California Press, 1999).

Chapter Twelve: The Radical Victoria Woodhull

Mary Gabriel, *Notorious Victoria: The Life of Victoria Woodhull, Uncensored* (Chapel Hill, NC: Algonquin Books, 1998).

Barbara Goldsmith, *Other Powers: The Age of Suffrage, Spiritualism, and the Scandalous Victoria Woodhull* (New York: Alfred A. Knopf, 1998).

Victoria C. Woodhull, *Free Lover: Sex, Marriage and Eugenics in the Early Speeches of Victoria Woodhull* (Seattle: Inkling Books, 2005).

Chapter Thirteen: Jane Addams

Jane Addams, *The Selected Papers of Jane Addams* (Urbana: University of Illinois Press, 2003).

Louise W. Knight, *Citizen: Jane Addams and the Struggle for Democracy* (Chicago: University of Chicago Press, 2005).

Rodger Streitmatter, *Outlaw Marriages: The Hidden Histories of Fifteen Extraordinary Same-Sex Couples* (Boston: Beacon Press, 2012).

SIDEBAR: *Lillian Wald and the Invention of Public Health*

Doris Daniels, *Always a Sister: The Feminism of Lillian D. Wald* (New York: Feminist Press at the City University of New York, 1989).

Marjorie N. Feld, *Lillian Wald: A Biography* (Chapel Hill: University of North Carolina Press, 2008).

Chapter Fourteen: Julian Eltinge

Kathleen B. Casey, *The Prettiest Girl on Stage Is a Man: Race and Gender Benders in American Vaudeville* (Knoxville: University of Tennessee Press, 2015).

Chapter Fifteen: Marie Equi

Michael Helquist, *Marie Equi: Radical Politics and Outlaw Passions* (Corvallis: Oregon State University Press, 2015).

Chapter Sixteen: Gladys Bentley

James F. Wilson, *Bulldaggers, Pansies, and Chocolate Babies: Performance, Race, and Sexuality in the Harlem Renaissance* (Ann Arbor: University of Michigan Press, 2010).

SIDEBAR: *Harlem: A Symbol of Freedom*

George Chauncey, *Gay New York: Gender, Urban Culture, and the Making of the Gay Male World, 1890–1940* (New York: Basic Books, 2008).

Chapter Seventeen: World War II

AN INTRODUCTION ABOUT THE WAR

Evan Bachner, ed., *At Ease: Navy Men of World War II* (New York: Harry N. Abrams, 2004).

Allan Bérubé, *Coming Out Under Fire: The History of Gay Men and Women in World War Two* (New York: Free Press, 1990).

Lillian Faderman, *Odd Girls and Twilight Lovers: A History of Lesbian Life in Twentieth-Century America* (New York: Columbia University Press, 1991).

PROFILE OF JOSE SARRIA

Nan Alamilla Boyd, *Wide-Open Town: A History of Queer San Francisco to 1965* (Berkeley: University of California Press, 2003).

Michael Robert Gorman, *The Empress Is a Man: Stories from the Life of José Sarria* (New York: Haworth Press, 1998).

PROFILE OF PAT BOND

Nancy Adair, *Word Is Out: Stories of Some of Our Lives* (New York: Dell, 1978).

Chapter Eighteen: Harry Hay

Will Roscoe, ed., *Radically Gay: Gay Liberation in the Words of Its Founder* (Boston: Beacon Press, 1996).

Stuart Timmons, *The Trouble with Harry Hay: Founder of the Modern Gay Movement* (Boston: Alyson, 1990).

Chapter Nineteen: Phyllis Lyon and Del Martin

Stephanie Coontz, *The Way We Never Were: American Families and the Nostalgia Trip* (New York: Basic Books, 1992).

Marcia M. Gallo, *Different Daughters: A History of the Daughters of Bilitis and the Rise of the Lesbian Rights Movement* (New York: Carroll & Graf Publishers, 2006).

Chapter Twenty: Pauli Murray

Patricia Bell-Scott, *The Firebrand and the First Lady: Portrait of a Friendship: Pauli Murray, Eleanor Roosevelt, and the Struggle for Social Justice* (New York: Alfred A. Knopf, 2016).

Pauli Murray, *Pauli Murray: The Autobiography of a Black Activist, Feminist, Lawyer, Priest, and Poet* (Knoxville: University of Tennessee Press, 1989).

Rosalind Rosenberg, *Jane Crow: The Life of Pauli Murray* (New York: Oxford University Press, 2017).

Chapter Twenty-One: Bayard Rustin

John D'Emilio, *Lost Prophet: The Life and Times of Bayard Rustin* (New York: Free Press, 2003).

Michael G. Long, ed., *I Must Resist: Bayard Rustin's Life in Letters* (San Francisco: City Lights Books, 2012).

Chapter Twenty-Two: Carl Wittman

Karla Jay and Allen Young, eds., *Out of the Closets: Voices of Gay Liberation* (New York: New York University Press, 1992).

D. E. Mungello, *Remember This: A Family in America* (Lanham, MD: Hamilton Books, 2016).

Chapter Twenty-Three: Rita Mae Brown

Rita Mae Brown, *Rita Will: Memoir of a Literary Rabble-Rouser* (New York: Bantam Books, 1997).

Chapter Twenty-Four: Gloria Anzaldúa

Gloria Anzaldúa, *Borderlands: The New Mestiza = La Frontera* (San Francisco: Aunt Lute Books, 1987).

Gloria Anzaldúa, *Light in the Dark = Luz en lo Oscuro: Rewriting Identity, Spirituality, Reality* (Durham, NC: Duke University Press, 2015).

SIDEBAR: *Holly Woodlawn: Any Gender Is Fabulous as Long as It Has Style*

Holly Woodlawn, *A Low Life in High Heels: The Holly Woodlawn Story* (New York: St. Martin's Press, 1991).

Chapter Twenty-Five: Sylvester and Anita Bryant

Anita Bryant, *The Anita Bryant Story: The Survival of Our Nation's Families and the Threat of Militant Homosexuality* (Old Tappan, NJ: Revell, 1977).

Alice Echols, *Hot Stuff: Disco and the Remaking of American Culture* (New York: W. W. Norton, 2010).

Joshua Gamson, *The Fabulous Sylvester: The Legend, the Music, the Seventies in San Francisco* (New York: H. Holt, 2005).

SIDEBAR: *HIV-AIDS*

Larry Kramer, *Reports from the Holocaust: The Making of an AIDS Activist* (New York: St. Martin's Press, 1989).

Susan Sontag, *Illness as Metaphor and AIDS and Its Metaphors* (New York: Picador, 2001).

Chapter Twenty-Six: Robert Hillsborough and Harvey Milk

Lillian Faderman, *Harvey Milk: His Lives and Death* (New Haven, CT: Yale University Press, 2018).

Randy Shilts, *The Mayor of Castro Street: The Life and Times of Harvey Milk* (New York: St. Martin's Griffin, 2008).

Chapter Twenty-Seven: Essex Hemphill

Martin B. Duberman, *Hold Tight Gently: Michael Callen, Essex Hemphill, and the Battlefield of AIDS* (New York: New Press, 2014).

Essex Hemphill, *Ceremonies: Prose and Poetry* (New York: Plume, 1992).

Chapter Twenty-Eight: Kiyoshi Kuromiya

Larry Kramer, *Reports from the Holocaust: The Story of an AIDS Activist* (New York: St. Martin's Press, 1989).

Chapter Twenty-Nine: Felix Gonzalez-Torres

Maurizio Cattelan, "Maurizio Cattelan Interviews Felix Gonzalez-Torres," *Mousse Magazine* 9 (Summer 2007).

Matthew Drutt, *Felix Gonzalez-Torres Billboards* (Santa Fe: Radius Books, 2014).

Nancy Spector, *Felix Gonzalez-Torres* (New York: Guggenheim Museum, 1995).

Chapter Thirty: Jamie Nabozny

ACLU, "Doing the Math: What the Numbers Say About Harassment of Gay, Lesbian, Bisexual, and Transgender Students."

Carlos A. Ball, *From the Closet to the Courtroom: Five LGBT Rights Lawsuits That Have Changed Our Nation* (Boston: Beacon Press, 2010).

Jordan Dashow, "New FBI Data Shows Increased Reported Incidents of Anti-LGBTQ Hate Crimes in 2016," Human Rights Campaign, November 13, 2017.

Chapter Thirty-One: Jack Baker and Michael McConnell

Michael McConnell with Jack Baker, *The Wedding Heard 'Round the World: America's First Gay Marriage* (Minneapolis: University of Minnesota Press, 2016).

"Pastor Reflects Back on Minn. Gay Marriage," KSTP, posted May 16, 2013, YouTube video.

SIDEBAR: *Marriage Equality and the Courts*

Nathaniel Frank, *Awakening: How Gays and Lesbians Brought Marriage Equality to America* (Cambridge, MA: Harvard University Press, 2017).

Chapter Thirty-Two: Sylvia Rivera

David Carter, *Stonewall: The Riots That Sparked a Revolution* (New York: St. Martin's Press, 2004).

Stephan L. Cohen, *The Gay Liberation Youth Movement in New York: An Army of Lovers Cannot Fail* (New York: Routledge, 2007).

Martin Duberman, *Has the Gay Movement Failed?* (Berkeley, CA: University of California Press, 2018).

Anna Klebine, "'Hell Hath No Fury Like a Drag Queen Scorned': Sylvia Rivera's Activism, Resistance, and Resilience," OutHistory.org.

Chapter Thirty-Three: Coming Out or Staying In

Human Rights Campaign, *Growing Up LGBT in America*.

Randy Shilts, *Conduct Unbecoming: Lesbians and Gays in the U.S. Military, Vietnam to the Persian Gulf* (New York: St. Martin's Press, 1993).

SIDEBAR: *Jason Collins*

Jason Collins, "Why NBA Center Jason Collins Is Coming Out Now," *Sports Illustrated*, April 29, 2013.

PHOTO CREDITS

PG. 89 Courtesy of the National Photo Company Collection, Library of Congress, Prints and Photographs Division

PG. 89 Courtesy of the Library of Congress, Prints and Photographs Division

PG. 95 Courtesy of the Library of Congress, Prints and Photographs Division

PG. 96 Wikimedia Commons

PG. 100 Internet Archive Book Images/Wikimedia Commons

PG. 102 Courtesy of the LOOK Magazine Photograph Collection, Library of Congress, Prints and Photographs Division

PG. 104 Courtesy of the National Child Labor Committee Collection, Library of Congress, Prints and Photographs Division

PG. 107 (both) Courtesy of the Billy Rose Theatre Division, New York Public Library

PG. 113 Wikimedia Commons

PG. 114 Wikimedia Commons

PG. 115 Courtesy of the Genthe Photograph Collection, Library of Congress, Prints and Photographs Division

PG. 117 California State Archives, San Quentin Prison Records

PG. 122 Schlesinger Library, Radcliffe Institute, Harvard University

PG. 126 (both) Schomburg Center for Research in Black Culture, Photographs and Prints Division, New York Public Library

PG. 127 Schomburg Center for Research in Black Culture, Photographs and Prints Division, New York Public Library

PG. 131 Schomburg Center for Research in Black Culture, Photographs and Prints Division, New York Public Library

PG. 140 San Francisco History Center, San Francisco Public Library

PG. 144 Manuscripts and Archives Division, New York Public Library

PG. 149 Photo by Dorothea Jacobsen-Wenzel, Schlesinger Library, Radcliffe Institute, Harvard University

PG. 159 Schlesinger Library, Radcliffe Institute, Harvard University

PG. 169 Courtesy of the New York World-Telegram and Sun Newspaper Collections, Library of Congress Prints and Photographs Division

PG. 171 Photo by Patsy Lynch © 2018, all rights reserved

PG. 176 San Francisco History Center, San Francisco Public Library

PG. 179 Photo by Diana Davies, Manuscripts and Archives Division, New York Public Library

PG. 185 K. Kendall/Wikimedia Commons

PG. 186 Charles L. Todd and Robert Sonkin Migrant Workers Collection, Library of Congress, Prints and Photographs Division

PG. 187 From the Russell Lee Photography Collection, courtesy of the Dolph Briscoe Center for American History, University of Texas at Austin

PG. 195 San Francisco History Center, San Francisco Public Library

PG. 199 Photo by Bettye Lane, Schlesinger Library, Radcliffe Institute, Harvard University

PG. 206 San Francisco History Center, San Francisco Public Library

PG. 209 Photo by Terrance McCarthy, courtesy of the San Francisco History Center, San Francisco Public Library

PG. 214 Photo by Robert Giard, © Estate of Robert Giard

PG. 218 Manuscripts and Archives Division, New York Public Library

PG. 221 Ansel Adams, 1902. Manzanar War Relocation Center Photographs, Library of Congress, Prints and Photographs Division

PG. 226 Photo courtesy of Peter Lien

PG. 239 Photo courtesy of Jamie Nabozny

PG. 243 Minnesota Historical Society

PG. 251 Photo by Diana Davies, Manuscripts and Archives Division, New York Public Library

PG. 262 Pax Ahisma Gethen/Wikimedia Commons

PG. 263 Steven Pisano/Wikimedia Commons

PG. 267 Keith Allison/Wikimedia Commons

PG. 272 Jon B. Lovelace Collection of California Photographs in Carol M. Highsmith's America Project, Library of Congress, Prints and Photographs Division

INDEX

ACT UP (AIDS Coalition to Unleash Power), 204, 217–18, 225. *See also*; HIV-AIDS; LGBTQ activism

Adams, Abigail, 31

Addams, Jane: antislavery activism, 101–2; background, early life, 97–99; Hull House/the settlement movement, 100–101; Nobel Peace Prize, 103; relationship with Smith, 102; relationship with Starr, 102; spinal tuberculosis, 98–99

Addams, John Huy, 98–99

African Americans: civil rights movement, xiv; community in Harlem, NY, 126; community in Hartford, Connecticut, 83–84; educational discrimination faced by, 160; and the enduring impacts of slavery, xviii; and the Ku Klux Klan Act, 238; LGBTQ, 213–19; military jobs during World War II, 130; stereotyping of, 90, 217; white supremacy, 215; women workers during World War II, 131. *See also* civil rights activism; Harlem, New York City

African Methodist Episcopal Church, 165

AIDS Coalition to Unleash Power (ACT UP), 204, 217–18, 225. *See also* HIV-AIDS; LGBTQ activism

Ajzenberg, Joseph, 191

Alcott, Louisa May, 73

Alice B. Toklas Democratic Club, 152

Allerton, Mary, 68

"alyha," defined, 17

American Communist Party, 138–39, 142–43, 173

American Friends Service Committee (AFSC), 166, 168

American Revolution, 30–34

"American," efforts to define, 88–90, 97, 196

androgynous minority, 139

Anthon, John Hone, 51

Anthon, Kate Scott Turner, 49–50, 52–53

antigay rhetoric and violence: by Balboa, 18–19; and HIV-AIDS, 203; and laws against homosexual behavior, 25, 27, 110, 124–25, 168; in the 1970s, 195–96, 198–99; ongoing, 212; and religious convictions, 267; Sarria's activism against, 132, 135; and the Stonewall riots, xiv. *See also* bullying; Hillsborough, Robert; Milk, Harvey

antisodomy laws, 27, 168

antiwar activism. *See* peace (antiwar) activism

Anzaldúa, Gloria: bisexuality, 187; *Borderlands/La*

*Friends from the Other Side/
Amigos del otro lado* (Anzaldúa), 189
friendships, romantic, 39–42,
44, 72, 105. *See also*
same-sex relationships
Fuller, Buckminster, 224–25
Fuller, Margaret, 54

Gandhi, Mahatma, 166
Gannett, Benjamin, 35
Ganymede myth, 23
Gary, relationship with Rivera,
250
gay: defined, 3, 5–6, 279; word
for describing gay men, 120
*Gay and Lesbian Poetry in Our
Time*, 216–17
Gay Community News, xvi
Gay Freedom Day Parade, San
Francisco, honoring of Hillsborough at, 208
"Gay is good" slogan, 6
Gay Liberation Front (GLF):
Brown's work with, 181;
formation of, xiv–xv; Philadelphia chapter, Kuromiya's
work with, 224; use of term
"gay," 3
gay liberation movement: antisodomy laws, 27; backlash
against, 195, 198; impact
on LGBTQ culture, 195;
and the Lavender Menace
"zap," 179; and the pressure
to come out, 259; as racist,
214–16; "Refugees from
Amerika: A Gay Manifesto"
(Wittman), 172, 175, 177.
See also the Gay Liberation
Front (GLF); Mattachine
Society
gay-straight alliances (GSAs),
xx, 234

Geer, Will, 142
gender/gender identity: defined,
280; as fluid, complex 8–9,
15; nineteenth-century
perspectives, 39–40; as
nonbinary, recognition of,
248; "normal," as cultur-
ally defined, 2, 8, 31, 58;
among North American
tribal societies, 14–16; and
pronoun preferences, 9,
31, 122, 159, 191; 249;
sexuality as distinct from,
7–8, 15
gender-variant people, 248–49
General Theology Seminary,
New York, ordination of
Murray, 162
Gernreich, Rudi, 138–39; 142,
144
Getty Center for the History
of Art and the Humanities,
Santa Monica, California,
219
Gilbert, Susan (Sue), 48–49,
52–53
Ginsburg, Allen, 224
Gonzalez-Torres, Felix: artistic
ideas and productivity, 227,
229; childhood, early life,
228; fame, museum exhibits,
230–31; handling of grief
through art, 230–31; move
to New York, 229; relation-
ship with Laycock, 229;
studies, 228
Grant, Cary, 6
Greenwich Village, New York
City, 192
GRID (gay-related immune
deficiency), 203
Griswold, Rufus Wilmot, 78
Group Material collective, New
York, 229

Hancock, John, honoring of Sampson, 35
Hardwick, Michael, 27
Harlem, New York City: acceptance of gender fluidity in, 126; diversity of cultures in, 126–27; drag balls, 128; Harlem Renaissance, 128; and the Jazz Age, 119; LGBTQ cultural leaders, 128; as symbol of freedom and independence, 127
Harpers Weekly, Woodhull as Satan cartoon, 95
Harry Hansberry's Clam House, Bentley's performing at, 120
Harry Potter and the Sorcerer's Stone (Rowling), xix
Hartford, Connecticut, African American community in, 83–84
Harvard Law School, refusal to accept female students, 160
hate crimes. *See* bullying; violence, hate crimes
Haudenosaunee Confederacy (Iroquois), 30
Hawaii Supreme Court, *Baehr v. Lewin*, 246
Hawthorne, Nathaniel, 72
Hay, Harry: early life and sexual awareness, 140–41; on gay people as spiritually unique, 145; illness and anxiety disorder, 142; Marxist ideas, 141; and the Mattachine Society, 138–39, 143; relationship with Gernreich, 142; relationship with Platky, 142; studies in theater and politics, 141; union card, 141
Hayden, Tom, 173

Hays, Matilda Mary, 71–72
Heart Mountain Relocation Center, Wyoming, 221
Heaven Grand in Amber Orbit (Curtis), 192
Hemphill, Essex: artistic productivity, 216; childhood and early life, 214; cofounding of Cinque, 216; financial struggles, 216; illness and death, 218–19; influence, 219; poetry chapbooks and other writings, 216; relationship with Jones, 215; self-outing, 213; sexuality, 214–15
Henry House settlement, New York, 103–4
hermaphrodite, 59, 280
The Hermaphrodite (Julia Ward Howe), 58–59
heterosexual/heterosexuality, 280
Hillsborough, Robert: murder of, 206–7; trials of Cordova and Spooner, 210
Hispanic students, view of as unintelligent, 186
HIV-AIDS: activism around, 201, 203–5; antiretrovirals and disease management, 204–5; first public recognition of, 201; marginalizing people with, 203, 217, 235; and opportunistic infections, 204; prevalence and death toll, 201, 204; and retroviruses, 203; widespread availability of information about, 274
Hodgers, Jennie. *See* Cashier, Albert D. J.
Hoffman, Abbie, 224
Holcomb, Betsy Bell (Bessie), 113

discrimination faced by, 234–35, 248–49; freedom represented by disco music, 194; impact of World War II on, 129; labelling of, 3, 10–11; laws protecting, 234, 239; new opportunities, 208, 275–76; number of, 2017, 263; reluctance to join the Mattachine Society, 143; safety of living in accepting communities, 126–27, 132; and the uniqueness of each group, 183; violence against, 18–19, 206–7, 235. *See also* HIV-AIDS; *each specific LGBTQ category*

Life (magazine), "The Defiant Voices of S.D.S," 226

Logue, Patricia, 238–39

Looking for Langston (Julien), 218

Look (magazine), "The Homosexual Couple," 243

Los Angeles, California: founding of the Mattachine Society, 138–39; Holly Woodlawn Memorial Fund for Transgender Youth, 192; laws against homosexuals, 138–39; laws against public cross-dressing, 110, 124–25

Louÿs, Pierre, 150

love: Free Love movement, 93–96; and the Gay Liberation Front, xiv; and Publick Universal Friend's beliefs, 29–30. *See also* friendships, romantic; Merrymount, Massachusetts

A Low Life in High Heels (Woodlawn), 192

Ludlam, Charles, 192

Lynn, Roger, 244–45

Lyon, Phyllis: background and early career, 147; lesbian activism, 152; publication of the *Ladder*, 151–52; relationship with, marriage to Martin, 148–49, 153

Mademoiselle (magazine), honoring of Murray in, 160

Maldonado, Maria Dolores, 133

maleness, masculinity: and the Civil War, 76; during the early twentieth century, 109; and expectations for athletes, 268; limits on emotional expression, 46; nineteenth-century gender norms, 39–40; and the rugged frontiersman, 30; as socially determined, 8; Whitman's redefinition of, 79, 82; and World War II, 130

Mann, Herman, 34–35

March on Washington for Jobs and Freedom, 161, 169, 222

maricón, 250

marijuana, medical, 226

Marlowe, Christopher, 23

Marquette, Jacques, 19

marriage: civil union vs., 246; between lesbians and gay men, 136, 148, 174; at Merrymount, 25; Native American traditions, 15, 18–19; same-sex, 153, 242, 244–47. See also *individual biographies*

Marshall, Thurgood, 161

Martin, Del: background and early career, 147–48; lesbian activism, 152; marriage, motherhood, and divorce,

behalf of social justice, 157, 159–60, 161; as a "girl-boy," 158–59; and the "Jane Crow" concept, 160; legal studies, 160–61; marriage, 159; and NOW, 161; ordination as an Episcopal priest, 162; relationship with Barlow, 162; relationship with E. Roosevelt, 157; *States' Laws on Race and Color*, 161; struggles defining sexuality, 158

music, cultural meanings, 194

Nabozny, Jamie: antibullying lawsuit, 238; bullying of, 235–36; childhood, 235–36; *Nabozny v. Podlesny*, 238–39; PTSD, 236–37

nádleehi, as Navajo term for nonbinary people, 16–17

Naegle, Walter, 170–71

National Association for the Advancement of Colored People (NAACP), 165

National Black AIDS Conference, 218

National Coalition of Black Gays, 215–16

National Coming Out Day, 260

National Organization for Women (NOW): Brown's participation in, 180; debates about inclusion of lesbians, 178–79; the Lavender Menace "zap," 178–79, 181; Lyon and Martin's work with, 152; Murray as cofounder of, 161

Native American tribes: diversity of cultures, 17; and nonbinary people, 16–17; role of women, 18;

spiritual practices, Hay's interest in, 141

Navajo, term for nonbinary people, 16–17

Navratilova, Martina, 260

Nelson, Gerald, 242, 245

Nethula Journal of Contemporary Literature, 216

New Bedford, Massachusetts, Equi family in, 112

The New English Canaan (Morton), 26–27

New Jersey Nets, Collins as player for, 267

New Left, limitations of, 174

Newsom, Gavin, 152

Newton, Huey, 224

New York City. *See* Greenwich Village, New York City; Harlem, New York City

New York Times: "Rare Cancer Seen in 41 Homosexuals. . . ," 201; story about Matlovich in, 258

Ninety-Fifth Illinois Infantry, Cashier's service with, 63

Nobel Peace Prize, awarding to Addams, 103

nonbinary, 277–78

nonmonogamy, 264–65

nonviolence: Rustin's commitment to, 166, 168–69. *See also* violence, hate crimes

normal: and the acceptance of difference, xix; as culturally defined, 1–2

Northern Paiute people, Hay's closeness with, 141

Obama, Barack, 171

Obama, Michelle, 266

Obergefell v. Hodges, 247

ONE (Mattachine Society), 143

open relationships, 241

opportunistic infections, 204.
See also HIV-AIDS

Oregon Daily Journal, praise for Equi's work in San Francisco, 115

OutWrite, xvi

Pacific Builder and Engineer, Lyon as editor for, 147

pacifism, Rustin's commitment to, 166

Panama, violence against homosexuals by conquering Spanish, 18–19

pansexual, 6–7, 264

"pansy performers," 120

Parker, Mary Ellen, 113

Parks, Rosa, 168

Passion Flowers (Julia Ward Howe), 55

Patterson, John, 34

peace (antiwar) activism: by Addams, 103; by Equi, 116; by Kuromiya, 224; by Rustin, 168; by Wittman, 172, 177

Perkins School for the Blind, 54–55

persecuting society, theory of, 27

the "personal is political" phrase, 162–63

Philadelphia, Pennsylvania, ECHO demonstrations in, 223

Pilgrims, rules and religious practices, 24–25

Platky, Anita, 142

Platt, Davis, 166–67

Podlesny, Mary, 236, 238

polyamorous people, 264–65

Prietita and the Ghost Woman/ Prietita y la llorona (Anzaldúa), 189–90

Primus, Rebecca: childhood and teaching career, 84; marriage, 87; relationship with Brown, 84–86

Progressive Era, 114

progressive movements, 96, 117

Proposition 6 (Briggs Initiative), 199, 201, 209

Protestant Reformation, 24

pseudohermaphrodite, 158–59

Publick Universal Friend (Jemima Wilkinson): freedom from gender expectations, 28–29, 31, 248; prohibition on sexual activity, 30; pronoun preference, 9; sermons, beliefs, 29; visions, religious conviction, 28; as young activist, 271

Pueblo people, gender and sexual traditions, 14–15

Puerto Rico, Gonzalez-Torres's studies in, 228

Puritans, rules and religious practices, 23–24

Quaker practice: Rustin's, 166; at Swarthmore College, 173; Wilkinson's, 28

queen, 282–83

Queensbury, Marquess of, 10

queer, 10, 37–38, 263–64

queer culture: blues songs, 122; and "A Gay Manifesto," 174; in Harlem during the Jazz Age, 119–21; Warhol's, in Greenwich Village, 192. *See also* LGBTQ activism; LGBTQ people

A Queer Little Princess and Her Friends (Eaton), 10

Queer Nation, 10

racial equality: Addams's work promoting, 102; and the Connecticut emancipation law, 83; Cushman's support for, 71. *See also* civil rights activism; slavery

Radicalesbians, 181–82

Radical Faeries, 145

Rainey, Ma, 128

Rally for Decency, Miami, 198

Randolph, A. Philip, 166, 169

rap music, 196

"Rare Cancer Seen in 41 Homosexuals...," 201

Reagan, Ronald, funding cuts for AIDS research and the arts, 202–3, 217, 230

Red Butterfly collective, 174

Red Scare, 117

Red Sox baseball team, support for Collins, 266

Redstockings, 181

"Refugees from Amerika: A Gay Manifesto" (Wittman), 172, 174–75

Reserve Officer Training Corps (ROTC) program, 165

retroviruses, 203

Revolutionary People's Constitutional Convention, Philadelphia, 224

RFD: A Country Journal for Gay Men Everywhere, 175–76

Riggs, Marlon, 218–19

Ripley, Sarah, 41, 46

Rivera, Sylvia: death, 256; founding of STAR, 253; identification as female, 250; parents, mother's suicide, 249; pronoun preferences, 252; trans activism, 255; as a young activist, 249, 272

Roberts v. City of Boston, 56

rock and roll, cultural associations, 195

Rockford Female Seminary, Rockford, Illinois, Addams at, 98

Rodriguez, Aminta, 191

romantic friendships. *See* friendships, romantic

Roosevelt, Eleanor, 157

Roosevelt, Franklin, 156–57, 220–21

Roscoe, Will, 16

Rowland, Chuck, 138–39

Rowling, J. K., xix

Rubyfruit Jungle (Brown), 182

Rustin, Bayard: background and childhood, 164–65; cruising and arrests, 167–68; death, 170–71; involvement with gay culture, 166; as an LGBTQ activist, 170; openness about sexuality, 166, 168, 170; parents, 164–65; as a political organizer, 166; relationship with Davis, 166–67; relationship with Naegle, 170; with the Southern Christian Leadership Conference, 169; work with the AFSC, 166; work with King, 168; as young activist, 272

Rustin, Florence, 164

sailors, homosexual relationships among, 81

same-sex marriage: activism around, 152–53, 240, 244–46; as an "impossible dream," 241; legalizing of, 246–47

same-sex relationships: criminalization of, 143, 235;

open relationships, 241; as sinful, 2. *See also* friendship, romantic

Sampson, Deborah (Robert Shurtleff): early life, 33; honorable discharge, 33–34; lectures, 36; marriage, 34; military pension, 34–36; military service, 33; posthumous honors, 36–37; as "queer," 37–38; tombstone, 36

San Francisco, California: crackdown on same-sex bars and club, 149; earthquake, 1906, 115; murders of gay men in, 207, 210–11; Tavern Guild, 135

San Quentin, Equi's imprisonment at, 116–17

sapphist, 4–5, 52

Sappho, 4–5

Sarria, José: background, early life, 133; drag performances, 132; election to public office in San Francisco, 133; enlistment challenges, 133; postwar activities, 134–35

Saturday Night Fever (movie), 200

Save Our Children campaign, 198

Scott, Kay, 124

Second Congress to Unite Women (NOW), 178–79

Sedition Act, 1918, 116

settlement houses, 100, 103

sex-reassignment surgery, 11–12, 283–84

sexual fluidity, 264

sexuality: as changing with age, 264; changing views on following the Civil War, 76; gender as distinct from, 7–8, 15; "normal," as culturally defined, 1–2; and public vs. private behaviors, 97

sex workers, 250, 252

Shakespeare, William, 23, 107

sharecroppers, 185

Shurtleff, Robert. *See* Sampson, Deborah

slavery: Addams's work to abolish, 101–2; and the Connecticut emancipation law, 83; enduring impacts, xviii; the Howes' opposition to, 29; Morton's views on, 25; Publick Universal Friend's views on, 29; Sumner's opposition to, 29. *See also* African Americans; civil rights activism; racial equality;

Smith, Bessie, 128

Smith, Mary Rozet, 102–103

social justice: Addams's enduring efforts of, 103; and changing approaches to activism, 273–75; the Howes' joint passion for, 55; intersectionalism, interrelated causes, 116, 173; Murray's work for, 161; and progressive goals, 96; role of the AFSC, 166. *See also* civil rights activism; racial equality

social purity movement, 88–89, 110

Society for Individual Rights, 133

Society of Fools, 140

Sodom, city of, 27

sodomy, sodomite, 4, 27, 283